MULTIPLE SELVES, MULTIPLE VOICES

The Wiley Series in

CLINICAL PSYCHOLOGY

J. Mark G. Williams *School of Psychology, University*
(Series Editor) *of Wales, Bangor, UK*

Further titles in preparation: *A list of earlier titles in the series follows the index*

MULTIPLE SELVES, MULTIPLE VOICES

Working with Trauma, Violation and Dissociation

Phil Mollon
Lister Hospital, Stevenage, UK

JOHN WILEY & SONS
Chichester • New York • Brisbane • Toronto • Singapore

Copyright © 1996   by John Wiley & Sons Ltd
                    Baffins Lane, Chichester,
                    West Sussex PO19 1UD, England

                    National   01243 779777
                    International   (+44) 1243 779777

Reprinted June 1999

Other Wiley Editorial Offices

John Wiley & Sons, Inc., 605 Third Avenue,
New York, NY 10158-0012, USA

Jacaranda Wiley Ltd, 33 Park Road, Milton,
Queensland 4064, Australia

John Wiley & Sons (Canada) Ltd, 22 Worcester Road,
Rexdale, Ontario M9W 1L1, Canada

John Wiley & Sons (SEA) Pte Ltd, 2 Clementi Loop #02-01,
Jin Xing Distripark, Singapore 129809

Library of Congress Cataloging-in-Publication Data

Mollon, Phil.
    Multiple selves, multiple voices: working with trauma, violation,
and dissociation / Phil Mollon.
        p. cm. — (The Wiley series in clinical psychology)
    Includes bibliographical references and index.
    ISBN 0-471-95292-3 (cloth). — ISBN 0-471-96330-5 (paper)
    1. Dissociative disorders. 2. Adult child abuse victims–
Psychology. 3. Post-traumatic stress disorder. I. Title.
II. Series.
    [DNLM: 1. Dissociative Disorders–etiology. 2. Multiple-
personality Disorder–etiology. 3. Stress Disorders, Post-
Traumatic–psychology. 4. Child Abuse, Sexual–psychology.
5. Recall. WM 173.6 M727m 1995]
RC553.D5M65 1995
616.85'23–dc20   96-1476
DNLM/DLC   CIP
for Library of Congress

British Library Cataloguing in Publication Data

A catalogue record for this book is available from the British Library

ISBN 0-471-95292-3 (hbk)
ISBN 0-471-96330-5 (pbk)

Typeset in 10/12pt Palatino by Saxon Graphics Ltd, Derby
Printed and bound in Great Britain by Biddles Ltd, Guildford and King's Lynn.
This book is printed on acid-free paper responsibly manufactured from sustainable
forestation, for which at least two trees are planted for each one used for paper production.

To the broken ones
and to all who are committed to a healing science

CONTENTS

ABOUT THE AUTHOR

Phil Mollon qualified in clinical psychology in 1976 (Leeds) and in psychoanalytic psychotherapy in 1985 (Tavistock Clinic) – and remains committed to *both* professions. He is registered with the British Confederation of Psychotherapists. He has worked in specialist psychotherapy units as well as general psychiatric services. Whilst at the Tavistock Clinic he undertook research into the dynamics and therapy of shame and other disturbances in the experience of self, resulting in his Ph.D. from Brunel University. His first book, *The Fragile Self,* derived from this work. He has served on British Psychological Society committees, including the working party on recovered memories.

SERIES PREFACE

One of the first challenges that the emerging science of psychology had to meet in the late nineteenth and early twentieth centuries was the clinical phenomenon of dissociation and multiple personality. Since that time, psychotherapists have often differed on how such phenomena should be viewed, but of the fact that there is something that desperately needs an explanation there is no doubt.

Mollon begins this book with the most striking case of dissociation. A client comes to therapy and sits in uncomfortable silence. Eventually, she comes out with the word 'hide' in a quiet and childlike voice. She says little more, and leaves. Later in the morning, the therapist receives a phone call from the same client, who apologises for not having been able to attend her therapy. As far as she is concerned, she had not attended, and she is puzzled when the therapist remarks that part of her had certainly come to her session. The author asks the question 'What is happening here?', and the remainder of the book is his quest for the answer. Ranging between writings of Janet and Freud on the one hand, through to current research on recovered memories on the other, Mollon illustrates at once the breadth of approach and the attention to detail needed to understand these phenomena.

As the twentieth century draws to a close, there has been a resurgence of interest in the potentially shattering effects that trauma can have on the personality. Mollon's book makes a major contribution to this field. It will be widely read and widely appreciated, for in it both lay readers and professionals will find the opportunity to share some of the insights from an experienced psychotherapist who thinks deeply about the issues that therapy presents.

J. Mark G. Williams

Series Editor

PREFACE

the analyses of narcissistic, borderline, and even neurotic cases have caused me to increasingly regard the phenomenon of splitting from the vantage point of dissociation and to suggest that the phenomenon of dissociation of personalities is more widespread and universal than has hitherto been thought.
(James Grotstein, 1981. *Splitting and Projective Interpretation*, p. 111)

When I completed training in analytical psychotherapy ten years ago, I believed the task of my work was to analyse the structures and conflicts within the patient's mind as they unfolded within the transference. In the last few years, as I have tried to help people more damaged than those usually attending a psychotherapy service, the cosy security of that tried and tested way of working has been shattered; my sense of reality and sanity has been repeatedly assaulted by communications of bizarre and horrifying memories, or apparent memories, for which my training did not prepare me. With these more injured and traumatised individuals, it is as if flashback *memory*, or *memory-like* material, violently intrudes, smashing the usual framework, assumptions and epistemological basis of analytic practice.

Sexual molestation and other forms of serious abuse of children, long covered over, began to invade our awareness in Britain in the mid-1980s, a little later than in the USA. In North America, after legislation was passed making reporting of suspected child abuse mandatory, there were 6000 cases of sexual abuse reported to protective agencies in 1976, whereas in 1992 there were almost 500 000 cases (Mendel, 1995).

Of course sexual and perverse abuse is a trauma, which overwhelms, distorts, or even 'breaks' the child's mind. (The *hearing* of perverse child abuse is also traumatic, evoking various emergency defensive reactions in the recipient of the unwelcome news.) The violation of the victim's body is obvious and may even leave physical evidence. The violation of the mind is more hidden and subtle. If we borrow Lacan's concepts of the three orders of the Imaginary (fantasy and dreams), the Symbolic (words and other symbols) and the Real (the actual external world), we can understand that normally there is a dynamic tension and fertile interaction between these. For the severely abused, something from the Real has smashed in, invading a sacred space, like a gang of Hell's Angels breaking into a church and raping the congregation. The boundary that separates the Real from the Imaginary is broken. The damage is invisible but profound.

Unmodified psychoanalytic work assumes an unviolated mind. Working with the violated is the challenge that I address in this book.

In spending many hours with severely disturbed traumatised patients I discovered something else that did not seem to be widely appreciated. Many of them experience hallucinatory internal voices, often extremely hostile; self-harm is often prompted by these voices. Usually these patients do not readily reveal their voices, for two reasons: first, the voices often forbid the patient to reveal their existence; secondly the patient is afraid of being regarded as schizophrenic. These people are not schizophrenic; they do not demonstrate thought disorder or delusions; they may however, experience brief periods of loss of contact with reality when traumatic memories or sensations from the past invade their current perception. Many of the characteristics of these patients can be understood in terms of the trauma theory and research which has developed in the United States within the last ten years – much of which is still relatively unknown in Britain. A good proportion of the chronic patients attending psychiatric services anywhere will be of this type. They do not respond well to medication, but tend to consume a lot of it.

Initially my only conceptual framework for understanding such patients was the notion of borderline personality disorder, as popularised particularly by Kernberg (1975). He viewed BPD as a condition resulting from high constitutional aggression and intolerance of frustration and mental pain, and a consequent reliance on splitting as a defence. On becoming aware of the American literature on dissociative disorders and on long-term effects of trauma (developed since the mid-80s), it became clear to me that many of the severely disturbed users of psychiatric services, who are not organically ill and are not schizophrenic, are suffering from a trauma-based dissociative disorder.

The most extreme form of dissociative disorder is the fully developed multiple personality disorder, recently renamed dissociative identity disorder. For some reason the existence of this diagnostic concept is highly disturbing to some clinicians and provokes fierce, and not always rational, hostility. Perhaps it is something to do with the idea of a personality based around pretence; or maybe it is threatening because it highlights the illusory nature of all sense of identity; or possibly it seems to make a mockery of psychiatric diagnosis since the MPD condition can mimic many other mental disorders. Regardless of how people feel about it, this severe dissociative disorder does exist and amongst a psychiatric population is not uncommon, although it may often be hidden, its manifestations covert rather than displayed openly. If we also consider the broader category of 'dissociative disorder not otherwise specified' – which really means a person's mental state has some characteristics of MPD/DID but not the fully developed picture – then it becomes apparent that trauma-based dissociative disorders are very common indeed.

Since I am in origin a psychoanalytic therapist, my understanding and use of theories of dissociation are inevitably strongly coloured by psychoanalysis. Indeed I believe that the analytic *stance* of listening receptively and responding thoughtfully and maintaining neutrality remains appropriate for work with the dissociatively disturbed, even if some altered parameters of technique may be necessary. However, I hope that what I have written will also be accessible to those whose main allegiance is to other frameworks. It will be seen that I attach great importance to addressing the distorted thinking and the deep schemas which are the domain of the contemporary cognitive therapist.

Since the book contains numerous clinical illustrations, a comment on confidentiality is necessary. Sexual abuse is about the violation of boundaries, and the unfolding and replaying of this theme within the therapy means that the experience of the therapist is often pervaded by guilt and shame. The sense of violating, betraying or abusing the patient is ever present. Therefore, the presentation of clinical material, although necessary, evokes particular unease in these instances. Needless to say, all the clinical examples presented here are heavily disguised in order to protect the boundaries of confidentiality. On the whole, the descriptions relate predominantly to events in the consulting room, unknowable to those other than the two participants. Some examples are composites of various patients. Whilst much material is my own, some is from colleagues elsewhere and I do not make clear which is which. Of course, clinical material is not scientific 'data' but merely illustrative of the application of an author's understanding; the implicit invitation is always for the reader to try the ideas in their own consulting rooms and form their own conclusion there.

Phil Mollon

Letchworth, August 1995

ACKNOWLEDGEMENTS

I would like to thank the following people for their help in the preparation of this book.

My parents. In working with victims of perverse and malevolent parenting I have become even more appreciative of my own.

My wife Ros and daughter Olivia, for their love and tolerance.

Dr Gail Price, for putting me in touch with the current American literature on trauma, for giving me access to her personal library, and for being a wonderful friend.

Mr C. for his consistent and thoughtful support.

Dr Phillips for first drawing my attention to dissociation.

My patients who teach me so much. In particular I would like to thank J and 'Barbara' for illuminating areas where I was completely in the dark.

Author's Note

In some cases psychological therapy with people who have been traumatised in childhood can be extremely difficult and potentially hazardous. Practitioners wishing to work with such patients are advised to ensure they have adequate experience and training, as well as an appropriate setting and support for the therapy. They are also strongly recommended to ensure that they are familiar with the literature on the inadvisability of attempting to recover repressed memories and the dangers of fostering false memories. Extreme caution is advised in all aspects of diagnosis and therapy with patients with dissociative disorders; respect for the patient's autonomy should be paramount.

Chapter 1

DISSOCIATION

A patient arrives for her psychotherapy session, silently comes into the consulting room and sits for some minutes without saying a word. She does not appear to respond to the therapist's gentle invitations to speak of what is on her mind. After about 15 minutes she suddenly shifts her body posture, looks frightened and moves around as if trying to escape into the corner of her chair. The therapist enquires what she is experiencing but in reply she repeats, in a quiet and childlike voice, the word 'hide' – this being said over and over in an eerie and imperative tone. She cannot or will not say what it is that she is frightened of, except at one point to say 'get hurt'. After some minutes of this she gets up and crouches down behind the chair, where she stays silently for almost the rest of the session. As the scheduled end of the session approaches, the therapist asks if there is another part of the patient who could take over at this point as they will have to stop in a moment. The patient gathers herself together and leaves without a word. At no point have patient and therapist engaged in any conventional exchange of words.

Later that morning the therapist receives a phone call from the patient who says that she is sorry she was not able to attend her session earlier but she could not face coming into the building and that she has been troubled by some bad experiences during the week. The therapist remarks that part of her had certainly come to her session. The patient seems puzzled by this comment and appears to assume that the therapist is not understanding correctly. She goes on to explain that she had driven to the hospital but could not bring herself to go in and so had sat in her car for the duration of the session.

What is happening here? The person speaking on the phone appears to be amnesic for her behaviour earlier in the day, or at least appears to have constructed a false version of events which she apparently believes. The therapist has remembered one set of events but the patient has presented quite a different set. Either the patient or the therapist appears to be deluded. How is such a problem to be addressed in the consulting room – and what experiences and mental processes could lie behind such a situation? Let us see what happened subsequently.

The following session the patient again apologised for missing the previous week and repeated the same explanation about sitting in the car. The therapist decided to try to confront the discrepancy and told the patient that another part of her, in her body, had indeed come in for the session the previous week. The patient appeared genuinely bemused and alarmed by this information and argued that this could not be true and that the therapist must be lying, although she could not imagine why he would want to lie. This debate went on rather fruitlessly for some minutes with the therapist trying different ways of explaining this. Suddenly the patient's demeanour shifted, her face looking directly at the therapist and appearing more self-assured; she said 'Tell her the name of the one who came last week'. The therapist asked what the name was and the reply was 'Tiny'. The patient then added that the therapist had done well with Tiny last week, especially in letting her hide behind the chair without intrusion. When the patient's demeanour changed again to the anxious head down posture, the therapist told her that the one who had come the previous week had been called Tiny. She agitatedly demanded to know how the therapist knew that name since it was a name only in her own mind, that only she should know.

So now three versions of the patient have been encountered: the designated patient; a frightened, childlike and inarticulate one called Tiny; and one who is rather calm and perceptive and seemingly helpful who does not so far have a name. This third one seems to know more than the others. Why have the patient's mind and personality become divided in this way? What is the origin of such processes of dissociation and what purpose is achieved by them? These are the problems that I set out to describe and answer in the rest of this book.

WHAT IS A DISSOCIATIVE DISORDER?

The patient described above is clearly suffering from Multiple Personality Disorder, more recently renamed Dissociative Identity Disorder. This is the most severe, complex and chronic dissociative state, although it is one which may be covert, hidden perhaps for years behind a variety of misdiagnoses. Contrary to the popular media stereotype, these patients do not usually display their dissociative phenomena flamboyantly, but carefully endeavour to conceal it. Because MPD/DID patients hear hallucinatory voices, they are often misdiagnosed as schizophrenic; however, they do not respond particularly well to neuroleptic medication in the way that schizophrenic patients often do. In fact, MPD/DID patients often experience a variety of Schneiderian symptoms, sometimes assumed incorrectly to be indicative only of schizophrenia (Ross et al., 1990). The differences are that MPD/DID patients usually experience their voices only as internally located, whereas schizophrenic patients may also experience them externally; MPD/DID patients do not show thought disorder, or delusions about present reality, although they may be temporarily disoriented by the intrusion of flashback memories into perception of the present. Schizophrenic patients do not reveal alter personalities, amnesia, occasional visual hallucinations, and the typical history of severe trauma that usually characterises MPD/DID. The MPD/DID patient may also experience recurrent severe headaches, often thought to be associated with the process of switching personalities – which again is not characteristic of schizophrenia.

Here are the DSM-IV criteria for MPD/DID:

A. The presence of two or more distinct identities or personality states (each with its own relatively enduring pattern of perceiving, relating to, and thinking about the environment and self).

B. At least two of these identities or personality states recurrently take control of the person's behaviour.

C. Inability to recall important personal information that is too extensive to be explained by ordinary forgetfulness.

D. Not due to the direct effects of a substance (e.g. blackouts or chaotic behaviour during alcohol intoxication) or a general medical condition (e.g. complex partial seizures).

There are also patients who show some degree of dissociative disorder but fall short of the full MPD/DID picture. These may be diagnosed as suffering from Dissociative Disorder Not Otherwise Specified (DDNOS).

DSM-IV also lists three other dissociative disorders: Dissociative Amnesia, Dissociative Fugue and Depersonalisation Disorder. In fact all these may be symptoms of the more inclusive MPD/DID; fugue states being like the phenomena of inter-alter amnesia, whilst depersonalisation – the experience of feeling detached from the body – is also a common feature of MPD/DID (Steinberg, 1991). (Of course, depersonalisation is also a common experience associated with phobic anxiety and panic disorder; consideration of the broader picture must precede diagnosis of a dissociative disorder.)

DSM-IV also allows for the possibility that Dissociative Identity Disorder may occur in the context of, or as a complication of, a personality disorder such as Borderline Personality Disorder. In this way DID, as an Axis I disorder, may coexist with an Axis II disorder.

Steinberg (1993a, b), in presenting a structured diagnostic interview, postulates five core areas of primary dissociative symptoms: depersonalisation; derealisation; amnesia; identity confusion; identity alteration. All these primary symptoms are usually covert; the patient does not reveal them unless asked. There may be a large and diverse range of secondary symptoms which are more overt, such as substance misuse, eating disorder, self-harm, mood swings, alcoholism, depression, phobic anxiety and many others.

I describe below a number of other forms of dissociation, including: psychotic dissociation, that between child and adult parts of the personality, between 'true' and 'false' self, and between different stages of life.

WHY DISSOCIATE? DISSOCIATION IS ABOUT DETACHMENT FROM AN UNBEARABLE SITUATION

Dissociation involves an attempt to deny that an unbearable situation is happening, or that the person is present in that situation. Thus dissociation involves the defence of denial, but in addition requires a degree of detachment of part of the mind from what another part is experiencing. This is like the 'hidden observer' phenomenon in hypnosis, described by Hilgard (1977, 1994). In Hilgard's experiment, a hypnotic subject was put in a trance and instructed to place their hand in ice cold water, whilst being given the suggestion that they would experience no pain; the person reported no pain, but it was possible to locate hypnotically another part of the person's mind that was aware of pain – the hidden observer. In this hypnotic state the more dominant part of the person's awareness is dissociated from the part that is aware of pain. Dissociation seems to be something like a state of self-generated hypnosis, developed to deal with unbearable pain or terror (Bliss, 1986).

A patient buries her head under a pillow on the analytic couch and begins to sob loudly, like a desolate and anguished small child. She appears to be re-enacting a childhood state of mind that was associated with severe neglect and abuse. Suddenly she sits bolt upright and says to the therapist 'I've got to stop or you are going to hit me!' She then reports that she feels unreal, as if she is not present, and describes how she is now completely out of touch with the feeling she was expressing in her crying just a few seconds previously.

About a week later she repeats a similar sequence, except she lets the drama in her mind unfold a little further. This time she stops her sobbing abruptly as before, but reports a vivid sensation of being hit repeatedly on her right side. As she thinks about this later, it occurs to her that her father was left-handed so that if he had hit her it would indeed have been on her right side.

What appears to be happening here is that as a memory (or memory-like fantasy) of abuse is approached, the patient employs the same process of dissociation in an effort to protect herself as she had in the past. She switches off from the experience and feels she is no longer present. However she later becomes able to undo the dissociation and to elaborate more of the experience through the sensations of being hit.

Children who are abused often develop dissociative mechanisms that are specifically aimed at escaping from the body which is being violated or tortured. A patient whose background apparently involved ritual abuse within a network of perverts, described how she had learnt to detach from her body during intensely painful circumstances, in such a way that she would then experience herself as positioned in a crack in the ceiling or in a lightbulb. This dissociation allowed her some relief, but led to further problems in that it could be difficult to return to her body; she described the agonising struggle to re-enter as being like a dog chasing its tail.

MEMORY, FANTASY AND PSEUDO-MEMORIES. A NEUTRAL STANCE

The much debated issue of recovered memory and pseudo-memory is discussed at length in a later chapter. However, since the study of dissociative disorders takes us directly to consideration of memories of childhood trauma – and since I have been part of the British Psychological Society working party looking at recovered memories (Morton et al., 1994) – it is appropriate that I should here make some preliminary brief comments about memory and technique.

First, I believe that detailed but false memories of childhood abuse can occur. Memory is inherently unreliable. As any analytic therapist will know, apparent memories of childhood events may be based upon real events, upon fantasy or dreams, or upon metaphorical representations, including representations of preverbal psychotic experience (Hedges, 1994). There is evidence that coercive therapeutic techniques can lead to the development of false memories. Moreover, traumatised patients tend to have a disturbed or defective sense of reality; they may be highly suggestible – especially if they are prone to dissociation, which may partly be thought of as a state of self-hypnosis. Hypnosis should not be used to recover memories. In the examples in this book, no coercive therapeutic procedures were used. In every instance I employed my usual analytic stance of listening receptively and responding thoughtfully.

This brings me to another general point. These patients are extremely vulnerable. They may have been severely traumatised in childhood and the potential exists for them to be traumatised again in therapy. Their sense of reality and perception of reality may have been undermined in childhood and the danger is that it could be again in therapy. The therapist must stay in the position of not knowing what went on in the patient's childhood – because he/she was not there. This is important not only because it is true that the therapist does not know objectively the historical situation, but also because the patient's own account may vary, and different parts of the patient may present differing accounts; it is not uncommon for one alter personality to describe an experience of abuse and for another alter to deny it and accuse the first one of lying. MPD/DID is a trauma-based disorder, but it is also based in fantasy and pretence; distinguishing what comes from reality and what comes from fantasy is inherently problematic.

The person who was abused or traumatised in childhood often has a very fragile sense of autonomy. False compliance with a therapist's view is always a danger – which may be followed ultimately by a violent repudiation of the therapy. Another danger is that of the patient being overwhelmed by reconnecting with warded off experiences of trauma. Through listening to my patients I have learnt to tread very carefully, gently and often slowly when facing experiences of trauma. I do not hold the view that it is always necessary or appropriate for childhood trauma to be faced fully and in detail in every case.

Intrusive investigations of childhood memory are not to be advised because (a) pseudo-memories may be encouraged; (b) the process of prematurely contacting memories of trauma may destabilise the personality system; (c) the patient's sense of autonomy will be threatened; (d) if and when the patient is ready and able to access or think about memories of trauma, then he/she will do so. On the other hand, a receptiveness and readiness, on the part of the therapist, to hear what the patient is consciously and unconsciously communicating of their early experiences is essential. The only responsible stance is to take seriously what are presented as memories and to consider these carefully with the patient, without rushing to a premature conclusion about their origin. I might add here that there is nothing essentially mysterious about amnesia for traumatic childhood experiences; to a large extent it is simply a matter of not thinking about a memory that is disturbing – and who has not done that?

One further point worth emphasising here is that there is a difference between a history and a clinical diagnosis. 'Childhood sexual abuse' is not a diagnosis of a mental state, nor a description of the adult patient's behaviour. Moreover, diagnosing a dissociative disorder does not rely upon knowing anything about a person's history. Whilst gradually coming to know a person's history may be important in understanding how he/she came to be in a particular mental state, the *goal* of therapy is the healing of a mental or behavioural disorder, not the unearthing of a traumatic history.

DISSOCIATION AND REPRESSION

The process of repression, the first mental defence described by Freud, refers to a state in which frightening mental contents are kept out of awareness on a relatively permanent basis, until such time as the 'return of the repressed' perhaps in the form of symptoms. What is implied here is that there is one main dumping ground, the unconscious, where unwanted mental contents are disposed of; this unconscious may speak, but only in the 'language of the unconscious', dreams, symptoms, parapraxes, etc. Dissociation, by contrast, suggests a fluctuating state of consciousness, wherein one part of the mind can know about and speak about, in ordinary language, matters which another part of the mind does not know about. In dissociation there can be many consciousnesses. Repression usually seems to be applied to internally generated mental contents, whereas dissociation is applied to externally generated trauma.

Davies and Frawley (1994) describe dissociation thus:

> dissociation is defined as a process by which a piece of traumatic experience, because it is too overstimulating to be processed and repressed along the usual channels, is cordoned off and established as a separate psychic state within the personality, creating two (or more) ego states that alternate in consciousness and, under different internal and external circumstances, emerge to think, behave, remember and feel. (p. 63)

Contrasting dissociation with repression, they state:

> Repression is an active process through which the ego attains mastery over conflictual material. Dissociation is a last ditch effort of an overwhelmed ego to salvage some semblance of adequate mental functioning . . . Repression brings about the forgetting of once familiar mental contents. Dissociation leads to severing of the connection between one set of mental contents and another.

Often dissociation and repression may be combined. A woman in her early twenties had begun to experience increasing flashback memories of sexual abuse, especially triggered during sexual activity with her husband. Part of the context for the intrusive re-emergence of the memories seemed to be the experience of having her own children, which was tending to put her back in touch with her own childhood. As she talked about this sexual abuse, she appeared emotionally somewhat detached, although her body was shaking. The interviewer had the impression that she was dissociated from her body, her head movements seeming quite lively but as if disconnected from the rest of her body which was relatively still albeit shaking. When asked how she felt about talking of these experiences, she replied that her attitude was one of trying to get the talking over and done with, which she said was like the way she used to try to get the abusive sex over and done with as quickly as possible. She was asked if there had been periods when she had been amnesic for the sexual abuse. She said that for a few years after leaving home she had put the abuse out of her mind. What if she had been asked at that time whether she had ever been sexually abused? She explained: 'I would have said no – and I would have believed that. I thought nothing had happened to me. I didn't want anything to have happened to me and so I thought that it hadn't.'

In this example there was clear repression, for a period of years, of the memories of abuse, the intentional forgetting of what was once known. The repression is also accompanied by the defence of denial: 'I did not want anything to have happened and so I thought that it hadn't.' This denial and repression of memories of abuse at the point of leaving home may be quite common. It is as if the abused adolescent decides at this point that he/she will put the past behind and will build a new identity on the basis of this repudiation of their past. The repression, in this example, follows the earlier defence of dissociation, the detachment from the experience of abuse and from the body that was abused. When asked about her childhood use of dissociation she said: 'It was as if there were two of me – the one that was abused and another one that it had not happened to.'

PSYCHOTIC DISSOCIATION

Dissociation is a central feature of psychotic processes, as Bleuler (1950) originally emphasised.

A schizophrenic patient complained of 'black lightning' emanating from her vagina, which she regarded as a 'septic sore', a source of pollution in her body. She wanted to cut her vulva away or else seal it up with a hot iron. She also described waking up with pains in her vagina. When the therapist suggested that these feelings might have something to do with unwanted sexual excitements, the patient replied that she did not consider that she had sexual feelings because she was not human but 'an alien'. Eventually it was possible to link these experiences to dissociation in the context of episodes of sexual abuse in her childhood, one of which had been by an alcoholic friend of the family. She wrote about this, stating starkly: 'I was molested by a drunk and I left my body.' It was as if she had reacted to her defiled body as people sometimes do on returning to find their house has been burgled who feel that they do not want to live there any more.

This patient had experienced sexual violation as exceptionally traumatic because of the schizophrenic fragility of the boundaries of her self and her sense of being easily invaded by other people. She had reacted by dissociating from her body and from her own sexuality, so that she thought of herself as an 'alien'. She defensively misclassified her sexual excitements as 'black lightning' and as pain.

As these experiences of abuse were explored in therapy she began to get in touch with her feelings of rage. She talked of wanting to kill the abusers and to fill them with pain and despair, just as she had felt emotionally poisoned by them. A recurrent dream vividly conveyed her wish to turn the tables on her tormentor. In the dream she and the abuser are seated at a meal table with other people. She has poisoned him and he is in agony and is dying and knows that she has done this but he cannot tell anyone. The dream captures the experience of something intensely damaging going on secretly within a seemingly innocuous scene of a social meal. In this way it can be seen that, as the dissociation that she had originally resorted to in the face of sexual trauma began to be undone through the process of therapy, she became more in touch with the feelings of rage and outrage and the wish for revenge, which were a natural accompaniment of these experiences.

Another common form of psychotic dissociation is the coexistence of sane and psychotic parts of the mind. At one moment the patient may be expressing perfectly sane or neurotic strands of thought, but at the next moment is displaying utterly delusional thinking. A schizophrenic patient represented this symbolically as follows: she hallucinated that there was a news flash on the television that half the government had fled the country. She was expressing vividly the way in which part of her mind was still being governed by sanity, whilst another part had taken flight from reality. This can also be understood as the coexistence of waking and dreaming states of mind, with the dreaming state intruding into the waking.

The fundamental dissociation in schizophrenic states often does seem to correspond to the process of 'decathexis' originally described by Freud (1911b). This is the fateful break with reality, the withdrawal of psychic interest from the world, and the subsequent creation of an alternative delusional world. The eventual psychotic break usually follows a childhood and adolescence of an increasing sense of personal failure often stemming from an inherent emotional vulnerability and sensitivity, perhaps combined with exacerbating dynamics within the family. Usually there is some 'final straw' kind of blow, perhaps seemingly mild in itself, but signalling to the person the collapse of any remaining hopes of being a viable adult person. In the face of an utterly shattered self-esteem, there is a giving up on reality. Part of the mind withdraws, leaving a much diminished garrison to deal with the external world. For the person who becomes schizophrenic the encounter with reality itself seems to be traumatic.

The 'decathexis' of reality then places part of the mind in a state akin to the withdrawal from the external world during sleep, resulting in dreams, which display thought processes that carry no respect for reality. Whilst 'dreaming' the schizophrenic person is still awake – and hence the interweaving of rational and dreamlike thought in this state of mind. This is the state which is itself represented by the patient's dream of half the government having taken flight.

The dissociation between a psychotic part of the mind, which has withdrawn from reality, and a sane part of the mind, which retains respect for reality, is described in some of Bion's writings (Bion, 1956, 1957). It is also implied in Freud's (1940b) account of splitting of the ego in his analysis of fetishism; in that state of mind, part of the ego accepts the reality that females do not possess a penis, whilst another part maintains the illusion that they do and looks to the fetish as a representation of this.

DISSOCIATION BETWEEN CHILD AND ADULT PARTS OF THE PERSONALITY

In people who have been severely traumatised or neglected, there is often a marked dissociation between child and adult parts of the personality. It is as if a precocious pseudo-adulthood had to be developed, superimposed upon, and in opposition to, an unintegrated child self. The inner child and the adult then are at war with one another, often each attempting to annihilate the other, each feeling that the other threatens their own existence.

For example, one patient had an angry child self that vigorously attempted to sabotage the adult's capacity to work; the background was that she had felt neglected and abused in childhood, her mother being out working excessive hours and the patient being left to take care of her siblings; for the angry inner child this patient's adult self that went to work was abusively abandoning her just as she had felt her mother had done. Often there was very little capacity for child and adult parts to cooperate in this patient; each was pursuing quite different agendas. Whenever the adult personality attempted to look for a job she would experience a loud and violent screaming of protest in her mind. This woman's capacity to work was indeed greatly jeopardised because although she could function as an adult and work competently for certain periods, she could not maintain this adult state and would find herself feeling, thinking and behaving like a small child with no access to her adult perspective and capacities. She would put on what she called her 'mask' in order to go to work, but would be terrified that the mask would slip and she would be revealed as a traumatised and disoriented child, lost in an adult world that made no sense to her.

A common clinical experience in working with people repeatedly traumatised in childhood is that he/she might appear in one emotional state during the session, but shift into quite a different and more disturbed state after the session. The patient may appear to be engaged in an analytic endeavour during the session, seemingly with a good working alliance with the therapist, whilst afterwards, or sometimes at the very end of the session, becoming very frightened and disoriented. This might be followed by extrasessional communications, such as letters or phone calls, which show much greater disturbance; these communications may be filled with incoherent rage or overtly psychotic material – which is then not easily addressed during the session. The problem here is that the relatively adult part of the patient that is 'out' during the session is dissociated from the traumatised child or psychotic parts. It is then as if these parts demand recognition and vehemently assert their presence later. Sometimes this phenomenon takes the form of the patient presenting to the therapist in different states of mind at different times, so that initially the therapist has the confusing experience of thinking at one point that he/she has a neurotic patient but at other times perceiving the patient as psychotic.

Where there is a marked dissociation between child and adult parts of the mind, there may be a considerable therapeutic problem of how to find meaningful access to the 'children'. The small child in the patient may not be able to make use of the adult oriented analytic session, which relies upon words and a rather austere atmosphere. To a child the stance of the adult analyst may appear strange and bewildering. For example, one patient complained that she simply could not follow the big words and long sentences that the therapist used. Another exclaimed angrily that there was nothing for a child in the consulting room. The availability of dolls, teddy bears or other toys may facilitate communication with the child. A classically trained analyst unwilling to modify his/her technique would have difficulty working with this kind of patient. Without some adaptation to the dissociation, on the part of the analyst, the child within the patient is likely to feel excluded, immensely angry, and will probably wreck the therapy.

DISSOCIATION BETWEEN 'TRUE' AND 'FALSE' SELF

Winnicott's (1960) description of a division between true and false self is not an account of repression but of dissociation. More than merely a social self or personna, Winnicott saw the false self as arising when the adaptation from the mother to the child is so lacking that the child is predominantly adapting to the mother. The mother substitutes her own gesture for that of the child. A false self of adaptation develops and the true self is held in abeyance.

A patient presents a lively personality to most people who know her, but brings her despair only to the therapist. To him she talks of hopelessness, loneliness and anguish. As she gets in her car to come to the session she feels her pretence dissolving and a sense of heaviness emerging. However, a recurrent fear in the transference is that the therapist will tire of her depression and want to get rid of her. Part of the background was that she experienced her mother as unable to tolerate her unhappiness; whenever she attempted to communicate feelings of misery, from whatever source, her mother would express disapproval and send her away. She learnt to be charming and cheerful, but this facade concealed despair – despair about ever being known and understood.

What evoked most anxiety in this patient's childhood was the wish to communicate to her mother the distress that her mother caused her. She perceived that her mother needed to be seen as glamourous and successful and worked to preserve her mother's self-image. Stolorow, Atwood and Brandchaft (1994), writing from a self-psychological point of view, describe this kind of situation as follows:

> One of the most noxious early pathogenic situations occurs when a child's attempts to communicate an experience of psychological injury by a caregiver result in a prolonged disruption of a vitally needed tie. When the

child consistently cannot communicate such experiences without perceiving that he or she is damaging or unwelcome to the caregiver, an invariant principle becomes structuralised that organises all subsequent experiences – the conviction that the subjugation of one's own distinctive affective experience is an absolute requirement for maintaining needed ties. (p. 125)

Thus this kind of quite common dissociation between true and false self is based not on gross trauma or abuse but on repeated painful interactions with a primary caregiver, involving partial rejection of crucial affective communications. Although serious, it represents a less severe dissociation than that which derives from gross and repeated trauma.

DISSOCIATION BETWEEN DIFFERENT STAGES OF LIFE

Most people's lives show some continuity and development through the progressive stages and tasks of the life cycle. The following is an example of someone whose life was constructed, by contrast, as a series of dissociative shifts.

A man sought help in mid life, presenting with depression and a general sense of turmoil. He had taken to dressing in army fatigues, had developed an interest in martial arts, and expressed desires to spend time living alone in a tent on isolated moorland or forestry. Prior to this he had worked for 20 years as a respected civil servant, wearing a conventional dark suit every day. He was married with three grown-up children. The shift in his mental state and life style had been preceded by a period in which he had been pursued by a rather predatory woman, with whom he eventually had an affair. Having initially strongly resisted the advances of this woman he subsequently became intensely attached to her and was devastated when she ultimately rejected him in a rather cruel way.

As he talked of his preference for living alone, his distrust of people generally, his hypervigilance and his new image of himself as a 'lone wolf', the therapist commented that he was sounding like somebody traumatised by war – like a Vietnam war veteran. He immediately responded to this analogy, agreeing that it was very apt. This led him to liken the way he felt now to an earlier period of his life, in his adolescence, when he had been sent abroad to a harsh military-style boarding school.

It was then possible to reconstruct the developmental sequence. His adolescence had been a period of trauma, involving loneliness, bullying and violence, with a sense of being essentially alone and having to fend for himself. He had developed character defences to deal with this, walling himself off emotionally, and developing a tough 'false self'. After leaving school he entered a period of heavy drinking, gambling and promiscuity which lasted about five years. Suddenly he stopped this way of life, embarked upon a respectable profession and made a conventional marriage, in which he assumed himself to be happy enough. In mid life he was insistently pursued by an attractive and predatory woman, offering a romantic, highly sexualised and exciting relationship. Whilst initially he rebuffed her in a manner consistent with his general view that it was not safe to let anyone get too close emotionally, the woman did eventually break through his defences, eliciting then an intense and needy attachment. Having gained his vulnerability, the woman triumphantly and seemingly sadistically rejected him, leaving him full of pain and shame. He was then left back in the same state of mind as the traumatised young adolescent at the military boarding school. As he and the therapist reviewed his life, he began to see that it had consisted of a series of discrete shifts rather than the more normal pattern of development with strands of continuity.

CHRONIC BUT SUBTLE DISSOCIATION

Sometimes dissociative states may be very pervasive but subtle and not immediately obvious to the clinician who is not attuned to these processes. Gradually a therapist may become aware that the patient seems to present in quite different moods and attitudes at different times, yet with enough continuity for the suspicion of gross dissociation to be dismissed. Analytic work may seem to be done, but resulting change is slow or non-existent; the patient may acquire important insight during one session, but in another session may talk as if this insight had not been achieved. The impression may be of a kind of stupefaction which prevents thinking and the linking of one piece of knowledge with another.

A patient would sometimes allude to terrible experiences that she may have had in childhood and appear very shocked by her own revelations, yet at other times talk as if her life had been quite uneventful. For the therapist it was rather as it might be if someone who had been in a Nazi concentration camp sometimes spoke in detail of the experience whilst at other times talked and behaved as if nothing like that had ever happened. Frequently she had dreams which represented idealisation of a situation, behind which was awful dereliction.

One day she reported a dream in which she was living in a log cabin in the woods and was looking forward to the winter, thinking how beautiful it would look when covered with snow. The therapist was somewhere in the picture and the patient gradually realised that the therapist was mad and had murdered someone. There were bunkbeds and the patient was underneath. She felt dampness and realised that blood was dripping on her and that the therapist had murdered a woman with a knife. She looked at the woman all cut up, with old stitches.

In her associations to the dream, she thought that her proximity to the murdered woman might be expressing the realisation that it was she herself who had in some sense been murdered; this represented some undoing of the original dissociation in which she had detached herself from the abused body. She recognised the idealisation and denial implicit in the musing about the beauty of the snow and how this gives way to a scene of utter horror. She also could see clearly expressed her terror of the therapist as a madman, not just in his transference role as a crazy father, but also as a lunatic who was attempting to return her to her ghastly and ghoulish memories. In the context of the content of recent sessions which had been concerned with considering her traumatic past, it was as if the dream was saying that anyone would be mad to want to go back to what she had been escaping from.

SUMMARY

Dissociation is the process whereby normally integrated streams of thought or consciousness are kept apart and communication between them restricted. This last ditch defence takes place in the face of repeated and overwhelming trauma. It begins with the child's self-hypnotic assertion 'I am not here; this is not happening to me; I am not in this body.' This pretence then becomes a structuring dynamic within the personality.

In its very nature, dissociation tends to be covert and easily overlooked. Some forms may be quite startling and dramatic when they do emerge, whilst others may be much more subtle. There may be stark dissociation between child and adult parts of the personality, between true and false self, and between sane and psychotic parts of the mind, and between different phases of life.

The defence of repression tends to apply to internally generated danger, whilst dissociation is brought into play against externally derived trauma, especially repeated trauma of sexual abuse. The notion of repression implies a single area of warded off mental contents, the 'unconscious', whilst dissociation implies multiple consciousnesses.

Chapter 2

A RECONSIDERATION OF FREUD'S VIEWS OF TRAUMA

EARLY TRAUMA THEORY: SEXUAL ABUSE; THE ECONOMIC MODEL; HELPLESSNESS; RETROACTIVE TRAUMA

The early writings of Freud were rooted in a trauma theory which in many ways is congruent with contemporary findings. In the following discussion I will introduce clinical examples to show the continuing applicability of some of these classic ideas.

Freud viewed neurotic disturbance as being the result of childhood sexual trauma, the effects of which might not be apparent at the time, but which acted like a kind of emotional time bomb, exploding after puberty when adult sexual desires and awareness threatened to reawaken the memory, now endowed with terrible meaning and overwhelming affect. The ego struggles to contain the trauma in the form of a symptom.

In *Draft K* (1896), Freud writes:

> The course taken by the illness in neuroses of repression is in general always the same: 1. The sexual experience (or series of experiences) which is traumatic and premature and is to be repressed. 2. Its repression on some later occasion which arouses a memory of it; at the same time the formation of a primary symptom. 3. A stage of successful defense which is equivalent to health except for the existence of the primary symptom. 4. The stage in which the repressed ideas return, and in which during the struggle between them and the ego, new symptoms are formed, which are those of the illness proper: that is the stage of adjustment, of being overwhelmed or of recovery with a malformation. (p. 222)

Freud maintained an *economic* view of trauma throughout his writings. By this term is meant the effect of the *quantity* of excitation which overwhelms the ego. In his Footnotes to the Translation of Charcot's *Tuesday Lectures* (1892), he wrote: 'A trauma would have to be defined as an accretion of excitation in the nervous system which the latter has been unable to dispose of adequately by motor reaction' (p. 137).

A little later, in his *Introductory Lectures* (1917), writing of trauma, he emphasised: 'Indeed the term has no other sense than an economic one. We apply it to an experience which within a short period of time presents the mind with an increase of stimulus too powerful to be dealt with or worked off in the normal way, and this must result in permanent disturbance of the manner in which the energy operates' (p. 275).

The purely economic dimension of trauma, the overwhelming with the *quantity* of excitation, is illustrated by a schizophrenic patient who described being in a state of overarousal due to the combination of anxiety about an exam and anticipation of a forthcoming holiday trip. She spoke of being paradoxically also on the edge of sleep – and agreed with the interpretation that she was trying to escape from the overarousal. She went on to describe how she felt very distant from her body and then expressed a thought of cutting her skin to examine the interior. She acknowledged that in this state of dissociation she was inclined to experience her body as alien and could feel a kind of detached curiosity about it and a wish to dissect it to see what it was made of – a recurrent delusion was that her skin was made of plastic. In this vignette can be seen a pattern which was characteristic for her: overarousal, followed by defensive dissociation, resulting in a sense of alienation from her body, experiencing of her body as not human, as made of plastic, and then cycling back to a wish to cut open her body partly in order to rediscover her humanity and aliveness. Her schizophrenic illness and associated difficulties in containing her emotions made her especially vulnerable to the traumatic aspect of overarousal. Strong emotions expressed by other people also tended to overwhelm and traumatise her. She could be said to have a poorly functioning 'stimulus barrier' or 'protective shield' (see Freud, 1920, 1926).

In *Inhibitions, Symptoms and Anxiety* (1926), Freud makes clear that he views the essence of trauma as the experience of *helplessness* in the face of an accumulation of tension or excitation which the ego cannot master. Children who are repeatedly sexually abused with the accompaniment of violence or threats of violence if they resist or tell, are chronically in this position of helplessness in the face of overwhelming excitation. Emergency mental defences are brought into play.

Freud implies that the trauma may impinge twice – first at the original moment and then later when the memory is revived. In *Further Remarks on the Psychoneuroses* (1896b), he writes:

the symptoms of hysteria can only be understood if they are traced back to the experiences which have a traumatic effect, and that these psychical traumas refer to the patient's sexual life . . . it is not the experiences themselves which act traumatically but their revival as a *memory* after the subject has entered on sexual maturity. (pp. 163–164)

In one sense Freud is surely wrong here. Sexual abuse certainly does disturb the child and often sets in train very severe mental strategies, often dissociative, in an attempt to deal with the repeated trauma. However he is making a very important point in emphasising the trauma inherent in the stimulation of memory of trauma. A patient whose therapeutic process involved her deeply in a spontaneous reliving of her childhood experiences of abuse, with associated feelings of terror and despair, complained that it was very unfair that she had to be traumatised twice, originally in her childhood and then again in her therapy as an adult.

It is a common clinical finding that when a patient recovers memories of childhood sexual abuse, whether within therapy or not, he/she may then feel much worse. I have often found that a patient may talk about a memory of abuse during a session, and after exploring its meaning and its associated affects, he/she appears to feel relieved and more hopeful as a result of the work done in that session – only to find that subsequently the patient feels more agitated, depressed and suicidal because other memories of abuse have been flooding into their mind. The patient then feels overwhelmed – traumatised as they were originally in childhood. At such times the patient may in some cases need to be hospitalised; then the containing hospital environment is carrying some of the functions of the 'protective shield' or 'stimulus barrier'.

As Freud described, the stimulation of memories of childhood sexual abuse as a result of the natural sexual developments of adolescence can provoke severe symptoms. This is the idea of *retroactive trauma*. The early experiences are given new meaning by the sexual desires and awareness of adolescence; the adolescent is capable of understanding the sexual significance of the abuser's activity and of appreciating the violation that was involved. The young woman who has been sexually violated in childhood is deprived of the opportunity to discover her own sexuality naturally and in her own time. It is as if a gift package has been opened and its contents spoiled before she receives it. Her inclination is to turn away and have nothing to do with it.

An 18-year-old woman had become suicidally depressed. She had also displayed some epileptic style seizures, which had been investigated and were felt to be of psychogenic origin. She disclosed that she had been sexually abused by a relative over a period of several years, ending at puberty, but she denied that this was of significance in how she was feel-ing now. She said she had no idea why she was feeling depressed and emphasised that she had not felt depressed as a child. Carefully and tact-fully the therapist explored her relationships with her peers and her thoughts about boyfriends. She revealed that she had attempted to avoid any interest in boys and had tried to associate with other girls who simi-larly had interests other than the opposite sex. She said that when neces-sary she had pretended to her peers to have a normal interest in boys. She knew that she was frightened of boys and that she had tried to tell herself that she need have nothing to do with them other than platoni-cally; the problem was that increasingly she knew that she did wish she could have a boyfriend like other girls. The therapist put to her that although she had downplayed the significance of the sexual abuse, it seemed very likely that her natural sexual interests at this stage of her life were threatening to remind her of her earlier experiences of abuse, leav-ing her with a sense of her sexuality having been defiled and spoiled – and that she would be likely to be left with despair and considerable rage at the realisation that although she might want to have normal relation-ships with the opposite sex this natural desire had been contaminated by the violations of her childhood. Her response was to agree that all of this was correct, but she insisted that she did not want to talk about the sexual abuse and that she would not continue with therapy if that was required. When asked if she felt better or worse as a result of the discussion she said she felt worse, more depressed and suicidal; she agreed that this seemed to confirm that her depression was associated with the implica-tions of her sexual abuse and that it was exacerbated as her memories were stimulated. The hysterical seizures were almost certainly a soma-tised expression of her rage about the abuse. Her insistence that she would not talk about the abuse indicated how intolerable, overwhelming and unmanageable (i.e. traumatic) she felt the experiences to be. This patient could be taken as an illustration of Freud's claim, as early as 1895 in his Project that 'a memory is repressed which has only become a trauma after the event. The reason for this state of things is the retarda-tion of puberty as compared with the remainder of the individual's devel-opment' (p. 413).

For these reasons it is common that when a patient begins to re-experi-ence memories of childhood abuse as a result of therapy – or begins to get in touch with the affect which had been dissociated from memories that had otherwise not been repressed – the patient unconsciously perceives the therapist as an abuser. The patient is retraumatised as the memories of helplessness in the face of abuse are re-encountered and perceives the therapist as responsible for this. Whereas the trauma originally was of external origin, the memories now provide an *internal* source of trauma.

The therapist *is* responsible in part for exposing the patient to trauma again.

At this stage of therapy the patient may complain that she used to be able to avoid thinking about the early abuse but as a consequence of focusing upon it in the therapy she now cannot get it out of her thoughts. She may feel utterly overwhelmed with memories and images of trauma, feelings of helplessness and rage, wishes for revenge, feelings of futility, and above all, suicidal impulses as she contemplates her lifelong attempts to pretend to herself that she was unaffected by the childhood experience.

A relatively mild example of this was shown by a woman in therapy who had recently begun to talk of childhood experiences of sexual abuse within the family – experiences which she had always remembered. She reported that she had begun to feel very much more anxious about coming to her sessions since talking of these events; she was also feeling more depressed. She commented that as she thought about her childhood it all seemed horrifying, all the more so because now she could understand what the abuse had been about in a way that she had not been able to as a child.

INTERNAL AND EXTERNAL SOURCES OF TRAUMA

Freud never abandoned the idea that sexual trauma in childhood may be common and that this may contribute to substantial psychological problems in some cases. He simply lost interest in such a specific environmental causation of neurosis that may apply to some children only. His concern was with universal features of the structure and dynamics of the mind. He had recognised that the encounter with repressed memory is traumatic, but he began to see that a more subtle source of internal trauma is the child's own wishes and fantasies, notably the Oedipus complex.

In *An Outline of Psychoanalysis* (1940a), he writes:

> Analytic experience has convinced us of the complete truth of the assertion so often to be heard that the child is psychologically father to the adult and that the events of the first years are of paramount importance for his whole later life. It will thus be of special interest to us if there is something that may be described as the central experience of this period of childhood. Our attention is first attracted by the effects of certain influences which do not apply to all children though they are common enough – such as the sexual seduction of children by adults, their seduction by other children (brothers or sisters) slightly their seniors, and what we should not expect, their being deeply stirred by seeing or hearing at first hand sexual behaviour between

adults (their parents) mostly at a time which one would not have thought they could either be interested in or understand any such impressions, or be capable of remembering them later. It is easy to confirm the extent to which such experiences arouse a child's susceptibility and force his own sexual urges into certain channels from which they cannot afterwards depart . . .

However instructive cases of this kind may be, a still higher degree of interest must attach to the influence of a situation which every child is destined to pass through and which follows inevitably from the factor of the prolonged period during which a child is cared for by other people and lives with his parents. I am thinking of the Oedipus complex . . . (p. 187)

Here Freud is pursuing the idea that trauma can be produced by the impingement on the ego of frightening instinctual impulses and associated fantasies.

Balint (1969) outlined some of the differences between Freud's early and later theory of trauma. The first concerned the economic impact of excessive excitation from an external source, whereas the later emphasis was upon dynamic tensions from within the mind. He wrote:

The new theory starts with assumption that the trauma, in spite of its appearance, is not an external event; it is produced by the individual himself as fantasy. It cannot claim easily that the individual was unprepared and was flooded by an excessive amount of excitation because after all it was he himself who produced the fantasy; on the other hand, it can claim the existence of very high intensity strains between the various parts of the mental apparatus, for instance, the id which forced the ego to indulge in fantasy making and the superego which orders that this activity should be suppressed. I hope that it will prove acceptable if I propose to call this new theory essentially structural. (p. 430)

The emphasis of most psychoanalysts since has been upon the traumatic collision between an external event and an internal fantasy. This is illustrated in the following example.

Dr Green, a young psychiatrist in therapy, always appeared very sensitive to any indication that the therapist might have crossed a boundary, for example a time boundary by being slightly late or by overrunning a session, or to any evidence that the therapist's functioning was less than optimum. Any such episodes would cause her to be extremely anxious and to be very preoccupied with the fantasy that she had omnipotently caused the therapist to act that way. She was also adamant that she could not use the analytic couch, with the implication that to have done so would have had some sexual connotation for her. Usually it seemed that her monitoring of the therapist's functioning was rooted in her experience of her father who had developed a brain disorder and had become confused when Dr Green was aged about nine. Often the impression was that Dr Green felt she had somehow caused this confusion.

Dr Green would always arrive late for her session, quite consciously and deliberately because her great fear was of arriving on time and finding that the therapist was late. Analysis of this often suggested that the therapist's lateness would mean that he was confused or drunk like Dr Green's father. On one occasion her worst fears were realised. The therapist overslept and having hurriedly got ready was somewhat dishevelled and slightly disoriented when he met Dr Green in the waiting room. Dr Green was profoundly shocked by this, deeply convinced that she had caused the therapist to react in this uncharacteristic way, and she was fearful that this confirmed that she could cause him to do almost anything.

During another session she presented an amusing narrative based around the grandiosity and slightly absurd behaviour of a colleague. In the next session she warned the therapist that she might have been exaggerating or distorting the account and expressed worries that she might not be perceiving situations correctly. She appeared very concerned that she might have given a misleading impression of the colleague. Eventually the therapist commented that this might be like the predicament of a child who wants to tell about something that has been going on but who is afraid of the implications if she is listened to and believed. In response Dr Green spoke of one of her own patients who had been talking of how her father used to play with her and tickle her and she had enjoyed this, but at a certain point she had no longer felt that this was safe; she had felt confused however about whether she was right to feel this and whether she should speak to her mother about it.

The therapist elaborated on some of the implied difficulties in the girl's experience. The situation was ambiguous. She did not know whether what was going on between her and her father was 'safe' or sexual. She could not be sure whether there was really something wrong about her father's involvement with her, or whether she was imagining (projecting) this. This was mirrored in the ambiguity in Dr Green's account of it – what was meant by the words 'play' and 'tickle'? Above all, the young pubertal girl did not even have the words and concepts with which to think about the problem. In talking to Dr Green the woman felt that as a child she had been afraid of telling her mother of her worries because she might have misperceived the situation, might have misunderstood and so might either be condemned herself or have her father condemned when he was actually innocent. The story raised clearly the question of whether the threat came from outside (father) or from inside (the girl's own sexual wishes). Finally the therapist commented that of course Dr

Green was perhaps using the reference to her own patient as a way of talking about aspects of her own conflicts.

In response Dr Green talked of how, as a child, she would rivalrously try to be a replacement for her mother when the latter was sometimes away for several weeks at a time. She would try to be a superior cook and homemaker – and, crucially, would sleep in her father's bed, even though her mother had expressly forbidden her to do so. She explained that there were occasions when her father would be confused due to alcohol and a neurological disorder; she surmised that there could have been times when her father might have mistaken his daughter for his wife in bed and have made a sexual approach to her. Dr Green began to recognise that she had probably experienced a terrifying, confusing and traumatic fulfilment of her Oedipal wishes – and that this had contributed to her recurrent fear that she could have an omnipotent effect on people and cause them to deviate from their normal behaviour and break boundaries. This meant that any disruption in the therapist's functioning threatened to traumatise Dr Green by stimulating her fantasies of omnipotently causing him to deviate from appropriate behaviour.

In this material, Dr Green experienced the therapist at times as the potentially confused and disorientated father with whom she might have a sexual involvement or in other ways bring about the terrifying fulfilment of forbidden wishes – and at times as the mother to whom she might wish to confess and who might condemm her. With regard to both she feared she had the power to control and mislead them and she looked fearfully for evidence that this fantasy was reality.

BEYOND THE PLEASURE PRINCIPLE. TRAUMA AND THE DEATH INSTINCT

Freud considered that most of mental life was governed by the pleasure principle (modified by the reality principle) – that pleasure was sought and 'unpleasure' avoided. However, in 1920 he described how trauma, impinging from outside, might overwhelm the pleasure principle and set in motion a quite different and more primitive line of reaction. He wrote:

> We describe as 'traumatic' any excitations from outside which are powerful enough to break through the protective shield. It seems to me that the concept of trauma necessarily implies a connection of this kind with a breach in an otherwise efficacious barrier against stimuli. Such an event as external trauma is bound to provoke a disturbance on a grand scale in the functioning of the organism's energy and to set in motion every possible defensive measure. At the same time the pleasure principle is for the moment put out

of action. There is no longer any possibility of preventing the mental apparatus from being flooded with large amounts of stimulus, and another problem arises instead – the problem of mastering the amounts of stimulus that have broken in and of binding them, in the psychical sense, so they can then be disposed of. (1920, pp. 29–30)

Freud goes on to discuss the function of traumatic dreams in which the frightening events are relived, which he notes are an exception to his formulation of dreams as wishfulfilling. These dreams are very distressing. Why does the dreamer dream them? He writes:

The fulfilment of wishes is, as we know, brought about in an hallucinatory manner by dreams, and under the dominance of the pleasure principle this has become their function. But it is not in the service of that principle that the dreams of patients suffering from traumatic neuroses lead them back with such regularity to the situation in which the trauma occurred. We may assume, rather, that dreams are here helping to carry out another task, which must be accomplished before the dominance of the pleasure principle can even begin. These dreams are endeavouring to master the stimulus retrospectively, by developing the anxiety whose omission was the cause of the traumatic neurosis. (1920, p. 32)

Freud considered that these dreams were trying to master the trauma by discharging the excessive excitation in the form of anxiety which had not been sufficiently expressed at the time of the trauma. It is worth noting that although the word 'mastery' is used, Freud did not appear to think the attempt was to achieve a *sense* of mastery – because he was not concerned with the sense of self and the strivings to repair a damaged sense of self resulting from experiences of overwhelming helplessness. His remained an essentially economic model of trauma.

Freud felt that he discerned in a variety of mental phenomena that were 'beyond the pleasure principle' the tendency to return to an earlier state, ultimately to an inorganic state of death. He postulated the existence of a 'death instinct' balanced against the strivings of the life instinct. In this theory, the death instinct is to a large extent fused with the life instinct and is turned outwards and in that way its destructive power is held in check.

In *The Ego and the Id* (1923) Freud adds the following comment:

Once we have admitted the idea of a fusion of the two classes of instincts with each other, the possibility of a – more or less complete – 'defusion' of them forces itself upon us . . . and we come to understand that instinctual defusion and the marked emergence of the death instinct call for particular consideration among the effects of some severe neuroses . . . (pp. 41–42)

A little later he makes the point that the death instinct is usually rather hidden and that the derivatives of Eros the life instinct are more obvious:

> Over and over again we find, when we are able to trace instinctual impulses back, that they reveal themselves as derivatives of Eros. If it were not for the considerations put forward in *Beyond the Pleasure Principle,* and ultimately for the sadistic constituents which have attached themselves to Eros, we should have difficulty in holding to our fundamental dualistic point of view. But since we cannot escape that view, we are driven to conclude that the death instincts are by their nature mute and that the clamour of life proceeds for the most part from Eros. (p. 46)

Beyond the Pleasure Principle is a study of trauma and its effects and also his first speculative postulation of the concept of the death instinct. Curiously he fails to consider the implicit point that perhaps trauma and the emergence of the death instinct are related. Certainly it seems to this author that the one circumstance in which the two instincts might be violently defused, releasing 'raw' death instinct, is that of overwhelming abusive trauma. It is not difficult to imagine situations in which great quantities of aggression are stimulated which are far too much to be neutralised by the available libido or Eros. The following might be an example of this.

A young woman who claimed to have been very extensively abused by her father throughout her childhood and adolescence, and who had used dissociative defences to cope with this, spent a therapy session talking about a particular experience of being tied to the bed and gagged by her father whilst he performed a variety of abusive and terrifying acts upon her. During this she described immense feelings of rage and hatred directed at her father. At the end of the session she reported feeling better and said that this had been her worst experience with her father. However, in the days following this she experienced a resurgence of dissociative hallucinatory inner voices shouting at her that she must kill herself, that she deserved to die, accompanied by a feeling of being overwhelmed by memories of abuse. She found great difficulty in resisting the impulse to kill or injure herself.

Her experiences of abuse, of being violated and tortured and completely humiliated, whilst being controlled and restrained and rendered utterly helpless, must have stimulated vast destructive rage which could find no external target – even though she had full consciousness of the object of her rage. There was no unconscious defence against awareness of the rage, as we might find for example in a state of severe depression, but the overwhelming affect could not be discharged. Her physical restraint during the abuse meant that even gross motor discharge through kicking, hitting or screaming was prevented. Neither fight nor flight was possible. Moreover there was no loving and comforting caregiver who could foster the Eros needed to bind or neutralise the death-seeking impulses. It is a common experience that if a person feels humiliated or wronged he/she is likely to feel rage, but if there is a friend, parent or lover who can offer empathy, sympathy and love, the violent feelings tend to subside as Eros is restored – but for the child isolated in her abuse this is not available.

Another example of trauma and threat to survival releasing overwhelming and dangerous aggression and 'death instinct' is the following case of a woman who had been greatly abused in childhood. One day the patient received a letter from her landlord saying that she was going to be evicted for getting behind with the rent. She had been expecting a letter of this kind and had been afraid to open it on her own and so had brought it to her session. On reading it during the session she did not react unduly but five minutes after the session ended the therapist received a desperate phone call from her, saying that she was at the railway station and was afraid she was not going to be able to make the journey home. The therapist had another patient about to arrive and so kept the call brief and promised to phone her an hour later; she appeared relieved. The next session the patient was extremely anxious, too afraid to enter the consulting room initially, and eventually explaining that she was afraid she would murder the therapist. She argued that he did not care about her because he had abandoned her in her terror and she could easily have been dead. She then made clear that her specific anxiety at the railway station had been that she would throw herself under a train and that she had been very frightened that she would not be able to stop herself doing so. She talked of feeling overwhelmed with terror and rage. She feared that it was not safe for her to leave the session with her murderous impulses still inside her because it might be herself that she murdered.

In this example can be seen how a threat to survival (the threat of eviction) evoked fundamental responses of fight and flight (rage and terror). But the aggression of the 'fight' response is deeper and more complex than an impulse to attack a perceived enemy. Her initial impulse was to kill herself. She sought help against this death drive within herself by phoning the therapist whom she hoped would be on the side of Eros and the preservation of her life – that he would be a 'protective shield'. On failing to find sufficient of this support she perceived him as an enemy who abandoned her to Thanatos, to the terror of the unbound death rage. She resorted to directing her 'death instinct' outwards, just as Freud and later Melanie Klein described; it was as though she then felt that either she or the therapist must die. Freud's comments in 1923 are relevant:

> the death instinct . . . can successfully be neutralised and the destructive impulses be diverted onto the external world . . . and the death instinct would thus seem to express . . . itself as an instinct of destruction directed against the external world and other organisms. (1923, p. 41)

THE DEMOLITION OF SIGNAL ANXIETY

In Freud's last great work on anxiety and trauma, *Inhibitions, Symptoms and Anxiety* (1926), he distinguishes a traumatic situation involving helplessness, the automatic anxiety that results from this, and the lesser 'signal anxiety' which is mobilised by the ego in the hope of avoiding a repeat of the original overwhelming anxiety.

> we go on to enquire what the essence and meaning of a danger situation is. Clearly it consists in the subject's estimation of his own strength compared to the magnitude of the danger and in his admission of helplessness in the face of it – physical helplessness if the danger is real and psychical helplessness if it is instinctual . . . Let us call a situation of helplessness of this kind that has been actually experienced a *traumatic situation*. We shall then have good grounds for distinguishing a traumatic situation from a danger-situation.

> The individual will have made an important advance in his capacity for self-preservation if he can foresee and expect a traumatic situation of this kind which entails helplessness, instead of simply waiting for it to happen. Let us call a situation which contains the determinant for such an expectation a danger-situation. It is in this situation that the signal of anxiety is given. The signal announces: 'I am expecting a situation of helplessness to set in . . .Therefore I will anticipate the trauma and behave as though it had already come, while there is still time to turn it aside.' Anxiety is therefore on the one hand an expectation of a trauma, and on the other hand a repetition of it in a mitigated form. (p. 166)

Where a child is being abused by a parent for the parent's sadistic pleasure, as in the example given above of the girl who was tied and gagged by the father, and where rendering the child utterly helpless is an intrinsic part of the perversion, then this sequence of the development of signal anxiety cannot occur – since there is no way the child can escape. Signal anxiety and traumatic anxiety collapse together. The child must resort to other forms of mental defence, ones which are more detrimental to contact with reality, such as multiple dissociation.

In this work Freud (1923) describes a series of anxieties centred around different kinds of loss, such as loss of the caregiver or loss of the caregiver's love. The implication is that the infant and child will naturally look to the caregiver as the protection against trauma, against danger and helplessness. This may be so, but what is completely overlooked here is the question of what it means if the caregiver is him/herself the source of the danger and the trauma. What if the giver of life appears as the threat to life ? The protector is the killer. Little surprise then if the child develops a perverse and sinister superego, or even a multiplicity of internal figures who beckon towards death. No wonder that severe and malevolent child abuse by a parent is so difficult for us to think about and so often seems to evoke emotional confusion!

SUMMARY

Freud regarded trauma as essentially an 'economic' problem – the ego is overwhelmed with affect and excitation. He proposed that childhood sexual abuse had a retroactive effect; the sexuality of adolescence stirring the childhood memories, now imbued with an alarming meaning. In his later writings on the 'death instinct' he considered the compulsion to repeat episodes relating to trauma. His argument suggests, but does not quite make explicit, the implication that trauma leads to 'defusion of the instincts' with the resulting release of unbound death instinct and consequent impulses towards self-destruction and intense anxiety. Many of Freud's views are compatible with contemporary understanding of the response to trauma.

Chapter 3

BACK TO JANET. EARLY STUDIES OF TRAUMA, REPRESSION AND DISSOCIATION

The theory of repression is the foundation stone on which the structure of psycho-analysis rests.

(Freud, 1914, p.16)

At the end of the nineteenth century, clinicians in various parts of Europe and the United States were studying disturbances of consciousness, and exploring hypnosis as a means of investigation and treatment. Amongst these, Janet developed an elaborate theory of dissociation stemming from trauma, which has remarkable relevance to many contemporary developments in this area. His theory fell largely into oblivion for the best part of a century, usually being quite misrepresented whenever it was referred to in textbooks. Janet's ideas have often been compared unfavourably with those of Freud, giving the misleading impression of a theory which rested essentially on an idea of hereditary weakness in the integrative powers of the mind. Freud's concept of repression and of the neuropsy-choses of 'defence' became the predominant paradigm for dynamic psychiatry and eclipsed the Janetian concept of dissociation. This meant that the study of trauma and the understanding of multiple consciousness went into obscurity. The concept of repression, as Breuer pointed out in his book coauthored with Freud (1893–95), implies a division of the mind, but not a splitting of consciousness; by definition the 'unconscious' is not conscious. Bound by the concept of repression, psychoanalysis could not accommodate the phenomena of multiple consciousnesses.

This direction of psychoanalysis is strange considering its origins in the case of Anna O, who is credited with the creation of the 'talking cure'. Anna O was described as having two states of consciousness, not a conscious and an unconscious mind:

Throughout the entire illness her two states of consciousness persisted side by side: the primary one in which she was quite normal psychically, and

the secondary one which may well be likened to a dream in view of its
wealth of imaginative products and hallucinations, its large gaps in memory and the lack of inhibition and control in its associations . . . [T]he
patient's mental condition was entirely dependent upon the intrusion of
this secondary state into the normal one . . . It is hard to avoid expressing
the situation by saying that the patient was split into two personalities of
which one was mentally normal and the other insane. (Freud & Breuer
1893, p. 45)

Thus in this case of Breuer's, a clear division or dissociation of the personality is described, which is also a division of consciousness – states of
awareness alternating or coexisting. This is presented even more clearly
in the following quote:

Nevertheless, though her two states were thus sharply separated, not only
did the secondary state intrude into the first one, but – and this was at all
events frequently true, and even when she was in a very bad condition – a
clear-sighted and calm observer sat, as she put it, in a corner of her brain
and looked on at all the mad business. (p. 46)

Here Breuer is describing the coexistence of a sane reality-oriented consciousness and a dreamlike 'insane' consciousness. It is like an idea of a
dreaming mind invading a waking mind. This is a far cry from the
Freudian notion which developed shortly afterwards, of instinctual derivatives, banished to the 'unconscious' (i.e. the 'without consciousness')
and pushing their way back through a repression barrier to form disguised expression in dreams or neurotic symptoms. Breuer's patient presents symptoms much more along the lines of multiple personality. This
is indicated in the following comment:

At a time when, after the hysterical phenomena had ceased, the patient was
passing through a temporary depression, she brought up a number of child-
ish fears and self-reproaches, and among them the idea that she had not
been ill at all and that the whole business had been simulated . . . When a
disorder of this kind has cleared up and the two states of consciousness have
once more become merged into one, the patients, looking back to the past,
see themselves as the single undivided personality which was aware of all
the nonsense; they think they could have prevented it if they had wanted
to, and thus feel as though they had done all the mischief deliberately. (p 46)

This is a good description of the view taken sometimes by patients who
recover from a multiple personality disorder or from a schizophrenic psychosis. It is as if the sane observing part of the mind has passively
allowed a mental illness to evolve – or at least believes itself to have done
so. We can again remind ourselves of Hilgard's (1977) notion of the hidden observer in states of hypnosis – a part that observes reality, such as
pain, and is not taken in by the hypnotic trickery.

Somewhat later in the text, Breuer makes the same point again:

> Many intelligent patients admit that their conscious ego was quite lucid during the attack and looked on with curiosity and surprise at all the mad things they did and said. Such patients have, furthermore, the (erroneous) belief that with a little good-will they could have inhibited the attack, and they are inclined to blame themselves for it. (p. 228)

Of course the impression of potential control over the mental state may be quite illusory. To give a contemporary example from this author's practice, a patient spontaneously shifted into the state of mind of a child alter, crouched on the floor near the therapist and began to speak of how her father kept hitting her. She spoke in the present tense as if she was actually a child. In the next session she talked of her sense of shock and embarrassment afterwards on her realisation of her behaviour. She said it had felt as though she was somehow acting, and yet it had also felt very real and spontaneous. She thought that perhaps she had been able to enact her childhood experiences in this way because she had come to feel safe enough with the therapist. This implies that the therapeutic environment was tried and tested enough for her to allow a regressive and disso-ciative enactment to take place. However, there had been other occasions when this patient had experienced no control over her spontaneous regressions into child states of mind, with consequent disasters in some areas of her life. It was quite unclear how much real choice and control over regression and dissociation this patient could have.

HYPNOID STATES

The early discussions of hysteria contained many comparisons with hyp-nosis and hypnotic-like states, including autohypnosis. Some, including Breuer, thought that those prone to hysteria had a natural tendency spontaneously to enter states of self-hypnosis. Breuer hypothesised that ideas developing in these dreamlike auto-hypnotic states, or reveries – 'delirium hystericum', were cut off from the reality testing that goes on in the normal waking state.

> What happens during auto-hypnotic states is subject to more or less total amnesia in waking life . . . The amnesia withdraws the psychical products of these states, the associations that have been formed in them, from any correction during waking thought; and since in auto-hypnosis criticism and supervision by reference to other ideas is diminished, and as a rule, disap-pears almost completely, the wildest delusions may arise from it and remain untouched for long periods. (p. 216)

The penetration of the hypnotic state into the lucid waking state was seen as like the intrusion of madness into an otherwise sane mind: 'The patient's mental condition was entirely dependent upon the intrusion of this secondary state into her normal one . . .' (p. 45).

A patient in the author's caseload would appear quite rational and sane but if allowed to talk freely would speak of her belief that the hospital was a church and that blood was bleeding from the radiators and that dead rats were lying all over the ward; it was as if her dreamlike state of 'delerium hystericum' would leak into her rational state of mind. In this patient, as in Breuer's Anna O, the 'delerious' state was not unconscious but at times took part freely in waking life; this is quite different to Freud's model of defence hysteria in which unwanted mental contents are banished to the unconscious mind, from where they force their way back, finding disguised expression, in dreams, parapraxes and neurotic symptoms. Basically there is no way that Anna O conforms to Freud's model of hysteria and her presence and fame sit uncomfortably at the very origins of psychoanalysis – as Freud acknowledges in remarks on page 285 of their joint work.

Paradoxically, this point is illustrated by Breuer's attempt to fit Anna O to Freud's concepts. The first published use of the term the 'unconscious' in a psychoanalytic context occurred in Breuer's description of his patient: 'Every one of her hypnoses in the evening afforded evidence that the patient was entirely clear and well-ordered in her mind and normal as regards her feeling and volition so long as none of the products of her secondary state was acting as a stimulus "in the unconscious" ' (p. 45).

The editor, Strachey, suggests that the fact that Breuer puts the term 'unconscious' in quotation marks may indicate that he attributes it to Freud. This seems very likely because in fact the notion of the unconscious makes no sense at all in this sentence; if the phrase 'in the unconscious' is omitted the sentence is actually more coherent. Breuer is not referring to an unconscious part of the mind but to an alternative consciousness.

Some parts of Breuer's description are very close to accounts of multiple personality: 'She used to hallucinate in the middle of a conversation, run off, start climbing up a tree, etc. If one caught hold of her, she would very quickly take up her interrupted sentence without knowing anything about what had happened in the interval' (p. 31).

Breuer juxtaposed two possible origins of hysteria. He thought that a crucial component of the hysterical state is the presence of an emotion-laden idea which is cut off from the normal processes of 'wearing away' through association with other ideas, through thinking and reality test-

ing. The result was that the idea is withdrawn from its 'associative contact' and, thus isolated, it retains its 'quota of affect' which might then
find expression through the hysterical symptom. Breuer suggested that
the affective idea could be excluded from its associative network either
through 'defence' – 'the deliberate suppression of distressing ideas which
seem to threaten his happiness or self-esteem' – or because the idea cannot be recalled because it occurred in an altered mental state similar to
hypnosis, a state he called 'hypnoid'.

Breuer suggested that 'pathogenic auto-hypnosis' could come about
when an affect is introduced into a state of hypnoid reverie. His example
was of how Anna O may have entered into this state in the twilight environment of the sickroom, a reverie that could then have become charged
with affect as a result of a particular train of thought. Anna O appeared to
have a particular disposition towards these dreamy hypnoid states of
mind – her 'private theatre' as she called it. Affect introduced in the hypnoid state could not then be 'worn away' through associations in the normal waking consciousness.

Breuer thought that some people may be more predisposed than others
to enter hypnoid states. He argued that when the reverie is repeated
again and again the person develops three main states of mind: waking,
sleeping and the hypnoid state. Breuer juxtaposes his own theory of hysteria arising from hypnoid states with Freud's theory of defence, accepting that both are possible routes to hysteria. What Breuer does not
consider here is the possibility that the hypnoid state is itself a defence
and perhaps a very fundamental one.

However, Breuer does hint that the hypnoid state may have something
to do with trauma. He does so by quoting with approval the following
remarks by Moebius, which he considers 'embody an important truth':

> The necessary condition for the (pathogenic) operation of ideas is, on the
> one hand, an innate – that is, hysterical – disposition and, on the other, a
> special frame of mind. We can only form an imprecise idea of this frame of
> mind. It must resemble a state of hypnosis; it must correspond to some kind
> of vacancy of consciousness in which an emerging idea meets with no resis-
> tance from any other – in which, so to speak, the field is clear for the first
> comer. We know that a state of this kind can be brought about not only by
> hypnotism but by emotional shock (fright, anger, etc.) and by exhausting
> factors (sleeplessness, hunger, and so on). (Moebius, 1894, quoted in Breuer
> & Freud, 1893–95)

Thus the hypnoid state is described here as a kind of detachment or
'vacancy'. This is precisely what is described by some articulate patients
with multiple personalities, who speak of extracting their awareness from

a situation of childhood trauma and becoming able to look on at the situation of abuse from a subjective position outside their body – such as the patient who described positioning herself in a crack in the ceiling or in a lightbulb. Other people describe moments of vacancy *between* personalities – a state of pure dissociation, a kind of empty mind state, prior to the emergence of a particular personality alter. One patient conveyed a sense of terror that could accompany these vacant moments, which we eventually likened to a dread of falling through the 'cracks' between personalities.

Even if a hypnoid state were not a *defence* against trauma, the state of detachment can certainly be a *response* to trauma, as is well known in relation to post traumatic stress disorder. Derealisation, depersonalisation and numbing are basic features of the response to trauma (Horowitz, 1986). Breuer actually implies something like this in a brief mention of 'traumatic neuroses': 'During the first few days after the traumatic event, the state of hypnoid fright is repeated every time the event is recalled' (p. 235).

SPLITTING AND REPRESSION

The term 'splitting' is used a great deal in Freud and Breuer's joint work, as is 'repression'.

Breuer contrasts their description of splitting of the mind with notions of splitting of consciousness. He argues that he and Freud are describing states in which ideas are divided into some admissible to consciousness and some inadmissible to consciousness. By definition therefore, this cannot be a splitting of consciousness but it is a splitting of the mind into consciousness and unconsciousness. This is the process that was later almost exclusively referred to as 'repression'.

Breuer acknowledges that other investigators such as Binet and Janet had found states of splitting of *consciousness*, which might currently be called multiple personality:

> It may be remarked that the findings of Binet and Janet deserve to be described as a splitting not merely of psychical activity but of consciousness. As we know, these observers have succeeded in getting into contact with their patient's 'subconscious', with the portion of psychical activity of which the conscious waking ego knows nothing; and they have been able in some cases to demonstrate the presence of all the psychical functions, including self-consciousness, in that portion, since it has access to the memory of earlier psychical events. This half of a mind is therefore quite complete and conscious in itself. In our cases the part of the mind which is split off is 'thrust into darkness', as the Titans are imprisoned in the crater of

Etna, and can shake the earth but can never emerge into the light of day. In Janet's cases the division of the realm of the mind has been a total one. Nevertheless, there is still inequality in status. But this too disappears when the two halves of consciousness alternate, as they do in the well-known cases of *double conscience,* and when they do not differ in their functional capacity. (p. 229)

Breuer agrees with Janet that 'splitting of psychical activity occurs in the more severe degrees of hysteria and that it alone seems to make a psychical theory of the illness possible' (p. 230). However, he states his 'complete opposition' (p. 233) to Janet's views regarding the origin of this splitting – which he also for the first time here calls 'dissociation'. He misleadingly claims that Janet considered that hysterical splitting rested entirely upon an innate psychological weakness and argued that the latter's views were formed from the study of 'feeble minded hysterical patients who are to be found in hospitals or institutions', in contrast to his and Freud's study of 'educated hysterical patients'. Clearly at this point there was great rivalry between the theories of Janet, on the one hand, and Breuer and Freud, on the other.

FREUD'S CONCEPT OF REPRESSION

After the *Studies on Hysteria,* Freud's interest moved away from environmentally derived trauma and towards the innate conflicts of the mind, especially the Oedipus complex, and the repression of instinctual impulses. In his 1915 paper on repression, he described the process as involving two components: first that of 'primal repression', in which the ideational representation of the instinct is denied access to the conscious mind, resulting in a fixation, drawing to itself related ideas; secondly there is 'repression proper', an 'after pressure' which pushes down mental *derivatives* of the instinct. He suggested that when the instinctual representative is withdrawn by repression from conscious influence it 'proliferates in the dark, as it were, and takes on extreme forms of expression'. Freud distinguishes the fate of the repressed idea from that of the associated affect; he believed that the affect itself, the instinctual energy, could not be repressed but only displaced to another idea.

In addition to his discussions of repression of an instinct and an idea, Freud also wrote of repression of various other mental contents:

of phantasies, in the *Fliess Papers* (SE 1) and in *Formulations on Two Principles of Mental Functioning* (SE 12);

of knowledge (sexual), in *The Sexual Theories of Children* (SE 9);

of envy (of the penis), in *On Transformations of Instinct* (SE 17);

of the Oedipus complex, in *Three Essays on Sexuality* (SE 7) and *The Ego and the Id* (SE 19);

of an identification, in *Moses and Monotheism* (SE 23);

of traumatic memories (of sexual abuse), in *An Outline of Psychoanalysis* (SE 23).

As Freud's theories developed, although he never entirely disregarded externally impinging trauma, they became increasingly a theory of innate phylogenetically programmed conflict and less of a trauma-based model of psychopathology. The concept of repression applies well to a theory of instinctual conflict, but less well to a theory of trauma. 'Repression' implies a mastery of an instinct by pushing it back down from whence it comes, whereas 'dissociation' implies an attempt to escape from some unbearable situation by denying, through a kind of pretence, that one is present.

JANET ON TRAUMA AND DISSOCIATION

> Man, all too proud, figures that he is master of his movements, his words, his ideas and himself. It is perhaps of ourselves that we have least command. There are crowds of things that operate within ourselves without our will. (Pierre Janet, quoted by Ellenberger, 1970, p. 370)

Writing at the same time as Freud and Breuer, Janet was developing a theory of a trauma basis of mental disorder, linked with dissociation as a crucial mental mechanism – a framework which is much closer to the recently emerging contemporary understanding of post-traumatic stress disorder (van der Kolk, Brown & van der Hart, 1989; van der Hart & Horst, 1989; van der Hart & Friedman, 1989). An important text for this was 'L'Automatism psychologique'(1889), which unfortunately has not been translated into English. Janet did encounter patients with full-blown multiple personality.

Janet considered that traumatisation resulted from the failure to take effective action against a potential threat, resulting in helplessness, which in turn resulted in 'vehement emotions', which interfered with memory storage. In this can be seen some similarity with Freud's view of trauma as being to do with the helplessness of being overwhelmed with excitation.

Janet suggested that memory itself is a kind of action – the action of telling a story. This action of creating a narrative, by attaching words to the experience so that it can be made sense of, forms part of the wider action of responding appropriately to a situation. He argued (1935) 'Making intellectual sense of an unexpected challenge leads to proper adaptation and a subjective sense of calm and control' (p. 409). The vehement emotions aroused by the frightening and overwhelming event prevent this process of adaptation and result in defensive dissociation. The traumatic experience is not lost from the mind, but persists as a 'subconscious fixed idea' which functions both to organise the memories of trauma and also to keep them out of awareness. Despite this attempt at mental defence, these highly emotionally charged 'fixed ideas' containing the memories continue to affect perception, mood and behaviour. The person behaves 'automatically' according to images and perceptions and emotions derived from the past rather than by realistic assessment of the present. In some ways this might sound like the Freudian idea of 'transference' where the perception of the present is coloured by childhood experience. However, it is much more like the phenomena recognised in patients who have been traumatised in childhood, where the dissociated experience of the past re-emerges in such vivid flashbacks that it *invades* the present, leaving the person temporarily psychotic and disoriented in relation to reality. An example of this is a patient seen by the author who would at times be almost certain that I was going to physically assault her and whilst in this state would carefully scrutinise me visually, trying to figure out whether I really was her father or not.

Janet thought that for adaptation to trauma it was necessary for a person to be able to talk to themselves and others about it, to form a narrative: 'It is not enough just to be aware of a memory; it is also necessary that the personal perception "knows" this image and attaches it to other images' (Janet, 1909b, p. 1557). In common with contemporary memory theorists Janet saw memory as a creative act in which the person organises and categorises their experiences and assimilates and accommodates into existing cognitive schemes and structures. In fact Piaget, whose work was concerned with the way the child structures his cognitive grasp of the world, was Janet's student.

For Janet, the 'schematisation' or 'narratisation' of the experience is disrupted by dissociation. Janet saw dissociation as involving a 'narrowing of consciousness' so that one experience cannot be associated with another – and so that thinking cannot occur. A patient with a multiple personality which had been partially resolved in therapy would often stare at me blankly for long periods during her sessions; she also would at times present one version of her childhood and at other times another, seemingly with little capacity to compare these and consider their incompatibilities. Eventually I began to appreciate her considerable difficulty in thinking; it struck me that she could only 'see' the surface of whatever was in the forefront of her mind; she could not look beyond this or 'into' this without help from the therapist. When this was articulated to her she agreed very emphatically that this narrowing of the field of consciousness was indeed very characteristic for her. Her dissociated pieces of experience formed isolated cores of consciousness, taking turns to emerge into the foreground of awareness, and which did not communicate with each other so that experience could not be thought about.

Janet made the crucial point that it was not sufficient for traumatic experiences, in the form of 'fixed ideas' to be made conscious. The fixed idea must be destroyed (as fixed idea) through assimilation and association with other ideas. In the case of the patient just described, there were a number of ideas that were conscious at different times; the problem was of linking one dissociated piece of consciousness with another. Technically it is a matter of reminding the patient of what he or she has said at different times. This is a clear difference from Freud's theory which emphasised the bringing of mental contents from the repressed unconscious into consciousness.

Janet was quite clear that dissociation took place for purposes of mental defence against anxiety. For example, he wrote of a 'phobia of memory' (Janet, 1919, p. 661). He considered that memories and 'fixed ideas' could be stored at various levels of information processing, as narratives, as sensory perceptions, as visual images in hallucinations and nightmares, and as 'visceral' sensations – i.e. memories in affect. These memories stored at levels less than narratives may return intrusively and 'automatically' disconnected from their context and from current reality. Janet's ideas are highly compatible with contemporary theories of information processing (e.g. Kihlstrom, 1984) which describe enactive, iconic and symbolic/linguistic modes, analogous to the stages of sensorimotor, preoperational and operational thinking described by Piaget.

The hypersuggestibility, often thought to be characteristic of hysterical patients, Janet believed to be the result of the narrowing of the field of consciousness. The dissociated parts of the mind lacked the higher mental functions of critical judgement.

Janet developed a concept of a hierarchy of mental functions with five levels. At the top is the 'fonction du réel' which is the capacity to grasp reality to the maximum, and at the lowest level are motor discharges. He considered that strong or 'vehement' emotions, such as are associated with trauma, disrupted this hierarchy resulting in a lower level of functioning:

> The individual, when overcome by vehement emotions, is not himself . . . I have shown on numerous occasions that the characteristics which have been acquired by education and moral development may suffer a complete change under the influence of emotion . . . Forgetting the event which precipitated the emotion . . . has frequently been found to accompany intense emotional experiences in the form of continuous and retrograde amnesia . . . They are an exaggerated form of a general disturbance of memory which is characteristic of all emotions. (Janet, 1909a, p. 1607)

The treatment approach advocated by Janet was a general one aimed at helping the patient achieve a higher level of functioning and mental integration. In addition to suggesting various uses of hypnosis, Janet recommended activities similar to contemporary art and occupational therapy.

Janet's was a balanced theory of neurotic and hysterical disturbance which would not be out of place today. He saw a place for both psychological dynamics and a biological substrate that could predispose some individuals towards an inherent mental weakness. It would not be surprising if, in an echo of Fairbairn's (1952) earlier plea 'back to hysteria!' for an understanding of splitting and dissociation, there might be an excited cry amongst contemporary trauma theorists of 'back to Janet!'.

In view of the superiority in certain respects of Janet's theory over that of Freud, why did the latter's view come to predominate? One reason might be that Freud, unlike Janet, continued to build on his insights in a number of interesting ways, illuminating dreams, social and cultural phenomena and the psychopathology of everyday life. Healy (1993) has also suggested that Freud's concept of repression, implying a top-down system of control, was more compatible with the prevailing biological and neurological ideas, such as Hughling Jackson's hierarchical model of brain functioning.

SUMMARY

At the end of the nineteenth and early twentieth centuries, a number of clinicians and theorists were studying disturbances of consciousness, dissociation, splitting of the mind and other phenomena related to hypnosis and hysteria. Predominant among these were Freud and Breuer, on the one hand, and Janet on the other. Breuer's thinking contained a number of interesting points, particularly the notion of hypnoid states, which have subsequently fallen out of popularity. Freud's notion of repression, resting upon the idea of splitting of the mind into consciousness and the dynamic unconscious, became the predominant framework for understanding psychodynamics for the best part of the next century. However, Janet's conceptualisations of trauma and dissociation, allowing for the possibility of multiple consciousnesses, with incompletely processed memories forming islands of consciousness as 'fixed ideas' which intrude 'automatically', all are much more consistent with the currently emerging understanding of trauma-based psychopathologies. Janet's theory is compatible with multiple personality disorder whereas Freud's is not.

It is interesting to note that one of the most famous cases in psychoanalytic history, that of Anna O, often credited as marking the origin of psychoanalysis, the 'talking cure', is not understandable in terms of Freud's (as opposed to Breuer's) own theory, Freud regarding this as a case of 'hypnoid hysteria' quite distinct from his own concern with 'defence hysteria'.

Chapter 4

THE EFFECTS OF TRAUMA AND ABUSE ON THE DEVELOPING SELF

TAXONOMY OF DISTURBANCE OF SELF

In an earlier book, *The Fragile Self* (Mollon, 1993), I described a taxonomy of seven categories of disturbance of the self – covering both the structure and the experience of self. This provides a useful framework for considering the devastating impact upon the developing self of childhood trauma and abuse.

Differentiation

The first category is *Differentiation of Self*. An abuser imposes his will on the child and imposes his version of reality, which may be a very distorted version. For example an incestuous father may tell his small daughter that what they do together is what all fathers do with their children but that it must always be kept a secret. The child's gradual discovery of reality is impeded by this; she cannot easily differentiate her perception from that presented by her father. The abusing parent treats the child as an object to satisfy his desire – or at least sets out sadistically to annihilate the child's potential to differentiate as a separate subjectivity.

The abused person even when grown up may continue to believe that the abuser has power to control her life. For example one woman continually feared that her father would cause her to be sacked from any employment; she also felt that he could somehow know what she said about him in her therapy and that he would have the power to influence the therapist. Frequently an abused woman may feel that she can only be free when her father is in his grave, but even then she may fear that he will come back to haunt her – and of course in her internal world he does so. It is as if the person continues to inhabit the version of reality presented by the abuser, that he/she will always be in control. The fact that the abuser may never be exposed or brought to justice emphasises his omnipotence in the mind of the abused; he is seen as beyond the law. If in normal development the father is seen as the representative of the law and of reality, and is the guardian of separation and boundary (Mollon, 1993), then the abusing father becomes the imprisoner of the child in a perverse world where the law is excluded.

James Glass (in *Shattered Selves: Multiple Personality in a Postmodern World*, 1993) writes:

> The abused daughter possesses no psychological avenues enabling her to create a seductive fantasy about the relationship; she has no internal space out of which to construct out of the father's presence a fantasized object of love and affection. He lives in her mind as a stark reality, without any modulation or softening by the power of internal object representations. The absolute perversion of human intentionality dominates their relationship. For this little girl, desire appears not as the sexual wish for love but as the disintegrating morbidity of death, the wish for nonbeing. There is no attraction, no life instinct, just fear of pain. What is 'desired' is not the father's penis but a liberation, a nirvana of spirit and body, a radical escape from the very physicalness of the father's body and his presence as an instrument of violence. (p. 69)

Subjective Self

The second category is *Subjective Self – Sense of Agency*. The potential to feel like an active agent in one's own life is severely damaged for the abused person who usually feels profoundly passive and helpless. Such a person experiences him/herself as at the mercy of other people. In therapy, the patient is highly sensitive to the struggle to preserve a fragile sense of autonomy. Attempts by the therapist to push the therapeutic process are strongly resisted. Sometimes the patient will feel so helpless in the face of their sense of dependence on the therapist that he/she will need to withdraw from the therapy temporarily in order to restore a sense of choosing the therapy – as opposed to a sense of being helplessly trapped in it. Any sense of pressure from the therapist may be experienced as further abuse.

One consequence of this is that the patient's sense of reality is disturbed. This is because being able to determine one's own perception of reality is a fundamental aspect of the sense of agency. The person who was abused extensively as a child has been frightened out of their own perceptions – and so in the most fundamental way their freedom to perceive has been mutilated. Such a person will feel genuinely unsure of what did go on in his/her childhood. The danger of suggestion from the therapist in reconstructing early events is therefore enhanced. Spiegel (1974) has found evidence that people repeatedly traumatised in childhood are more suggestible; thus those who have been abused may be more prone to distorted memories of abuse.

I have a patient who sometimes tells me of childhood abuse, and sometimes denies this – adopting different positions at different times. I find that if I challenge whatever position she is adopting, she becomes very brittle and defensive, and clams up like a sullen adolescent. My reaction has been to emphasise to her that the therapeutic process is under her control; that I can only respond to the pieces of communication she gives to me, which are like pieces of a jigsaw puzzle; that I cannot know what the whole picture will look like – that *I* cannot know whether or not her father abused her; that I can only consider the pieces she gives me and see how they might fit or not fit together, and where there might be missing pieces. She appears to find this reassuring.

Ray Wyre, who has interviewed a great many sexual offenders, has described how these people, whether they are rapists or incestuous abusers within the family, very often go to great lengths in their strategies leading up to abuse (Wyre, 1987, 1989, 1990, 1995; see also Salter, 1995). The incestuous father may have been preparing his victim over a period of many years, just as the rapist may stalk his victim over a great period of time very carefully. He is often, by his own admission in interview, endeavouring to control his victim's mind, emotions and behaviour at all levels with great skill and complex strategies, so that the abused person does feel helplessly controlled. The victim's sense of being controlled mirrors the precise strategies of the abuser; the abused one feels helpless and controlled because he/she is, but they do not understand how.

Very often this damage to the sense of agency leads a person to be preoccupied with asserting power over others, identifying with the aggressor. One form this may take is to become aggressively promiscuous; a woman may pick up men and then discard them so that *they* feel used and abused, projectively evoking in them the experience of exploitation. Therapy with the abused patient frequently becomes chaotic and stormy as she tries to cross all manner of boundaries, all reflecting the way in which the confused boundaries and perverted authority of the original family is replayed in the transference. One abused patient would oscillate between states of feeling a frightened vulnerable victim, and manic states in which she would feel powerful and triumphant; in these latter states she would be promiscuous, wear revealing clothes and behave in a sexually provocative manner in her sessions, and declare her determination to seduce the therapist sooner or later.

Another patient menacingly told the therapist that if he did not agree to have sex with her, ostensibly in order to help her sexual anxieties, she would kill herself because this would indicate that he did not care about her. In this way she was perhaps repeating in the transference an early experience in which she was emotionally blackmailed into sexual activities; but now it was she who was the aggressor.

Objective Self

The third category is *Objective Self*. This concerns the person's 'objective' view of the self – self-concept and self-esteem. The images that an abused person has of themselves are negative in the extreme – of the non-human and of excrement. If the person has dissociative internal voices they may scream that he/she is filth and deserves to die. An abused child almost always reasons that he/she must be very bad for the abuse to have taken place. Moreover, a skilful abuser will ensure that the child feels responsible for the abuse as an active participant. This may be particularly a problem for the child when there has been sexual arousal and hence pleasure during the abuse, resulting in immense shame and guilt.

Although the child is genuinely a victim, helpless and controlled by the abuser's superior strength, power and capacities to threaten and deceive, he or she will blame the self for the abuse. The reasoning may be that the child should have said no, or should have made more effort to tell someone, or should have resisted no matter what the consequences – very much along the lines of an adult rape victim. The child will hate him/herself for being weak and vulnerable and abusable.

The abused child will identify with the image that the abuser has of him/her. The mechanism of projective identification is important here. A major part of the motivation of the abuser is projectively to evoke in the abused the unwanted images of the self, to make the abused feel utterly helpless, humiliated, shamed, violated and rendered 'abject' (Price, 1994). For example, a patient reported that her abuser would urinate into her mouth and make her eat pieces of faeces, telling her that she was a toilet and should be treated as such. In seeking a projective solution, the abused becomes the abuser of the next generation and so on. What drives the abuser is not sexual desire itself, but rather the sadistic wish to control, violate and humiliate, to take possession of the self of the other; it is this malevolent intention towards the other that forms the fuel for the sexual excitement. The consequence for the abused is a near annihilation of the self and the creation of images of the self that are negative, to an extreme that is quite intolerable, generating panic measures of dissociation and projection.

The abused child will also draw conclusions about the meaning and implications of the abuse for the value of the self. A patient suffered a resurgence of depression after she heard from an older brother that he too had been abused. We drew out her underlying thought that her mother must have been in a position to know about the abuse if it involved other siblings as well, and that she must have turned a blind eye to it. Her semi-conscious reasoning then was that if her own mother could not be concerned to protect her then she could not be worth very much. She described how in fact her behaviour tended to reflect this view of herself because she would always put other people first as if her own needs were of no importance.

One patient declared that she felt better because she had decided she would forget about the past and become an entirely different kind of person. This reflects the desperate attempts at cure through dissociation, and represents a repudiation of an intolerable image of the self, substituting a new 'conjured up' self-image. In the extreme instances of multiple personality disorder this becomes a kind of continual murder of the self, as more and more images of the self have to be repudiated as others are created. The more positive self-images of the traumatised person who resorts to dissociation may not be based upon experience but on wishful fantasy. It is as if the person thinks: 'I can decide I am not an abused person at all, but instead am strong and happy and have not experienced abuse.' Multiple personality disorder is about playing tricks with reality, in the face of a reality which is intolerable. The problem is that images of the self which do bear the imprint of reality, and also of the projective fantasies of the abuser, do not forever vanish but continually threaten to re-emerge into consciousness.

Structure-organisation

The fourth category concerns the *Structure and Organisation* of the self. In a previous book I wrote about the 'fragile self' in patients whose early development had been distorted in various ways, often involving a non-mirroring mother and/or an affectively absent father. By contrast, the person who has been extensively traumatised or abused in childhood may have a *shattered* self. Such functioning as they have is achieved through splintering of the self, dissociation and warding off of experiences of trauma. An apparently high level of adult functioning may be unstable and deceptive. Some people may show a pattern of moving from job to job, maintaining a functioning facade for limited periods of time and moving on when this starts to crumble. The maintenance of this functioning false self may require that other parts are allowed expression at other times; the person may go home after work and binge eat, or drink excessive alcohol, or indulge in self-cutting. Engaging in therapy can be hazardous to the fragile false-self functioning that a person has achieved; giving expression to warded off parts of the self can weaken the capacity to keep them warded off – a patient might then find him/herself leaving a session in the state of mind of a small traumatised and frightened child. With patients who have employed dissociation extensively it is important for the therapist to keep in mind that changes in mental state are not, for these people, gradual but abrupt – at least until substantial integration has been achieved.

The self state of a person who has experienced severe childhood trauma is often chaotic, as the frantic use of dissociative and manic defences plays havoc with integration and stability. At one moment the person is an abused and frightened child, at another moment a triumphant aggressor, and then an adult in denial of any abuse, and so on. During therapy the patient may oscillate wildly between personality states even within one session. In some ways this chaos may reflect that of the original family. Frequently the clinician working with this client group will hear of families of origin characterised by a confusion of boundaries and a generally sexualised atmosphere; this may leave the person with a lack of clarity about what was going on in the family, an uncertainty about the distinction between fantasy and reality. The patient may at times express all kinds of fantasies and speculations about who was having sex with whom; whatever the literal truth in such ideas, they reflect an experience of a family where the normal boundaries and structures, including the generational boundaries, have been violated or are non-existent.

In the 'self psychology' developed by Kohut (1971) and extensively discussed in my earlier work (Mollon, 1993), the structure and organisation of the self is seen as dependent upon the responsiveness of empathic 'selfobjects' during childhood (and to a lesser extent during adulthood); the selfobject is a figure who provides a function which supports the development of the self. This is consistent with the everyday observation that when we are in the presence of those who accept and empathically understand us, we feel more held together and more coherent and calm, whereas in the presence of hostile and unempathic figures we may feel disorganised and incoherent. The abusing figure is par excellence an unempathic 'anti-selfobject' (to coin a neologism!).

Instead of the soothing, calming selfobject providing experiences needed to build up the structure of the self, along the metaphorical lines of digestion of nutritious food, the anti-selfobject violently intrudes, forcing itself into the vulnerable developing self as an indigestible foreign body. The experience of abuse simply cannot be digested mentally without assistance from an understanding selfobject, whether in the form of a relative, friend or therapist. The abused child not only fails to experience the empathy necessary for building a coherent and cohesive self, he/she also does experience a violation which smashes the potential structure of the self.

The experience of having a foreign body inside is illlustrated by a patient who would at times scream in her therapy: 'Get him out of me!' She talked of an experience of a relentlessly persecutory and punitive figure in her mind, and also of a sensation of something stuck in her vagina. Another frequent pattern in her experiences was that whenever she cried in the presence of any male companion, including the therapist, she would fear that she would be hit. This constellation appeared to derive from childhood experiences when someone would hit her if she made a noise crying. In this kind of example can be seen what amounts to a perversion of the normal experience of a selfobject; instead of a 'nutritious' experience the child is presented with emotional poison.

Balance between Subjective and Objective Self

The fifth category concerns the *Balance between Subjective and Objective Self*. This is to do with the delicate balance and movement of attention between awareness of the self from inside, feelings and wishes, etc., and awareness of the other's view of the self from outside, that is required for effective social intercourse and relationships. This balance can be skewed in either direction. Too much anticipation of the other's view and an excessive desire to accommodate to the other leads to a marked false self position with reduced awareness of the person's own thoughts, feelings, wishes and perceptions. On the other hand an exclusive concern with the person's inner experience means a failure to relate to others as human beings.

The abused person has had to accommodate excessively to the demands of the abuser and to disregard his/her own feelings and desires. One could say that the image of the abusing other has fallen like a dark and all-encompassing shadow over the psyche of the abused, blotting out awareness of the self.

The abused person exists against a background of chronic terror, constantly scanning the environment for danger. For example, a patient in therapy would spend much of her sessions staring suspiciously at the therapist, sometimes asking angrily what he was wanting. The whole idea that the sessions were for her to speak of whatever she chose was very difficult for her to grasp; if asked what she was thinking or feeling, she would say that she was trying to figure out what the therapist was thinking or wanting. She was not easily able to direct her attention inwards away from the constant external scanning.

The background of terror makes attention to the inner world of feelings and fantasies very frightening. Such a person attempts to keep the inner world under control and surveillance just like the external world. His/her consciousness is suspended between two worlds of terror. Communication between these worlds is feared as madness, as is letting go of control.

Optimum social communication, especially in intimate relationships, involves an exquisite and continual exchange between an empathy with the self and an empathy with the other. How terrifying to empathise with the malevolent intention of the abuser and to realise that one is the object of that intention; and how unbearable to empathise with the self that is that object! The abused can reach out neither to the other nor to the self, but remains forever frozen between.

Illusions of Self-sufficiency

The sixth category is concerned with *Illusions of Self-sufficiency*. The person who has been extensively abused in childhood naturally feels that other people in general cannot be trusted. Indeed it may be that one result of abuse is particularly rigid schemas or beliefs regarding relationships, which are relatively immune to new information. The person will feel that it is safest to trust no one. Attachment to another person may evoke great anxiety and a wish to withdraw. In therapy the patient's awareness of dependence may stir rage and manic fantasies of being stronger than other people.

One abused patient would sometimes enter manic states of mind in which she would believe that all those in her life were now weak and dependent upon her. She would declare her intention of training in counselling and of providing treatment for her therapist.

One chronic problem for a person who has been abused is that if he/she attempts an intimate relationship, any behaviour by the other person which remotely or paradigmatically resembles that of the abuser will stir up all the overwhelming affect of the original experience. The response then will probably be a wish to withdraw protectively. This may be

THE SEARCH FOR HEALING 49

accompanied by despair at the prospect of the future being merely a continuation of the abuse of the past.

The perverse solution of avoiding intimacy and dependence is another resort of the abused person. Exploitative and cynical sexual relationships may be pursued in which the person is discarded in favour of sensory excitement. Genital pleasure is used to fill the hole left by the absence of intimacy. The abused man may resort to overtly perverse practices, including homosexual adventures.

Sense of Lineage

The seventh category is the *Sense of Lineage*. This is to do with the sense of being part of a family or cultural line, ultimately to do with acknowledging one's lineage as a product of parents in intercourse. The person who has been abused by someone in the family will often wish to deny their lineage which will be associated with immense shame. This may be part of the reason why some abused people go through periods of wanting to cut off completely from their family.

A normal sense of lineage may depend upon a sense of a parental couple, whose intercourse has led to a subsequent generation. If the family has been generally disordered in its boundaries, with much sexual confusion, if the sexual couple has been a parent and child, then instead of a sense of a line there will be a muddle. The sense of who one is and where one comes from will be blurred and confused. Accurate recollection of what has gone on in the family is often much more difficult under these circumstances because there has been no clear family framework. As in the experiments on 'field dependence', in which the subject sits in a tilting room and has to judge horizontal and vertical axes, when the framework is unreliable and moving, our capacity to gauge reality is impaired. Thus a disturbed sense of lineage may be associated with an impaired sense of reality. This is perhaps why people who have been abused and traumatised in childhood often give a very confused and confusing account of childhood, in which it is difficult to sort out who was doing what to whom.

THE SEARCH FOR HEALING OF THE TRAUMATISED SELF IN THE SELFOBJECT DIMENSION OF TRANSFERENCE

We may conceptualise broadly three dimensions of transference: the historical – the repetition of relationships and experiences of the past; the projective – the projection of internal objects and parts of the self into the relationship with the therapist; the selfobject dimension elucidated by Kohut's self psychology. The selfobject dimension concerns the way in which the patient is unconsciously seeking the responses from the therapist that are needed to restore the derailed development of the self. In this dimension the patient is quite genuinely dependent for his/her development on the provision of these development-enhancing functions by the therapist (see discussion in Mollon, 1993). Healing does not occur through insight alone. In general these selfobject functions are in the realm of empathy.

The abused and traumatised patient will certainly bring much to do with trauma and the experience of malevolence in the historical and projective dimensions of transference, but in addition, when the conditions are favourable, will seek out the therapist's empathy, recognition and affirmation where it is needed to facilitate the unfolding of the smashed developmental potential. The patient will have 'another go' at developing and healing, a venture requiring tremendous unconscious courage, as failure by the therapist would compound the damage and magnify the despair.

CLINICAL ILLUSTRATION SHOWING THE STRUGGLE FOR A SENSE OF AGENCY

There are very many dimensions to complex clinical material. I will tease out just a few themes relevant to my concerns here. My focus is upon the way in which the patient represents and re-enacts traumatic experiences of the past but also seeks out a new corrective experience in the present with the therapist. The corrective experience is not deliberately staged, but arises from the therapist's attempts to understand the patient's communications of her experiences and of her needs, and from the conveying of this understanding to the patient. This lies in the selfobject dimension of the transference.

Miss T is a very disturbed Scandinavian woman in her mid twenties, in analytical therapy several times per week, who sought help because of feelings of desperation, despair, panic, failed relationships, and tendencies to be either out of touch with her feelings or else overwhelmed by them. She had left her country of origin because she felt she could not survive whilst in any contact with her family. She had worked in a variety of jobs including a travelling circus, but had not been able to sustain any of these; nevertheless she displayed intelligence and a number of creative talents.

From the beginning she behaved in rather unusual ways in the consulting room – jumping up and down on the couch, screaming loudly, hiding in a corner and jumping on the spot, all the time appearing to be in great distress. Nevertheless all of this was also interspersed with lucid accounts of her experiences. She felt she needed to behave in this way, but did not know why, except that she suspected that she was in some way re-enacting scenes of abuse from her childhood. She was afraid that I might shout at her or attack her. She was also afraid that I was not affectively present for her. She complained of a sense of being completely alone – this was especially so when she removed her glasses, and it emerged that as a young child she had been extremely short-sighted but this was not discovered until she was five years old, so that presumably she lacked visual contact with her mother in the early stages. Often she complained that the therapy was too intense for her and talked of stopping and finding some other more suitable kind of therapy. After some weeks she quietly remarked that she had come to make some noise today, and got out various pots and pans and a wooden spoon. Rather bemused and slightly alarmed by this, I asked jokingly if I should get my ear plugs. She ignored my remark and proceeded to bash the pans, making a most appalling noise in my small consulting room for several minutes. Clearly she wished to make some kind of impact on me! In her subsequent remarks she associated to her mother working night shifts and being asleep on the sofa whilst Miss T played alone alongside her.

Following this she turned up for her subsequent session and stood anxiously by the door, saying that she had just come to tell me that she was not coming any more; she said that the therapy was too intense and was a form of abuse and that she had initially told the referring agency that she wanted therapy once a week, not several times a week and that her wishes had been disregarded. She then left, having stayed about two minutes. I found myself in some state of shock.

I wrote to her, indicating that I was giving much thought to her communication, wanting to understand more and that, since I would like to give her the opportunity to explore the issues further with me, I would be there during her session times for the following week and she could turn up to any of these without notice. She returned. I invited her to consider whether to lie on the couch or sit and she chose the chair. I also offered her a choice of positioning of the chair and she chose to have the chair moved nearer the door so that she could escape if necessary. Later she was to tell me that more than anything, it was my moving the chair for her that gave her an increased sense that she could trust me. What emerged was that she had been developing increasing anxiety about me and that she had developed a near delusional idea that I would attack her and rape her; thus during her lying on the couch, with minimal visual data about me, a psychotic transference had been quietly fermenting. She decided to continue. What made the difference, according to her, was that I listened to her and gave her an accurate reflective account of what she was saying and feeling, that I let her choose her position in the room, that I put to her that whilst we had established a certain structure of sessions per week it was up to her how many of those sessions she chose to come to – i.e. that in these different ways I was letting her establish a sense of control. She missed one session in the next few days and told me she thought she had chosen not to come in order to demonstrate to herself that she did not have to come. Following this she hardly missed a single session.

Miss T commented on my reference to getting ear plugs in the session before she took flight. In a more neurotically structured patient, the meaning would have been more unconscious, but for her it was transparent – I could not bear to listen to her and I wanted to close my ears to her. She had felt profoundly rejected. We gradually came to a greater understanding of her need to know that I am in touch with her affective state and that I am open to what she needs to communicate affectively. When she suspects that I am not, she reacts with rage and terror.

Miss T is extremely sensitive to whether or not someone is in touch with feelings – both hers and their own. If she suspects that someone is not in touch with their own feelings she avoids them. She has a dread of antidepressants and anyone who is on them because she perceives those people as avoiding their feelings. She also dreads anyone who has any kind of addiction, whether it is to drugs, alcohol, work, compulsive caring for others, or any kind of manic defence. She believes that her mother used to abandon her a lot by working excessively in a caring profession; when she herself goes to work she feels she is cutting herself off from her own affective child self just as her mother did in relation to her – and feels rage towards herself. The impression is that both her parents were significantly lacking in their ability to be in emotional contact with her. One dilemma in the therapy is that if I talk to her in a way that puts her in touch with her feelings she can then feel overwhelmed and perceive me as dangerous and abusive; on the other hand if I go along with her own distancing from her underlying affects, she perceives me as behaving like her mother and emotionally cutting off from her.

Miss T's sense of self is truly fragile. She is immensely sensitive to any criticism or hint of criticism, or any threat to her autonomy. To these she reacts with haughty rage, violent discharges of affect, and retreats to an aloof certainty of the validity of her own point of view. Behind this stance she experiences enormous shame. If I fail to agree or to affirm fully her position on some matter, she experiences this as what she describes as a threat to her reality. She then fears she is going mad. The impression I have of her early relationships is that she was not allowed her own perceptions and thoughts but was made to accept the version of events given by her parents; thus as well as involving the sense of agency, this struggle concerns the first category of differentiation of the self. Regarding category 5, the balance between objective and subjective self, Miss T cannot easily negotiate between her own perceptions and feelings from inside, and the perceptions that others may have of her; she feels either that she must impose her own view on others or others will impose their view on her.

Miss T may or may not have been physically and sexually abused as a child. Neither she nor I have yet come to any conclusion about this, but certainly it is a recurrent theme. She not only fears that I will fly into a rage and attack her and perhaps rape her, but also she has fantasies of attacking me, of pulverising me and of throwing me around the room – the latter idea seems to represent a turning of the tables on an experience she thinks she had of being thrown around by her father. Early experiences of physical and sexual abuse would certainly give partial explanation of these fears and impulses. However, I think there is another component to this. I have noticed that her paranoid perception of me, her wish to attack me and her fears that I will attack her are often associated with her feeling that she cannot convey her pain and desperation to me or indeed to anyone. When I give her an indication that I am hearing her and registering her pain and fear then she seems to become calmer. I have talked to her of how it is crucial to her to feel heard and understood, to feel that I am receptive to her, and that when she does not feel that, she becomes frantic and enraged, and then expects that this anger will come back at her, that I will attack her.

Discussion

It seems clear to me that Miss T was able to continue in her therapy only because I understood and accepted her need to preserve some sense of autonomy and of having some degree of control over the process – i.e. that I supported her sense of agency. When I discussed this work with analytic colleagues, some, but not all, emphasised the way in which she appeared to control me. Some have seemed to feel irritated, even outraged, by Miss T's failure to behave like a conventional analytic patient, and have urged me to insist that she put her feelings and impulses into words rather than action. I have always felt that I must follow her, let her lead the analytic process, and try to understand as best I can what she is trying to communicate, what she is repeating from the past and what she needs of me. I do not mean that I think I should be endlessly malleable, not at all, but that I should remain calm, consistent, attentive in the face of her chaos, and tolerant of her attempts to communicate in whatever way she is most able. In this way I think I am offering an analytic contrast to a subjective world in which authentic affect is blocked, manic denial prevails and autonomy is smashed by the imposition of power by those who are stronger. Above all I think I am gradually understanding more about how her sense of self, and particularly her sense of agency depends upon her feeling that she can communicate effectively and affectively – and about how she is struggling with an internal object that is hostile to affective communication.

I do not know whether Miss T was sexually abused as a child, but I think it is quite possible. Sexual abuse by a father may have a particularly damaging effect on a child's sense of agency, since, if there is validity in Lacan's ideas (see discussion in Mollon, 1993), the father has an unconscious function as representative of the 'law', essentially the law against incest. The 'law' guards against the arbitrary imposition of power. An incestuously abusing father is like a corrupt policeman who delivers the child into a precivic anarchy, in which there is no space for her experience of self as subject, but only as object. The patient with this kind of background experience will look for evidence that the therapist is bound by the 'law'; for example it has been important for Miss T to discover over a period of time that whatever she says or does the therapist continues to sit in his chair, listen, think and try to understand. Almost certainly, if the therapist were to vary his approach from one session to another, Miss T would be so alarmed that she could not stay. She can at times speak of a wish to be held physically by the therapist precisely because she knows that this would not happen.

SHAME IN THE COUNTERTRANSFERENCE

Many of the effects of sexual abuse on the sense of self are closely allied to shame (Mollon, 1993). Shame is inherent in sexual abuse. Indeed, sexual abuse is the ultimate shame, and probably that is its purpose – to transfer projectively shame from the abuser to the victim, a strategy which has to be addictively repeated. By definition we are talking of intensely private, intimate and shameful experiences. If the abuse has not been private but has involved several abusers in a network of paedophiles or a cult, then the shame and humiliation are intensified. The natural privacy of the self has been violated and autonomy has been mocked. The reaction is to want to hide the abuse. Shame is for the self and for the connection to the abuser.

Shame is the hidden affect. Shame gives rise to shame about shame. Shame is contagious. If we connect empathically with another's shame we feel shame. Not surprisingly, both patients and therapists have tried to avoid contact with shame, preferring instead to focus on feelings of guilt, aggression and sadism – all of which can actually be fuelled by shame. These 'strong and bad' feelings associated with aggression can be used to counter and cover the 'weak and pathetic' feelings of the shame constellation.

The affect of shame tends to block empathy. Therapists do not want to feel this most toxic of emotions. I notice certain defensive reactions in myself if I present work with a particular shame-prone, and perhaps abused, patient in a seminar to colleagues. I feel afraid of being regarded as a fool if I believe the patient has been abused. I fear a scornful reaction if I describe empathy with the patient's experience. This leads me to emphasise the patient's aggression, her efforts to control me, and my scepticism and uncertainty regarding the question of whether she was sexually abused. I find that in presentations where I emphasise her aggression, my colleagues seem more at ease than when I emphasise her position as a possible (shame-ridden) victim of abuse; I too can then feel tough-minded, not a fool, not 'taken in', but vigilantly rooting out destructiveness wherever it may be hidden.

In these days of debate on true and false memory, we can all be fools.

To accept the patient's perception is to risk shame in analytic circles. We may be seen as no more than an empathy-ridden counsellor. Unless we are decoding and revealing a hidden text, at odds with the patient's conscious account, we perceive ourselves as analytically impotent. In this way we strive to view ourselves as master(mistress) of the analytic theatre, interpreter of the script, translator of the dream – not as mere audience or witness. Why, of all the psychological therapies, is it psychoanalysis that is so fearfully shame-ridden? In analytic seminars and scientific meetings the tension so often seems to focus upon demonstrating what the analyst has missed, upon how he/she has been taken in. Is this a legacy of Freud's having felt a fool when he changed his mind about patients' accounts of sexual abuse? We now know that he really *was* a fool over the Emma Eckstein episode.

If we empathise with the abused patient we experience shame vicariously. Because shame is aversive we may block our empathy. However, there is another means by which we may be forced to experience shame.

The field of therapy with patients who have been sexually abused may be full of shameful cases – the ones we do not talk about, the ones where the boundaries become somehow violated. Re-enactment of boundary violations in the transference is probably ubiquitous, if not inevitable, in the therapy of those who have been abused. When struggling against the shameful state of victimhood the patient may place the therapist in the role of abused and shame-ridden victim.

CLINICAL ILLUSTRATION OF THE PROJECTIVE COMMUNICATION OF SHAME

Mrs Y, whom I had been seeing for several years, in a hospital setting, often complained that she could not really let go during her sessions because she might break down in tears and need me to comfort her with a hug, but she knew I would not do this. She said she could not bear it if she were in tears and I just stared at her. Immediately we can see here a shame dynamic; she could not bear the shame inherent in being looked at when she was emotional – rather like those infants described by Broucek (1982) who show an early version of shame-withdrawal when faced with a mother's blank face.

One day she came to her session and said she needed to ask me something. She asked me if I would give her a hug. She insisted that she could not tell me why and was totally unprepared to engage in any exploration of why this was so important at that point. She said that she had made a decision and also a promise to herself that hinged on whether or not I would agree to her request. She had promised that she would take a particular course of action. She also said that she promised she would not come back to see me if I did not give her a hug. She had often referred to her belief that a promise, no matter in what circumstances it was made, was absolute and inviolate. All my attempts to reason and interpret failed. Her manner was urgent and somewhat threatening. I felt highly pressured, manipulated, controlled and confused. I did not understand what was going on. I did not give her a hug. She said she was not able to continue her therapy and handed me a letter to read after she had gone. When I read the letter it contained a desperate message alluding to suicide, eventually if not imminently.

I wrote to her offering her a further appointment in spite of her 'promise'. She declined the appointment but telephoned. She said that she was missing her appointments with me very much but she could not break her promise not to come back. I commented on the perverse nature of this promise but to no avail. She talked of her intention to kill herself when her currently very ill uncle died, something she had often spoken of. She said she was not particularly depressed but in fact relieved at her decision. She said she was getting the house in order and was generally preparing her affairs. She then alluded to having persuaded another patient to be with her at her death so that she would not be alone. I asked if this was someone known to me and she indicated that it was. She said her proposed method of suicide was to be by injection of a lethal over-dose of a medicine which she had stolen. She said she would have a bot-tle of the same substance for this other patient too. She remarked that I might then have two dead patients. I said to her that if she planned to murder herself – and I hoped profoundly that she would not – this was one thing, but to be involved in the murder of another patient would be even more terrible. She seemed somewhat chastened by this and said that she felt guilty. I said that her feeling of guilt was perhaps appropriate and she agreed.

She then talked angrily of her belief that none of us at the hospital really cared about her or took her seriously – another basis for shame, the sense of not mattering – and that I did not believe she meant what she was say-ing. She declared that she would prove to us all that she did mean it. I assured her that I did take very seriously what she was telling me and that I knew she meant it. She complained that even though I was saying that I took her seriously I had still refused to give her a hug when she had asked for one. She talked of a desperate need for a hug. Eventually I said to her that I would gladly give her a hug if it would save her life. She immediately said that this would not be right because it would be black-mail. I asked her to explain and she said it would be as if she was saying to me that if I did not do what she wanted, which I felt to be wrong, then she would kill herself. She then added that she had been placed in that position lots of times and she knew what it was like. I asked her what sit-uations she was thinking of and she replied that she thought I knew very well what situations she was referring to. I said to her that this was exactly the point, that she had been unconsciously re-enacting for me a situation of somebody being pressured to agree to do something which was felt to be wrong – that this was the situation that she had been trying unconsciously to communicate to me through placing me in this position. She immediately agreed with this interpretation and her attitude seemed to shift. She agreed to come back to see me. She thanked me with much feeling for telephoning her.

A couple of weeks later another patient told me of Mrs Y's intention to inject herself with a large amount of medicine and deposit herself in a dying state in my consulting room. I was told that Mrs Y seemed very determined to do this. When Mrs Y did arrive she told me she had been stopped in the act of stealing the medicine from a friend. However, she had taken a number of tranquilliser tablets and continued taking them in front of me during her session. She talked and behaved in a way that I found horrifying. She spoke of a wish that her uncle would die but also said that she wanted to kill herself first in order to punish him – and also in order to punish me. She wanted to punish people for not caring about her. When I drew her attention to the impact of such action upon those who did care about her and also her attempts to involve another patient in her death and to encourage that patient to kill herself, she declared that she did not care about other people because nobody cared about her. She took a syringe out of her pocket and began to play with it, jabbing it into her arm repeatedly, as if it were a dart board. She expressed hopelessness and despair because she believed that nobody cared about her. She said she felt that somehow she could not accept that anyone cared about her unless they gave her a hug. She said she believed that I found her disgusting because of her childhood sexual experiences. As blood poured down her arm she asked mockingly whether I thought the blood meant that she was human. I said to her that I thought one of the fundamental problems she was struggling with was her view of herself as inhuman; because she had been treated inhumanly as a child, she was looking to me for validation of herself as human. When she asked me again for a hug I gave her one, fully aware of the complexities of such a communication, yet believing it was appropriate at that point since it might help her to stay alive – bearing in mind that I would not be able to interpret the meaning of her behaviour to a dead patient. She clearly appreciated the hug but then said that this left her very confused because it did not fit her belief that I did not care about her.

She indicated that she was intending to drive to work. I tried to dissuade her, pointing out that she was in no fit state, having taken so many tranquillisers, either to drive or to work. I offered to order a taxi. She insisted she was going to drive. Later that day she telephoned to say that she had been sent home from work and that she had got home safely.

My countertransference experience of being with her was of horror and disgust at the destructive and perverse state of mind that she appeared to be in the grip of. I felt like I needed to have a shower afterwards, having been in contact with something revolting. She had managed to give me the experience of being violated, manipulated, made to witness and participate in something perverse. I was party to something shameful which I would not readily wish to reveal to colleagues. If I put aside my analytic work ego, I would wish to dismiss the experience and pretend it had not happened. In retrospect I think this was part of the way she was unconsciously placing me in the position of the recipient of something monstrous, just as *she* may have been in her childhood. In this state of mind she appeared to be identified with a perverse abuser, whilst placing me in the role of victim of this. In this way her behaviour towards me could be . understood as a communication of her own early experiences of shame.

Shame is toxic. It makes us feel yucky. We try to avoid being in touch with it, in ourselves and in others. As patients and as therapists we try to cover it with a distracting focus upon aggression. The person who has been sexually abused in childhood is saturated with unmetabolised shame which can often be communicated only by enactment and projection in relation to the therapist.

SUMMARY

Childhood trauma and abuse affect all seven categories of disturbance of self outlined in my earlier book *The Fragile Self*. These disturbances can also be considered as various aspects of the impact of shame. Sexual and perverse abuse is the ultimate in shaming experience. The dynamics of abuse and shame will be enacted in the transference and countertransference; sometimes the therapist may be placed in the role of the victim who is filled with shame.

Chapter 5

THE EFFECTS OF TRAUMA AND ABUSE UPON INTERNAL AND EXTERNAL OBJECT RELATIONS, BELIEF SYSTEMS, AND PSYCHOBIOLOGY

THE NEGATIVE THERAPEUTIC REACTION

One paradoxical result of psychotherapy with the abused person is that he/she may appear to get worse as a result of the therapist making emotional contact with needy parts of the patient's self. It is as if the therapist is rewarded for his/her efforts by the patient's deterioration and rage – perhaps even by paranoid accusations against the therapist. Traditionally this is called the negative therapeutic reaction.

Drawing on Fairbairn's theory of internal object relations, and particularly his concept of the rejecting object and the antilibidinal ego which derive from identifications with rejecting aspects of early caregivers, Seinfeld (1990) describes the negative reaction as follows: 'the negative therapeutic reaction comprises the patient's unreceptivity to an alien, unfamiliar positive object, reinforced by his active rejection of his own need for a positive object in identification with the original external rejecting object' (p. 13).

Thus Seinfeld describes first the point that a person who has experienced little nurturing and caring in childhood will find the benign attentiveness of the therapist to be unfamiliar, puzzling and perhaps frightening. He/she may have no existing schema to which such positive experience can be assimilated. One patient, whose background was of severe abuse, commented on the therapist's strange behaviour, that he acted 'like a perfect gentleman'; on the other hand she once screamed that he obviously did not care about her because he did not abuse her.

The promise or threat of contact with a good object arouses great anxiety. This anxiety may be of the danger of overwhelming neediness being evoked, or it may relate to the fear of losing, or being abandoned by, the newly found object – or more commonly a combination of these. To be met emotionally, to have a baby self connected with and then to be sent away at the end of the session and not be allowed contact outside of session times, and not to be allowed physical contact such as cuddling, may be experienced as cruel and abusive.

At these times the 'rejecting internal object and antilibidinal ego' is activated and is used to suppress the patient's libidinal dependent strivings for contact with the therapist. To put it in rather simpler terms, the patient turns from love to cruelty.

A patient would often talk to the therapist of her wishes and plans to damage or kill herself, sometimes playing provocatively with a syringe full of poison. She also often spoke of her desire to find someone to beat her up. She seemed to delight in tormenting herself and the therapist. Often when in these states of mind it would be very difficult for the therapist to find a way of contacting her and releasing them both from this chamber of torture. On one occasion she sadistically taunted him by telling him that he would have to suffer with her in not knowing whether she would still be alive by the next session. After the therapist had drawn attention to her preoccupation with cruelty, she then acknowledged how she could often be obsessed with desires to be held and cuddled by the therapist, longings which she found humiliating and frightening. She agreed with the interpretation that when experiencing these intense desires emanating from the infantile parts of her mind, which threatened to overwhelm her, and particularly when faced with the limited availability of the therapist, she turned from her neediness and distracted herself with cruel excitement. The wish to have someone beat her up could be seen as wanting the vulnerability to be beaten out of her. Her cruel rejection of the therapist's attempts to reach her and of her own dependent strivings also clearly expressed her rage at the frustration of these needs.

THE RELATIONSHIP TO THE MALEVOLENT OBJECT

A young man indicated that he was feeling increasingly afraid of the therapist, but was not clear why. He spoke of fears that the therapist would suddenly reject or abandon him or would launch a devastating critical attack on him; he was aware that the therapist had not so far behaved in any of these ways. As this anxiety was explored he began to associate to his mother's unpredictable behaviour, her violent rages, and her occasional assertions of her wish that she had aborted him and flushed him down the toilet. It then became clear that the patient was faced with a terrible conflict and dilemma; his natural wish to reach out for contact with a nurturing object, re-experienced in the therapy, led him to the dread of being murdered, flushed away, by this same malevolent object. The mother that is expected to nurture life is perceived as murderous. This core conflict left him often feeling despair about the possibility of ever having a good and lasting intimate relationship; this fundamental approach–avoidance conflict left him feeling forever stranded on the outside of the human race. A less integrated patient would have made more use of splitting of the object, so that good figures would be kept separate from bad ones.

Hedges (1994) refers to the 'organising transference', by which term I understand him to mean an infantile state of seeking contact with an object which is simultaneously experienced as malevolent; at this level of relating the infant, and the infantile parts of the adult in the transference, are attempting to reach out and make contact in order to form the basis of organisation of the self and object world. This is perhaps the most fundamental and primitive level of transference. Hedges describes it as follows:

> This earliest of transferences represents learning experiences of the infant that occurred whenever he or she emotionally extended or reached out and was somehow turned away, not met or negatively greeted. The questing activity was met with environmental responses that taught the infant not to strive in that way again. The 'never go there again' experience effectively marks organising experiences that later on can be identified as transference. (p. 187)

A woman patient repeatedly and in a variety of ways communicated her need to feel properly recognised by the therapist. Often this took the form of needing the therapist to greet her by name in a very clear way. Without this she complained that she felt he did not know who she was and that she did not know either. Her parents had become old and ill and it became apparent that she particularly dreaded the prospect that her parents would die without her ever having felt recognised by them. There were many indications that she had somehow not felt properly greeted and welcomed into the world at the beginning of her life. Often she complained angrily that the therapist did not do enough to meet her emotionally, that he kept his distance from her, that he hid behind words and so on. However, if the therapist, who struggled as best he could to be in emotional contact with her, went further in his interpretations than she herself had conveyed, then she would erupt with rage and anxiety. She would complain that she felt violated. She had in fact accused a previous therapist of sexually abusing her during an LSD therapy session many years ago in the USA. This is an example of a patient who desperately seeks contact and recognition, but who experiences contact as intrusive and traumatising. Therapeutic methods designed to facilitate access to unconscious or warded off material, such as LSD and other forms of chemically-assisted abreaction, are often experienced unconsciously as violating, even if consciously asked for by the patient.

The person caught at this level of conflict fears that any contact will turn bad. Contact is longed for but is felt to be dangerous. As Hedges (1994) puts it: 'people living organising experiences are terrified of interpersonal connection. At every moment of longed for and sought for contact, some image or experience of a traumatising other suddenly intervenes to make sustained contact impossible' (p. 188). Although Hedges himself seems to relate this transference only to infantile impingements, of the kind described by Winnicott (e.g. 1960), this relationship paradigm seems equally applicable to later childhood experiences of abuse and trauma.

A woman had great difficulty sustaining relationships, felt profoundly distrustful of almost everyone, and was often preoccupied with dangers of being sexually attacked. She may have been sexually abused in childhood. During one session she talked of how she would really love to have children of her own but felt she could never trust herself not to abuse a child in some way. She spoke of a relative's little boy and of how cute he was and of how she wanted to pick him up and cuddle him all the time; then she added that she felt this desire to cuddle him was wrong because it might be, or might become, sexual in some way. She then talked of her amazement that some people might allow their children to appear semi-undressed in front of visitors, arguing that one never knew who might be a child molester. Then she went on to say that she did at least trust the therapist, but then added in a flippant and free-associative manner that for all she knew he might be a wife-beater who could not actually be trusted. She further added that she quite often would look at people and think that they seemed nice but then think to herself 'but I wonder what they are really like at home!' In this sequence of thoughts can be seen her very fundamental anxiety that the seeking of a loving connection, either from her to the other or from the other to her, may start out as good but would become derailed and turn into something bad, often into something abusively sexual. This anxiety captured much of her pervasive inhibitions in relationships and no doubt reflected aspects of her early experiences in relationships, some of which may have been sexualised.

In work with patients who suffer from this kind of fundamental conflict, in which the sought for object is also perceived as malevolent, it is extremely important that the process should be at the patient's own rate. If the therapist tries to hurry or take short cuts, or in some way bypass the natural resistance and anxiety about contact, the patient will, unconsciously if not consciously, feel violated and abused. There is always, with patients who were abused by a caregiver, the potential for development of a psychotic transference where the therapist is experienced as malevolent; this danger is greatly intensified if the anxieties about contact are insufficiently addressed and if the therapist does not allow the patient to keep him/her at a distance. For these people, maintaining an area of inner privacy, of being unknown, is felt to be vital to psychological survival; to be known can be felt to be terrifying.

Hedges gives a vivid example of a patient's unconscious experience of a therapist's intrusive intervention as abusive even though at the time it was felt to be helpful. The patient arrived at her session in a state of extreme suicidal despair, leading the therapist to feel very great concern for her life. After asking her permission, the male therapist sat next to her on the couch and comforted her with an arm around her. No sexual or other form of contact that would be generally regarded as improper took place, and indeed the patient seemed supported by this at the time and survived this suicidal crisis without the need for hospitalisation. Some years later after therapy had ended, she filed a lawsuit against the therapist alleging that he had spent the session having sex with her. Whilst this was not literally true, the psychic reality of the psychotic transference was that the therapist had sex with her. The 'abuse' was that the therapist had violated her need to be kept out of contact, to be unreachable. A therapeutic dilemma indeed; does one let the patient commit suicide or 'violate' her by making contact and seducing her into staying alive?

Another aspect of understanding this patient might include the possibility that, in suing the therapist, she had identified with the malevolent predator and had thereby moved into the psychopathic position. This state of mind is well described by Meloy (1988) and involves a particular kind of identification with the aggressor. Drawing on Grotstein's (1982) work, Meloy suggests that the psychopath has identified with the 'stranger selfobject' (actually a rather idiosyncratic use by Grotstein of the Kohutian term 'selfobject'); Meloy describes this as 'a preconceived fantasy that helps the infant anticipate the presence of the predator in the external world, or the prey to whom the infant is to be eventually the predator' (p. 46). The psychopath becomes the predator in his/her primary identification; for the dedicated psychopath this identification becomes part of a grandiose self-concept. It seems quite possible, however, that people who are not completely and consistently psychopathic, but who have been the prey of predatory abusers, may at times move into this state of mind where the predominant identification is with the predator and the position of prey is projectively located in the other – thus the therapist may become the prey.

FROM DEPENDENCE ON THE ENVIRONMENT TO SURRENDER TO THE INTERNAL CONTROLLER

Winnicott described how the infant and child is normally dependent not only on the person of the mother and other caregivers but also upon all the caregiving functions provided by the environment. This is clearly an absolute dependence, especially in the early stages of life. It is more than just an object relationship. The absolute dependence is there whether the infant is aware of it or not. According to Winnicott's formulation, the task of the caregiving environment is to protect the infant from excessive stimulation and to harmonise the responses from outside with the needs and desires arising from inside – and in this way to act as a barrier against 'impingements'.

What happens if the environment fails in this function – if the protectors seem themselves to be abusive? What if the protector is also the enemy? Then there is nowhere in the external world to turn. The infant is forced to resort to internal solutions. One solution is to block awareness of the abuse from the caregiver so that attachment can be maintained; this is the strategy described by Freyd (1993) in her 'betrayal-trauma theory'. Related to this there may be dissociative splits in the mind, such that one part knows of the abuse and other parts do not.

Another kind of response, often deeply hidden, is the development of an internal controller, or 'control centre'. This part of the mind claims ultimate authority over the person and aims to guard against the danger of being devastated again as a result of dependence on another human being. It may be experienced as an internal voice, sometimes non-human, which instructs and prohibits at times of crisis. Dependence on others is permitted only within certain limits. Emotional contact with others beyond these limits is followed by internal punishment. Disclosure to others of the existence of the controller is similarly followed by punishment. The organisation is like a military junta that takes over a country during an emergency, with all the paraphernalia of secret police, control and distortion of information, and rule by terror. If the therapist begins to discern the presence of the controller and speaks about it to the patient, the latter may become extremely agitated and frightened. Extreme caution is advisable in approaching this kind of internal organisation.

The mental structure described here may have something in common with the internal 'mafia' outlined by Rosenfeld (1971), Fairbairn's 'internal saboteur', and the internal organisations of terror described by Meltzer (1973).

THE COLLAPSE OF THE DIMENSION OF IMAGINATION

In discussing the countertransference to the sexually abused patient, Bollas (1989) comments:

> I know I always feel a depression when I hear this news, and this mood is not, I confess, an act of empathy. It is not because I feel sorrow for the victim. Instead I am disappointed over the (apparent) ending of the analytic. I am out of work. Redundant . . . it is fruitful to consider how my response to this news is, in my view, similar to the despair and fury of the victim of incest. When the father violates the child, the child can no longer play with the father in her mind. He terminates the imaginary. (p. 180)

In normal development where the incest barrier has not been breached and where the caregivers have more or less functioned as protectors preserving a safe developmental space, the inner world of fantasy and desire could elaborate without the danger of merging and collapsing with the dimension of the real. Between inner fantasy and external reality there could be the transitional area where play could take place. But where there has been incest or other severe trauma in which reality closely mimics primitive fantasy, this transitional area has been foreclosed; there is literally no space between fantasy and reality where imagination could play. Where there could have been fantasy there now is reality; the mind has been raped.

A patient in psychoanalytic therapy rapidly began to experience very concrete fears that the therapist would rape her or in other ways physically assault her. She enacted scenes of assault by screaming and fighting and engaging in much physical activity in the consulting room. She seemed to need to do this; words alone appeared inadequate to convey her experience. For a long time the analytic space was filled with action and terror. It was not a safe place; often she experienced a need to leave the door open and position herself near the door in case she had to escape from assault. The usual experience of the analytic session as a space in which imagination and play can roam free, framed off from reality, was not present; fantasy and reality were confused and the transference was 'psychotic', barely holding its 'as if' quality. One of her comments about her childhood was that she had no recollection of play-ing and that 'it was never safe to play'.

This patient was nevertheless determined to create a space for play and began to bring dolls and toys and paint and paper. The sessions were reminiscent of play therapy with children. During one session she talked of a wish for the therapist to play on the floor with her and for them to paint together. Then she added that she was afraid to say that because of what she had said in a previous session about an uncle abusing her; she feared that this would have given the therapist ideas and that he too would then abuse her. Apparently this uncle had been a paedophile who cultivated relationships with many children, being willing to play with them for hours. It then became possible for therapist and patient to see that she was making another attempt at becoming able to play but was very frightened that again this would become perverted by abuse; almost certainly the uncle played on the floor with her just as she had wanted the therapist to. The interpretation was that she was trying to create a space in which it was safe to play, but her fear was that the analytic work was all a prelude to abuse, just as the play had been with the uncle.

What about the situation with patients who are less determined in their efforts to create a transitional space? Often it is as Bollas describes above. The sessions are filled with boredom, both parties wondering what there is possibly to say. The narrative of abuse has been told and that is that. Apart from uncovering more memory of abuse what is there to be done? This is the despairing state of mind into which therapist and patient both may fall. The analytic space is collapsed, near dead, and revived only slowly and with much effort. The patient may sit or lie in silence, as if looking for direction or perhaps desire from the therapist. The sessions may feel very difficult and persecutory to both participants. Dull, repeti-tive and deadening narratives may occasionally be punctuated by highly disturbing communications of trauma.

OTHER LONG-TERM EFFECTS OF REPEATED CHILDHOOD TRAUMA

Post-traumatic stress and borderline personality disorder

There have been several reviews summarising research findings regard-ing the long-term outcome of childhood sexual abuse; e.g. Briere (1989, ch. 1); Brown and Finkelhor (1986); Trickett and Putnam (1993). Most of these focus on female victims; for a discussion of the equally severe impact on males, see Mendel (1995).

Naturally it is extremely difficult to tease out specific effects of sexual abuse since these experiences would be likely to be embedded in a matrix of a generally disturbed environment. However, the following features of adult psychopathology have frequently been reported as sequelae of childhood abuse, including sexual abuse:

Depression, involving feelings of hopelessness and helplessness.

Suicide attempts and other forms of self-harm.

Anxiety, panic, nightmares, intrusive flashbacks of trauma.

Numbing, dissociation and multiple personality.

Sleep problems.

Low self-esteem; negative self-images.

Difficulty in trusting others.

Problems in parenting.

Tendency to be revictimised.

Sexual problems: anxiety, guilt, dissatisfaction, non-orgasmic, greater than average number of sexual partners.

Promiscuity.

Substance abuse, alcoholism.

Distorted thinking and other cognitive disorders.

Most of these disturbances are characteristic of adults diagnosed as having a borderline personality disorder – as described by authors such as Gunderson (1984), Kernberg (1975), Mack (1975), Perry and Klerman (1980). As Herman and van der Kolk (1987) point out, most studies of borderline personality disorder identify disturbances in five major areas: affect regulation; impulse control; reality testing; interpersonal relationships; self-concept or identity. The understanding of post-traumatic stress disorder which developed in the 1980s, partly through studies of Vietnam combat veterans who had suffered prolonged trauma, allowed some clinicians to begin to recognise that many features of PTSD are similar to those of borderline personality disorder. This link has been carefully and persuasively argued by Herman and van der Kolk (1987), Briere (1989), Herman (1992) and Waites (1993) amongst others. Thus it has been argued that childhood trauma gives rise to long-term PTSD and also that borderline personality disorder is a kind of PTSD; in some cases, borderline personality disorder may be a result of childhood trauma.

Anxiety, panics, nightmares and intrusive flashbacks of images of trauma are well recognised symptoms of PTSD. These correspond to the 'overwhelmed' stage of the response to trauma (Horowitz, 1986). The states of dissociation are characteristic of the stage of numbing, which is the defence against the overwhelmed state. Dissociation can be an automatic response to trauma, but with repeated trauma can also progress to a more intentional and partly conscious strategy of denial in which the child says to him/herself 'I am not here, not in this body – this is not happening to me – this is happening to someone else'. In extreme instances this dissociation may progress to multiple personality disorder; studies have shown a very high percentage of severe abuse or trauma in the backgrounds of patients with MPD (e.g. Putnam, Post & Guroff, 1986).

Many patients with histories of abuse devote much energy to not remembering or thinking about the traumatic events. When faced with the non-directive and free-associative quality of the analytic consulting room, they may become extremely anxious in struggling against the thoughts, images, impulses and affects which threaten to emerge. Self-harm, violent self-stimulation or other forms of distracting action may be resorted to in order to keep away from these threatening mental contents. The therapist need do no more than listen attentively in order for the patient to be traumatised by what is in his/her mind. Outside of the consulting room, such patients may spend much time in creating present day drama and engaging in alcohol and substance abuse as continual distractions from past trauma.

Cognitive distortions; core beliefs and conflicts

A number of cognitive distortions can be observed in patients with a history of childhood abuse. The person comes to view self and others and the future in highly negative ways. For example, the person will view the self as bad, worthless and as responsible for the abuse; he/she will see themselves as helpless; the future will be viewed as hopeless; there may be a belief that others can never be trusted. These may be similar to the cognitive distortions found in the thinking of depressive patients and those with anxiety disorders (e.g. Beck, 1967; Beck, Emery & Greenberg, 1985). However, the cognitive distortions of those traumatised in childhood seem to be particularly rigid and immune to influence. In working with such people it is possible to discern deep-rooted core beliefs that profoundly structure their experience of self and other. Examples of commonly found core beliefs are as follows:

I am responsible for the abuse that I suffered.

I must have been very bad for this abuse to have been done to me.

I deserve to die for allowing this abuse to take place.

I will always be abused.

I have never been loved and never will be.

It is never safe to trust anyone.

I can only be desired as an object of abuse.

Anyone who loves me is a fool worthy only of contempt.

There are only two kinds of people in this world – abusers and victims.

Some of these beliefs may be woven into very disabling conflicts. For example, a woman could only feel safe with a gentle and unassertive man; however, she also believed that a 'real man' was one who would dominate and control a woman, just as she had experienced her father.

It is also possible to discern recurrent core conflicts in abused people. For example:

WISH: I want to have a close and intimate relationship with X.

FEAR: I will be abused and controlled by X.
          Then I will be overwhelmed with rage and one of us
          will be destroyed.

DEFENCE: Therefore I will avoid X. If I find myself being drawn to X
          emotionally, I will run away, or I will distract myself with
          cruelty and hurt myself physically.

A review of cognitive distortions found in abused children is provided by Fish-Murray, Koby and van der Kolk (1987).

The functions of self-harm

A patient with a multiple personality disorder who had been severely abused in childhood explained to me the problem she experienced with dissociation. She said it was a very effective way of escaping from pain, but the dilemma then was how to get out of this state and back into the body. She described it as being like a dog chasing its tail, never quite catching it. Thus dissociation can be a successful defence against trauma but it leads to further anxiety, a dread of being forever lost outside the self.

Self-injury is often employed as a means of recovery from dissociation. A violent assault on the body is a way of returning to the body. Although appearing violent, it is actually a means of self-soothing. As Herman (1992) points out, abused children will discover that dissociation can be effectively terminated by a major jolt to the body, inducing an autonomic crisis or a state of extreme autonomic arousal. Cutting the body does this perfectly. People who deliberately cut themselves often describe this as highly relieving and gratifying. The act of self-harm may be highly addictive because it is very reinforcing, being immediately pleasurable. For this reason it may be extremely difficult for people to give up. Similarly purging and vomiting can have these effects, as can compulsive sexual activity, exposure to danger, and use of stimulant drugs.

Self-injury may also be prompted by the state of helplessness. The person who is deliberately cutting the body has entered a private world of omnipotence in which he/she is both abuser and abused. When the whole world around seems chaotic and abusive and the person feels no sense of control over his/her own life, cutting or otherwise hurting the body can provide an illusion of control. Overwhelming rage is in this way discharged on the body, which is thereby 'punished' for being a victim of abuse. In a hospital setting this behaviour may be experienced by staff as manipulative, but often it is not so in its motivation; self-inflicted injuries to the body may frequently be concealed rather than displayed as a communication to others.

Biological addiction to trauma

The psychobiology of the trauma response has been reviewed by van der Kolk (van der Kolk & Greenberg 1987; van der Kolk 1994). Kolb (1987) first proposed that excessive stimulation of the CNS during trauma may result in permanent neuronal changes, resulting, for example, in hyperarousal and hypervigilance – evidenced in such indicators as accoustic startle response which fails to habituate. It is suggested that this chronic physiological hyperarousal is due to long-term alterations in central neurotransmitter systems (van der Kolk, Greenberg & Boyd, 1985). Traumatised people may appear normal in some circumstances but may respond abnormally to stress; high states of arousal seem to evoke traumatic memories and sensations and behaviours associated with the trauma (van der Kolk, 1994). In attempts to compensate for the aversive hyperarousal, traumatised people may enter states of chronic numbed responsiveness, alternating with states of intense anxiety and rage.

The possibility of addiction to trauma is indicated by the fact that stress and injury give rise to elevated levels of plasma beta endorphins. Van der Kolk and Greenberg (1987) argue that repeated environmental trauma can give rise to an endogenous opioid response producing an effect similar to that of exogenous opioids – leading to a reduction in anxiety, rage, depression and paranoid feelings. This effect may be what is produced by self-cutting.

Apparent addiction to trauma may also result from the perseveration that is characteristic of states of high arousal. Under normal circumstances an animal will seek pleasure and avoid what is aversive. However, when hyperaroused the animal seeks what is familiar even though it may be highly aversive. Mice that had been locked in a box where they were exposed to electric shocks returned to those same boxes when they were subsequently stressed again (Mitchell, Osborne & O'Boyle, 1985). This means that when subject to high levels of stress, instead of following the usual response of avoiding pain, the animal will appear to seek it out – a profoundly paradoxical response which closely parallels the 'repetition compulsion' noted in humans.

SUMMARY

Succeeding in making emotional contact with the needy part of the abused patient may result in a negative therapeutic reaction. The patient's original object of need was a malevolent object – thus the patient is caught in a profound approach–avoidance conflict. Scenarios of the relationship to the malevolent object are a frequent theme in the therapy with the patient abused in childhood. It is crucial to address the patient's distorted thinking – the abuse-related cognitions. In recent years the long-term forms of post-traumatic stress disorder resulting from childhood abuse have been understood much more than previously. It can be seen that many features of borderline personality disorder can be understood as trauma-based. Trauma and abuse lead to chronic changes in psychobiology. Hyperarousal alternates with states of numbing. For the traumatised, self-harm may have a relieving, and thereby addicting effect. There are mechanisms for the biological addiction to trauma. In addition, animal studies show that the traumatised organism will compulsively seek out the trauma when hyperaroused.

Chapter 6

REMEMBERING, FORGETTING AND CONFABULATING: TERROR IN THE CONSULTING ROOM

The idea that our minds can play tricks on us, leading us to believe in a distorted reality, even in fantasy and confabulation, is deeply disturbing. If we can't trust our own minds to tell us the truth, what is left to trust?

(Loftus & Ketchem, 1994, p. 68)

The present debate about memory, recovered memory and pseudo-memory is thoroughly contemporary, reflecting many societal anxieties, fantasies and projections. It is also a very old debate, taking us right back to the origins of psychoanalysis – and it is probably no easier for us now than it was for Freud then. All manner of problems arise when the intimate material of the consulting room spills out into the wider social world, becoming a whirling storm gathering the legal system, the media and a variety of lobbying groups into its wake. Sexual abuse begins with an explosive violation of boundaries – and the explosion continues as the trajectory enters the consulting room and on outwards.

The debate is interesting in a number of ways. In particular it forces psychoanalysis and cognitive psychology to meet and attempt communication – difficult though that may be. Neither can reach an adequate understanding of these problems on their own. Moreover, we are compelled to recognise our own ignorance, both individually and collectively. Whilst a superficial examination may lead to an apparent understanding of what is going on – either in favour of the False Memory Society position, or against it – the issues are actually deeply murky and confusing. Beware of anyone who claims to understand what this is all about! In what follows, I offer no comfortable answers or certainties.

An earlier and shorter version of this chapter appears in Sinason (1996).

'UNFATHOMABLE, UNCATEGORISABLE, UNASSIMILABLE'. PSYCHOANALYTIC STRUGGLES WITH NARRATIVES OF TRAUMA AND ABUSE

In Freud's Vienna, knowledge of incest and of perverse and sadistic child abuse was largely in a state of repression. For example, Wolff (1995) describes two court cases within the same month involving parents alleged to have tortured and murdered their own children. Wolff comments: 'For the Viennese of 1899 these two trials were compellingly interesting – but they were also unfathomable, uncategorisable, unassimilable, for there were no references or precedents to help make sense out of such horror' (p. 4). After this brief and intense publicity, child abuse again fell out of public awareness in Vienna.

It was against this background about 100 years ago that Freud was struggling with the narratives of child abuse that were emerging in his consulting room, in response to his novel medical treatment based around talking and listening. He became greatly preoccupied with assessing the relative importance of reality-trauma and fantasy, and the truth status of recovered memory.

For example, in a letter to Abraham, he wrote: 'A proportion of the sexual traumas reported by patients are or may be phantasies . . . disentangling them from the so frequent genuine ones is not easy' (Abraham & Freud, 1965). As we know, Freud's attention moved from the impact of actual sexual abuse, and memories of this, to the role of the instincts and fantasy and, in particular, to the Oedipus complex. Blass and Simon (1994) describe the stages in Freud's development and discarding of his original seduction-trauma theories and his painful struggle with issues of evidence and truth. Simon (1992), in commenting on the decline of psychoanalytic interest in actual trauma and sexual abuse, in a paper entitled 'Incest – see under Oedipus Complex: The History of an Error in Psychoanalysis', writes:

> I believe much of what Freud had begun to observe and theorise about incest, and much of what he might have elaborated, migrated to the area of the primal scene, the psychoanalytic trauma par excellence . . . Primal Scene thus served as a distraction from, or defence against, the further awareness of the trauma of actual sexual abuse of children by parents. (p. 971)

It may be that Freud did find narratives of perverse abuse of children to be 'unfathomable, uncategorisable, unassimilable'. The evidence for this lies in the fact that although he wrote a great deal about sexuality, including a certain amount about more benign forms of perversion, he nowhere considered the question of what drives the person who abuses children.

In their discussion of knowing and not knowing massive psychic trauma, Laub and Auerhahn (1993) point out that in the last chapter of *The Interpretation of Dreams*, Freud (1900) describes a young woman who appears to have memories of sexual penetration in childhood, but she does not know what they mean; Freud labels these as 'hysterical fantasies'. They comment: 'In this case we see a man totally committed to knowing who does not know, does not recognize what he sees and, instead, discounts recall as fantasy . . .' (p. 288).

Meanwhile Ferenczi continued to emphasise trauma in the genesis of mental disorder, and the modifications of analytic technique which he felt were necessary to reach these deeper levels of warded off experience. This conflicted with Freud's position. In a letter to Freud in 1929, Ferenczi summarised his views:

> In all cases where I penetrated deeply enough, I found uncovered the traumatic-hysterical basis of the illness. Where the patient and I succeeded in this, the therapeutic effect was far more significant. In many cases I had to recall previously 'cured' patients for further treatment. (p. xxi)

He also complained of a trend in psychoanalysis towards 'overestimating the role of fantasy, and underestimating that of traumatic reality, in pathogenesis . . .'

On the whole, analysts who have emphasised actual trauma have been criticised, often fiercely, as Ferenczi was by Freud. Greenacre, in commenting on the response to her earlier writings on pre-Oedipal trauma, which were not specifically concerned with incest, wrote:

> The amount of resistance to my findings took me by surprise, especially the attitude expressed several times by colleagues that my work attempted to undermine the importance of the Oedipus complex. (quoted in Simon, 1992, p. 980)

Winnicott's views on the facilitating environment and on environmental failure, written in reaction to the emphasis of Melanie Klein on innate fantasy, stirred controversy and considerable hostility, but were perhaps more accepted because he was emphasising inadvertent trauma rather than gross and deliberate abuse.

Contemporary analysts still vary considerably over what credence is given to suggestions of actual sexual abuse and trauma. For example, I have found that analysts who hear material from the following psychoanalytic therapy are quite divided over whether the patient may have actually been sexually abused or not.

The patient shows the following characteristics. She frequently experiences terrors that the therapist will sexually assault her. For this reason she will not lie on the couch. Instead she sits in a chair which she requested be moved near the door for ease of escape. She often insists on leaving the door open so that she can run away easily if the therapist were to attack her. She is very afraid of men generally. She avoids wearing any clothes that might be seen as sexually provocative. Sometimes she enters a dissociative state and reports in a childlike manner experiences of sexual abuse and violent assault. On occasion she resorts to action and screaming rather than words, and will appear to be enacting scenes of sexual assault. She describes what she calls flashbacks of sexual assault – evoked for example by the sensation of a toothbrush in her mouth – and she becomes very frightened and flips into a state of dissociation and disorientation. She has presented a series of dreams in which men are breaking into the house she is in; in one of these a pole is thrown through the window; in some dreams she develops amazing strength to repel these men – and in one dream she thrusts an umbrella violently down someone's throat. She believes she may have been sexually abused as a child, but has no clear and visual memories of this.

Was she sexually abused or is the imagery of sexual attack a sexualised form of the patient's own violent wish to intrude and to control the therapist, now experienced in projection as coming back at her? It is the question of who thrust the umbrella down whose throat first. Other possibilities have also been suggested, but the idea that she may have been literally sexually abused has tended to be the least favoured option. Recently the patient has obtained corroborative evidence from a cousin suggesting that she was indeed sexually assaulted as a child.

This ambivalence amongst analysts about the reality or otherwise of sexual abuse is mirrored by that amongst patients. Van Leeuwen, in a paper entitled 'Resistances in the treatment of a sexually molested 6 year old girl' (1988), describes how the impulse to tell may occur in sudden bursts, unexpectedly, and may be followed by retraction and denial. Nonverbal re-enactments were more frequent in the case she describes.

CONTEMPORARY TRAUMA THEORY AND THE FALSE MEMORY DEBATE

An early precursor of contemporary trauma theory was the book edited by Krystal (1968) which looked at survivors of Nazi concentration camps, describing, amongst other effects, the extreme states of numbing which developed in these severely traumatised people. Most of what constitutes our current understanding of trauma has developed during the 1980s (predominantly in the USA) with the increased awareness of post-traumatic stress disorder, partly arising from studies of Vietnam war veterans; although psychodynamic this is outside the psychoanalytic mainstream. Van der Kolk, with his 1987 book *Psychological Trauma*, is foremost amongst this group of researchers and clinicians who have brought an understanding of how mental disturbance can have roots in childhood trauma. Judith Lewis Herman, who wrote the landmark *Trauma and Recovery* (1992), is another major figure who has developed the clinical implications of these insights. Ulman and Brothers wrote *The Shattered Self* (1988) which looks at trauma from a Kohutian self-psychological point of view. Levine edited *Adult Analysis and Childhood Sexual Abuse* (1990); whilst reflecting the increasing awareness amongst analysts of CSA, this volume does not take full account of the emerging studies of trauma. Davies and Frawley have recently written *Treating the Adult Survivor of Childhood Sexual Abuse* (1994) which is also from a psychoanalytic point of view and is excellent and fully informed by the recent trauma studies. Also related to these trends is the extensive American literature on dissociative states thought to result from severe childhood abuse.

Van der Kolk and Fisler (1994), summarising much of this work, describe a constellation of five areas of disturbance, clustering in people who suffered interpersonal trauma at an early age: '1. alterations in regulating affective arousal; 2. dissociation and amnesia; 3. somatisation; 4. chronic characterological changes in the areas of self-perception, perception of others and relationship with the perpetrator; 5. alterations in systems of meaning' (p. 147). Clearly this is a description of many non-psychotic chronic psychiatric patients who suffer from a variety of somatic, affective and interpersonal problems.

Just as we were beginning to arrive at some understanding of the trauma-based nature of severe personality disorders, the 'false memory' debate exploded around us, with numerous newspaper articles, threats of litigation, and special working groups of both the British and American Psychological Societies.

The memory debate began in 1991 when Pamela Freyd, under the pseudonym of Jane Doe, wrote an article in *Issues in Child Abuse Accusations*, entitled 'How could this happen? Coping with a false accusation of incest and rape', describing the impact on a family of an adult daughter's recovered 'memories' of abuse. She then sets up the False Memory Syndrome Foundation (FMSF), with a group of sympathetic academics and mental health professionals. Subsequently, the Freyd's daughter, Jennifer, who was the subject of the Jane Doe article and who is herself an academic cognitive psychologist, joined in the debate with a vengeance (Freyd, J. 1993). In vivid and emotive language she accused her parents of a variety of boundary violations. Having heard Pamela Freyd's account of their experiences with their daughter (personal communication), I am left as confused as ever, since both narratives seem plausible and both are pervaded with profound pain.

Who is telling the truth? Whose version of reality will prevail? In scenarios like these, somebody is knowingly lying or their perception of reality is seriously distorted – but whose?

Psychotherapists face a puzzle, involving clinical, ethical, legal and public image dimensions, over accounts of false memory narratives of childhood abuse. The problem is not confined to those who might use specific memory recovery techniques, but is an issue for all whose adult patients tell of childhood abuse. Few psychologists or decently trained psychotherapists would assume that memories of childhood events are necessarily accurate. However, some emerging anecdotal evidence is that memory narratives of childhood abuse may develop which are detailed and persuasive but are essentially untrue (whilst others may be essentially true).

The implications of this are so serious that inevitably the debate has become highly emotional and at times itself abusive. Some of the reporting and commentary in the press has been inflammatory, generating considerably more heat than light. Although the recent (1995) BPS report on recovered memories takes the position that false memories of abuse are a possibility to be considered very seriously, some of the media coverage misleadingly asserts that the report dismisses the possibility. As a result psychologists become seen as supporters of something called 'recovered memory therapy', a term actually invented by the False Memory Societies. In the murky maelstrom of this debate, what is clear is that the problems around memory in psychotherapy are profoundly important, deeply disturbing and extraordinarily confusing.

The evidence suggesting the occurrence of false memory of childhood abuse lies mainly in the following areas:

1. Many families claim false allegations.
2. Experiments show that false memories, including those of past lives and abduction by aliens, can be implanted through hypnosis. Hypnosis can elicit both true and false memories, but with enhanced belief in their accuracy. Some forms of therapy may have hypnotic-like components, including suggestion, influence of authority, peer-group pressure, etc.
3. Experimental studies, especially by Loftus, show how easily memory can be distorted. It is widely recognised that memory is reconstructive rather than photographic.

4. Experimental studies have shown that the creation of completely false memories is possible.

The argument of the False Memory Societies (in both the USA and Britain) is that false memories are fostered by the following factors: (a) a culture or subculture preoccupied with child sexual abuse, resulting in a mental set to expect memories of abuse; (b) 'survivor groups', often with strongly feminist agendas, create environments where participants inadvertently suggest narratives of abuse to one another; these provide single self-exculpating and comforting explanations of participants' problems; (c) naïve views of memory as being like a videotape are widespread; (d) powerfully suggestive and aggressive techniques are used in therapy to elicit 'memories'; (e) there is an inappropriate use of the concept of repression, when there is little unequivocal research evidence that repression of traumatic memory is possible.

Examples of the better academic writings emphasising the dangers of false memories emerging in psychotherapy are: Lindsay and Read, 1994; Ceci and Loftus, 1994. These and other authors have emphasised some of the misleading assumptions about memory which may be prevalent amongst some therapists.

A typical quote from the FMS literature is as follows:

> In less than a decade, new fields of law and psychotherapy have sprung up around the theory that children can repress memories of sex abuse and later, as adults, retrieve them.

> Actually, recovered memories of sex abuse only gained increased acceptance by psychotherapists in the early 1980s, providing a means of explaining eating disorders, difficulties in forming relationships, low self-esteem and sexual dysfunction. They theorised that the trauma of sex abuse could cause children to repress temporarily all memory of the abuse. (Loftus & Rosenwald, 1993)

Whilst it is true that the awareness of the prevalence of child sexual abuse only emerged in the mid 1980s, the knowledge of traumatic amnesia has been known for over 100 years and is part of a well established tradition in psychiatry. The idea of recovered memories is not new. However, the determined, even frenzied search for memories of childhood sexual abuse, which has been described as characteristic of some therapists in the USA (Loftus & Ketcham, 1994) may be a recent, hitherto unknown phenomenon. The reconstruction of childhood experiences, through assembling the clues in transference, countertransference, free-association and dreams, is an extremely complicated undertaking, requiring extensive training in analytic work – a training which many therapists do not have.

Whilst there can be no objection to the point that memory is only partially reliable and can be subject to a number of errors, I believe it is misleading to suggest (as much of the FMS literature does) that the idea of being abused as a child can be a comforting solution to mental distress. In my experience recovered memories do not make people feel better – at least not initially. Approaching a traumatic memory may put a person in a state of terror, with disorientation and temporary psychosis. It may provoke extreme self-harm and suicidal acts, especially cutting as illustrated in the following example.

Clinical illustration 1

The following account, given by a colleague in the United States, covers a period of about four years. The setting is a general psychiatric clinic.

This very difficult case illustrates how the struggle with spontaneously emerging thoughts of childhood trauma can lead to an alarming worsening of a patient's mental state.

Mrs S, an African American woman in her early forties working in a profession in pharmacological science and with an excellent career record, presented with a complaint of total inability to tolerate intercourse, although she did experience sexual desires for her husband. The marriage, of several years duration, was in fact unconsummated. Previous behavioural therapy, of standard format, had been unsuccessful and therefore she was referred for psychotherapy. The patient presented a lively account of herself, but an initial consultation was inconclusive, other than indicating considerable fears of sexual attack – including a quite literal anxiety that the male interviewer would assault her. In the hope of understanding more, she and the therapist embarked upon further extended consultations. These became further extended – as each time they hoped to arrive at some clearer understanding of the nature and roots of her problem, even if only partial. A pattern developed in which she would present much material which strongly hinted of sexual abuse in childhood, but would block any attempt to explore this further and would complain that she had no memories of any such experiences. However she did explain that she put great effort into not hearing, reading or viewing any material which might trigger thoughts about sex.

They went on like this for months, unable to stop and reach any conclusion, and unable to continue with productive therapy. She was as afraid of her mind being penetrated as she was of her vagina being raped. She acknowledged that there were 'guards' in her mind, which at times could be extremely hostile towards the therapist. She would stare at him suspiciously and ask what he was looking for. She would shout at him not to push her into a corner – although from his point of view he was simply trying to listen and understand. She became aware that her life was pervaded by a profound distrust of everyone and a constant fear of being sexually attacked by men.

The work was at a prolonged stalemate. She was profoundly distressed but seemed unable to allow the therapist to have much access to her mind. A great many lines of interpretation and understanding were attempted but none led to any break in the impasse. Frequently she asserted that there was no reason for her state of mind, it was simply the way she was. At her own initiative she sought help from a hypnotherapist at another clinic, specifically with the aim of recovering early memories (a practice clearly not to be recommended). During each session with him she managed to engage him in so much discussion of other issues that no hypnosis took place; again she experienced conscious anxieties that he would rape her. She and her husband sought marital therapy and there was some improvement in their relationship and she experienced him as genuinely supportive, but still there was no intercourse. She could not allow vaginal penetration in spite of a desire for this.

Her failure to achieve intercourse even though she had a new and better relationship led her to feel ever more depressed and despairing. Increasingly she communicated despair, suicidal thoughts and fears of becoming out of control and hurting herself or others. This steadily progressed to a state in which she was regularly cutting herself. States of dissociation were apparent. She had little capacity to think about what might be behind her agitation. She would phone in considerable anxiety, needing to speak to the therapist, but would then storm out of his office without anything being discussed. Sometimes she would indicate that something was troubling her deeply but she did not know what it was. The therapist felt helpless, aware of her distress, unable to help her, and yet witnessing her rapidly deteriorating mental state. His only understanding of her was to speculate that some as yet undiscovered early trauma, which had originally filled her with terror and rage, was pushing its way to the surface of her awareness with explosive force, resulting in the overwhelming affect that she was presenting. She continued to be extremely hostile to any attempt to explore what might lie behind her anxiety – always resorting to an insistence that she was just made that way. She was referred to a psychiatrist colleague but she refused medication. Mrs S and the therapist were able to clarify and agree upon one point; that throughout her sessions the fundamental question that informed his communications to her was 'Why?', and this was the question that she always wished to avoid because it made her anxious.

She became unable to go to work. Her behaviour became increasingly disturbed and she talked frequently of overwhelming suicidal urges and described attacks on her body with knives, razor blades and burns with a hot iron. She also experienced powerful urges to attack other people. Her moods oscillated wildly, she began to lose track of time and appeared very frightened and confused about herself. What was going on? The team did not know. Eventually they admitted her to hospital. None of the clinicians felt they had much idea how to help her. She was not psychotic but was clearly deeply troubled and disturbed and dangerously suicidal.

Gradually, in the safer and more contained atmosphere of the hospital, Mrs S produced much material relating to early abuse and terror. She became extremely anxious about these thoughts, at times dismissing them all as lies. She became very anxiously preoccupied with whether or not she was a liar, and whether a relative had abused her. She was tormented by the uncertainty; many indications of early abuse had been revealed, but much remained inconclusive. The difficult therapeutic task at this point was to support her in her struggle with the uncertainty, to make clear to her the problems of distinguishing literal truth, metaphorical truth and fantasy, and to avoid pushing her to a premature conclusion about these matters.

She became even more suicidal and bent on self-harm. She complained that she could not bear the thoughts and images and memories that were emerging in her mind. During her sessions with the therapist she would be preoccupied with her wish to damage herself. She would be busy looking around the room for something to cut herself with. She told him that she always carried razor blades in her pocket in case she needed to cut herself. On one memorable occasion, she began by mentioning that she had a terrible nightmare which she did not wish to talk about. When the therapist asked her if she would like to tell him anything at all about this, she got up and began pounding her head violently against a wall. He attempted to restrain her. She fought with him, kicking a table and its contents flying, attempted to smash her fist through the window and began to reach in her pocket for her razor blades. In the end it required three men to restrain her, pinned to the ground.

It became clearer to the therapist that these states of mind in which she was preoccupied with self-harm functioned as distractions from whatever thoughts and memories were troubling her. For example, in the incident just described, she had been escaping from her nightmare – the content of which she felt related to childhood experiences. In addition to the distraction, the self-harm states also seemed to involve unconscious re-enactments of scenes of abuse – thus in that instance she ended up being held down by three men, an experience which she consciously associated with rape. From this point whenever she showed any signs of being in a self-harm state of mind, the therapist firmly and clearly interpreted this function of distraction. He also pointed out that it was not her memories per se which disturbed her and caused her problems; rather it was her attempts to avoid these memories – this was true obviously of her original presenting problem of inability to have intercourse, especially since she had by now become clear that she was afraid to attempt intercourse in case she had a flashback of abuse (her own insight). She began to get this message and actually calmed down a bit.

The point about this example is that whatever the truth of her thoughts and images about her childhood, the patient did not find the idea that she had been abused to be in any way relieving or reassuring. The idea was associated with immense anxiety. Indeed it appeared to be the pressing emergence of this idea (whether true or fantasy), and her attempts to avoid its emergence, that had been disturbing her in the first place.

REMEMBERING AND REPRESSING

Repression has never been experimentally demonstrated in the laboratory. However, there is nothing novel or implausible about the notion of motivated amnesia (or simply denial) for memories of trauma, which reemerge into awareness at a later stage. Clinical and naturalistic research, as opposed to that based in a laboratory, which has looked at survivors of abuse has indeed found evidence of amnesia for trauma (e.g. Herman & Shatzow, 1987; Briere & Conte, 1989; Feldman-Summers & Pope, 1994; Loftus, Polonsky & Fullilove, 1994; Williams, 1994). Few in the field deny that motivated loss of memory is possible. The debate is about the reliability of recovered memory.

There are some memory images which inherently suggest traumatic amnesia. For example, a woman has a memory of going up to her schizophrenic father's bedroom and coming out crying and screaming, but does not remember what went on in the bedroom. In another example, a man claims to have almost no memory of his childhood; however, he reports that when he thinks of the decade of his pre-adolescent childhood, he imagines it as like looking down from an aircraft over a city shrouded in cloud, knowing that below this covering was crime, pollution and corruption.

Is the concept of repression misleading? In a widely quoted paper, Pope and Hudson (1995) argue that a requirement for a satisfactory test of repression is that 'psychogenic amnesia' should be distinguished from those 'cases in which victims simply tried not to think about the events, pretended that the events never occurred . . .' (p. 122). However, as I listen to patients talking about their experience of forgetting and remembering traumatic childhood events, what is striking is that the amnesia often does seem to be based upon a partially conscious attempt not to think about something awful, or upon a wish to deny that something happened. A person may report that on talking about childhood, not necessarily to a therapist, a painful event is recalled; he/she might say 'It wasn't that I had really forgotten – I just hadn't thought about it for years – I guess I hadn't wanted to think about it.' Another way of understanding the amnesia is that the memory of trauma acts like an internal phobic focus; the person learns to avoid thinking of something which leads to anxiety, just like any other phobic behaviour. The phenomenology of remembering and forgetting is not of some mysterious process completely beyond consciousness.

It is quite often argued by advocates of the FMS position that if an adult patient reports emerging memories of childhood sexual abuse, the therapist should seek corroborative evidence. This is a curious argument because it seems to deny the fact that the patient is an adult. Whilst it may be appropriate for the therapist to help the patient think about the nature of an apparent memory and the question of whether there exists any independent evidence or possible corroboration, the therapist clearly has no right to seek this him/herself without direction from the patient. The therapist's primary task is to address the patient's thoughts and is not to become involved in family disputes. Very few patients who disclose childhood sexual abuse to a therapist seem concerned with taking any legal action against the abuser. The wish is usually for acknowledgement and an expression of remorse. My impression is that where an adult patient privately confronts a parent or relative with having abused them, the possibilities of healing, of dialogue and of arriving at the truth are greatly diminished by the parents' rushing to a legalistic protestation of their innocence.

ILLUSTRATIONS OF THE EXPERIENCE OF FORGETTING AND REMEMBERING

The following two accounts describe patients who sought therapy *because* they were experiencing flashback images of childhood abuse. Both narratives were presented in single initial consultations.

Clinical illustration 2

In an initial consultation, a patient described extensive sexual abuse in her childhood, involving a number of perpetrators in what sounded like a very disordered family. She had referred to these events in her application form, filled out before attending the clinic; she had not seen any other therapist or counsellor, nor attended any 'survivor groups'. Her initial comments were about what she called 'blackouts' which appeared to be brief periods of dissociation when she lost awareness and was amnesic. After she had gone on to give a lengthy narrative of abuse, I enquired further about dissociation, explaining that sometimes when children are repeatedly abused they try to cope by pretending it is not happening. She replied: 'Oh yes – I did that – it was as if there were two of me – the one who was getting the abuse and another one that it wasn't happening to.' She also then spoke of how she has a tendency to switch off now, like in these 'blackouts', perhaps when she is watching television. I asked whether these periods of dissociation might be triggered by material on TV which reminded her of abuse. She thought this was the case. She also gave an example of how she had recently dissociated during a conversation which had contained a reference to sexual abuse.

She said it was the first time she had told anyone about *all* the abuse, adding that she had felt very anxious about coming to the consultation but knew she needed to talk about these experiences; she wanted to get the talking over and done with, which she felt was rather like the way she had wanted to get the abuse over and done with whenever it took place. She said she had begun to remember more and more since beginning to talk about these matters to her husband a few months ago. I asked if there had ever been a time when she had not remembered these events. She replied that there definitely had been such periods, especially for a few years after leaving school. During this period 'it was as if nothing had happened to me – I didn't want to think anything had happened to me.' I then asked what she would have said at the time if she had been asked if she had ever been sexually abused. She replied that she would have said no. I asked if she would have believed this. She said: 'Yes – I didn't think anything had happened to me until recently when things started coming out.' She then explained that her memories were quite detailed, sudden flashbacks involving various sensory modalities, including smell. She added that partly she did not want to remember and wanted to forget again. She wanted to get the telling over and done with so that she could put it out of her mind. She added that she thought the memories had been returning much more since having her own children.

Clinical illustration 3

This patient was a woman in her thirties, briefly admitted to a psychiatric ward. The following account was given to me in a single consultation. Her memories of abuse emerged spontaneously and not in the context of therapy.

She told me that she had been extensively abused between the ages of six and fourteen. This had involved a family of five brothers who lived nearby. They would take her places and threaten that if she did not do what they wanted, or if she told anyone, they would abuse her younger brother. She said she recalled experiences in which three of these young men were having sex with her at the same time, vaginally, anally and orally, whilst one watched and the other kept a look out.

She said she had begun to have flashback memories of these experiences about two and a half years previously and as a result had started seeing a sexual abuse counsellor at a local clinic. As a result more memories of abuse came to her awareness. She said the flashback memories were very vivid – 'like being there again'. She described how she would remember them and then forget them again. Eventually she found the emergence of these memories to be too painful and overwhelming and had stopped seeing the counsellor and had 'shut it all out'. She had managed to do this for about a year but then the memories had started to emerge again.

She said that after recovering the memories of the five boys, she had begun to recall highly abusive experiences with her disturbed mother. For example, she described how her mother would hang her upside down with her hands tied and suspended from the ceiling of the coal shed and would leave her there.

She said she had been afraid to speak about the abuse from the brothers because she thought her father would kill them and would end up in prison and she would be left with her mother. She emphasised how frightened she was of her mother and described an occasion when her mother had chased her down the street with a carving knife. She had hidden under a stationary lorry and her mother kept jabbing at her with the carving knife. Her father happened to be driving past at this point and she managed to attract his attention and he got out and took her to the police station. At the police station they found she was covered in tiny punctures from the carving knife and a police woman put plasters over these. They took her mother back to the psychiatric hospital where she was a patient. She then explained that her mother had MPD, which must have been a rare diagnosis at that time, and that she had five personalities, one of which was a loving mother, whilst 'the other four were all evil'. She said her mother would torture her by sticking pins underneath her toenails; if she showed pain her mother would do this more and so she learned to cut off from pain. She also spoke of her mother involving her in perverse sexual activity.

She had previously had a period of hospitalisation 20 years before, because she had spontaneously undergone a prolonged regression to a childlike state; she had been given many ECTs at this time, which she felt had contributed to her blocking out her childhood memories.

She thought this most recent admission to hospital had been precipitated by flashback images of 'Dad doing things to me'. These images had been horrifying to her, she said, because her Dad had been the one good figure in her life. There had been two images which disturbed her: one was of her father bathing her in a bowl of water, washing her private parts and the water being red coloured; the second image was of being in bed with her father. She had struggled with these images, but when she had come into hospital had decided she would 'let it all come out'. When she did so she experienced a realisation that the images were to do with her father washing her *after* she had been abused by the others – that he was putting her to bed afterwards and in this way had been trying to look after her. I asked if she thought he knew about the abuse. She said she thought he must have known and she felt angry with him about this but felt that in his own way he had been trying to protect her.

She remarked that when she had told people about some of these events, she felt that they did not want to believe her because the accounts were so awful. She thought this had been another factor that had inhibited her speaking about her experiences. She said she had not wanted to believe herself.

After some unhappy earlier relationships she is now happily married to a man she finds very loving and supportive. I wondered aloud whether it may have been partly her happy marriage that had enabled her to feel safe enough to begin to remember. She became thoughtful about this and said she thought this might be so.

I talked to her about the problems of assessing the truth of childhood memories. She seemed to appreciate fully that memory is not always reliable and can be misleading. She said that her own changing interpretations of the images of her father had persuaded her of this.

This account is particularly interesting, first because of the vivid way in which she describes the trauma of remembering, and secondly her changing interpretations of the images involving her father. The visual image flashes into her consciousness, but she gives two quite different meanings to it – and who knows whether either of them is correct ?

LOFTUS AND TERR

In 1994 two books were published by memory experts: *Unchained Memories* by Lenore Terr, who is a psychiatrist who has made longitudinal studies of the memory of trauma victims; and *The Myth of Repressed Memory* by Elizabeth Loftus and Katherine Ketcham – Loftus is an academic psychologist specialising in memory research, and Ketcham is a journalist. The books are strikingly similar in style, both highly readable – and both describe the same murder case where the crucial and sole piece of evidence was an adult's flashback memory of her father bludgeoning a child to death. Terr, for the prosecution, argued there was every reason to believe the memory was true, and claimed that traumatic memories are retained in particularly vivid detail. Loftus, witness for the defence, disagreed, arguing there was every reason to doubt the reliability of the apparent memory, and claimed that her research showed that trauma particularly interfered with the accuracy of memory. The jury believed Terr. Two memory experts, two divergent views. The terrible reality is that we do not know who is right.

Commenting on experiments by Loftus and others which indicate ways in which memory can be falsified in the laboratory, Terr (1994) writes, rather dismissively:

> Despite the interesting points in the Loftus research, psychological experiments on university students do not duplicate in any way the clinician's observation. What comes from the memory lab does not apply well to the perception, storage, and retrieval of such things as childhood murders, rapes or kidnappings. Trauma sets up new rules for memory You can't simulate murders without terrorising your research subjects. Experiments on college students do not simulate clinical instances of trauma. And they have little to do with childhood itself. (p. 52)

Loftus disagrees, arguing that experimental psychologists study the basic processes of memory formation, storage and retrieval which *can* be generalised to real life. She emphasises the essential permeability of memory, described as 'flexible and superimposable, a panoramic blackboard with an endless supply of chalk and erasers' (1994, p. 3). Actually I find Loftus to be the more cautious of the two writers, sensitive to the dilemmas of the clinician, but emphasising uncertainty in evaluating memory.

Whilst Terr certainly believes that false memories are possible, she argues that if recovered memory is associated with signs and symptoms of trauma, then this is evidence that the memory may contain truth.

> If a child is exposed to a shocking, frightening, painful or overexciting event, he or she will exhibit psychological signs of having had the experience. The child will re-enact aspects of the terrible episode and may complain of physical sensations similar to those originally felt. The child will fear a repetition of the episode, and will often feel generally and unduly pessimistic about the future . . . If on the other hand, a child is exposed only to a frightening rumour, . . . to the symptoms of another victim of trauma, the child may pick up symptom or two . . . but will not suffer a cluster of symptoms and signs. (1994, p. 161)

Perhaps so – but the fact that an apparent memory is consistent with a cluster of symptoms and signs does not prove that the particular memory is true. The 'memory' could be a fantasy, congruent with a deep schema of the mind but not containing literal truth. Such a memory could be *structurally* or *thematically* true but literally false.

EXPLICIT AND VERBAL MEMORY VS IMPLICIT AND ENACTIVE MEMORY

It is a commonplace of memory theorising (ever since Bartlett, 1932) to emphasise that memory is reconstructive, like repeatedly telling a story to oneself, and that it is assimilated to and organised by schemas. Thus according to this assumption, memory of the 'raw' and unprocessed event is never available. Moreover, according to Piaget (1945), until there are available *representations* of events, predominantly words, which can be manipulated within the mind, there can be no memory: 'There are no memories of early childhood for the excellent reason that at that stage there is no evocative mechanism capable of organising them' (p. 187).

Certainly, if we consider only memory that can be recalled and communicated in words, then we are led to emphasise the essential unreliability of memory and the impossibility of recalling anything from the earliest years. We might regard our remembering of our own past as little more than a continual personal mythmaking. Indeed, some psychoanalytic theorising emphasises just that (e.g. Spence, 1982), viewing the analytic endeavour as arriving at only 'narrative truth'. However, this would be to ignore the whole area of implicit, behavioural or enactive memory, excellently reviewed by Share (1994). These may not be accessible to conscious recall or to representation in words, but may be startlingly accurate; by contrast verbal memory is dependent on conscious awareness and is subject to a great many distortions and creative embellishments.

For example, Terr (1991) found that amongst 20 children with documented histories of early trauma, none could give a verbal description of events before two and a half years, but 18 of these showed evidence of a traumatic memory in their behaviour and play; e.g. a child who had been sexually molested by a babysitter in the first two years of life, could not at age five remember or name the babysitter and also denied any knowledge of being abused, but in his play he enacted scenes that exactly replicated a pornographic movie made by the babysitter. In another example, a five-year-old child who had been sexually and pornographically abused in a day centre between age 15 and 18 months, was amnesic of these events, but reported a 'funny feeling' in her 'tummy' whenever a finger was pointed at her; photographs confiscated from the centre showed an erect penis pointing at her stomach. Terr (1988) concludes that 'literal mirroring of traumatic events by behavioural memory (can be) established at any age including infancy' (p. 103).

Similarly, Dorpat and Miller (1992), writing of 'enactive memories', review a case presented by Pine (1985). The patient was an intelligent eight-year-old girl who repeatedly engaged in unprovoked aggressive behaviour involving charging through a group of her peers, knocking them over. She had been hit by a truck and badly injured at 18 months of age, but had no conscious memory of this. During each therapy session she would begin by dropping to the floor as if dead, or would make a beeping sound like the horn of a truck.

Another example of enactive memory is provided by Piontelli (1988) who described her work with a two-year-old psychotic child, whose play was pervaded by what appeared to be 'memories' of foetal experience. It was known that the child had stopped moving in the womb at 5 months and was born with the umbilical cord wrapped tightly around her neck. In her highly repetitive play she wore a heavy chain wrapped around her neck and refused to remove it, she pressed an object against her navel, and wrapped herself up tightly in a curtain like a mummy – and in these ways seemed to want continually to recreate the experiences in the womb. Piontelli (1989) has also studied foetuses using ultrasound and has documented the continuities in behaviour and temperament between the child's behaviour inside and outside the womb. In the context of these studies of foetuses, the repetitious behavioural enactments of her two-year-old patient seem less surprising.

A truly startling example of a 30-month-old child's accurate and verbal memory of his own birth, by caesarian section, is given by Laibow (1986).

The child's development was exceptional, for example, lifting his head, focusing and following with his eyes on day 1, speaking recognisable words at 3 months and sentences at 5 months. One day, aged two and a half, whilst sitting in the bath, he suddenly asked his parents why the lights were so bright 'when I was new'. On being asked what he meant by 'new', he explained that he meant 'being born' and said there were many things he did not understand about this. He then proceeded to ask: why the light was circular and intense where he was but dim elsewhere; why the bottom half of the faces were missing, with a green patch there instead; why someone had felt his anus with their finger; why he was put into a plastic box and taken somewhere; why liquid was put into his eyes so that he could not see; what was inserted into his nose that made a loud sucking sound. He also described many other features of his birth and experiences in the womb. Laibow commented that he had never seen a surgical unit, nor seen surgical green masks, nor known that silver nitrate solution is routinely used in the eyes of newborns, nor seen or heard a suctioning device used in the nostrils – except on the occasion of his own birth. It would appear that this child had an unusually developed and organised sensory awareness before and at birth, and was able to retain these experiences in a way that could later be linked to the (also precociously developed) linguistic system. Those who argue that memories of birth are inherently impossible have the onus of explaining instances of this kind – and these are just a few of the examples scattered through the psychoanalytic literature.

It is not surprising that academic memory theorists and researchers have largely ignored behavioural or enactive memory, since it is mainly the psychoanalytically trained observer who is likely to be attuned to these unconscious modes of representation, and who studies infants and children in relatively unstructured situations. This is essentially psychoanalytic data, the unconscious representation of trauma. Share (1994) provides an extensive discussion of the representation of infant trauma in dreams. Drawing upon suggestions by Mancia (1981), she hypothesises that earliest experience can be processed through REM states, long before a linguistic system is available.

In these days of concern about pseudo-memories and false allegations of childhood abuse, it should be needless to add that of course no dream or behavioural enactment can give definitive evidence of an event in infancy or early childhood. Moreover, the exploration of the unconscious meanings of dreams and behaviour is extremely complex and demanding and should not be attempted by those with inadequate training.

It is clear from the above that the experience of trauma may be processed and stored in memory in modes which may not be accessible to language.

The theorising of cognitive psychologists such as Schactel, Bruner, Postman, Neisser, Piaget, suggest that in the earliest months, memory is encoded in sensorimotor, enactive and iconic modes, as opposed to linguistic (see discussion in Greenberg & van der Kolk, 1987). This reveals the possibility of a blocking of the processing of trauma into the symbolic language necessary for cognitive retrieval – either for defensive reasons or because of the immaturity of the neurological system. In 'recalling' such trauma, a person could then experience affect without words, 'unspeakable terror' or 'nameless dread', which is in fact often described by traumatised patients. We might expect the possibility of the partial reliving of affective and somatosensory components of traumatic memories, without the symbolic and linguistic representations necessary to place the trauma in its historic context. Such partial flashbacks could be reactivated by affective, auditory or visual cues; for example the way a person may be precipitated into a state of rage and terror whilst having intercourse with their partner. Reviewing the evidence, van der Kolk (1994) concludes:

> Conceivably traumatic memories could emerge, not in the distorted fashion of ordinary recall but as affect states, somatic sensations, or visual images (for example nightmares or flashbacks) that are timeless and unmodified by further experience. (p. 261)

However, the caution must be added that as soon as the person attempts to make sense of their experience in words, distortions and confabulations may begin.

TRAUMA PATHWAYS IN THE BRAIN

Neurocognitive psychologists (e.g. LeDoux, 1989; van der Kolk, 1994) suggest that two areas of the limbic system are particularly involved in the processing of emotionally charged memories, the amygdala and the hippocampus. The amygdala is thought to play a part in the evaluation of the emotional meaning of incoming stimuli and may be thought of as the affective learning system in infancy. This part of the brain matures earlier than the hippocampal system which is thought to record the spatial and temporal dimensions necessary for the storage and retrieval of declarative or explicit memory. The slow maturation of the hippocampus may be the essential reason for infantile amnesia. It seems quite conceivable that blocking of the processing from the amygdala to the hippocampus may be one possible mechanism for severe repression of traumatic experience

– whether this is motivated defensively, or simply a consequence of the trauma itself. Van der Kolk (1994) comments:

> Various external and internal stimuli, including stress-induced corticos-
> terone production, decrease hippocampal activity. However, even when
> stress interferes with hippocampally mediated memory storage and cate-
> gorisation, some mental representation of the experience is probably laid
> down by means of a system that records affective experience but has no
> capacity for symbolic processing or placement in space and time. (p. 261)

Memories established through the amygdala appear to be highly immune to modification. LeDoux, Romanski and Xagoraris (1991) studied fear extinction in rats. The conditioned stimulus was visual, a flashing light, and the unconditioned stimulus was a shock grid. In those rats whose visual cortex had been lesioned, the learned fear responses were far more persistent than in rats with an intact visual cortex. What this means is that when the affective learning takes place subcortically, probably via the amygdala, the emotional learning is more or less indelible. Moreover, LeDoux, Romanski and Xagoraris (1991) found that a single intense stimu-lation of the amygdala in mature animals will produce lasting changes in neuronal excitability and behavioural changes towards either fight or flight. Adamec, Stark-Adamec and Livingston (1980) used kindling experi-ments with cats to show that growth in the amplitude of amygdaloid and hippocampal seizure activity led to permanent increases in defensiveness and predatory aggression – the direction of these changes being deter-mined by the prior temperament of the cat.

These studies suggest that preverbal emotional memory of trauma may be deeply persisting – perhaps linked to what Terr (1988) calls 'burned in' visual impressions. Terr suggests:

> When a trauma or series of extreme stresses strikes well below the age of 28
> to 36 months, the child 'burns in' a visual memory of it, sometimes later
> becoming able as years go on to affix a few words to the picture . . . On the
> other hand, when trauma strikes after the age of 28 to 36 months, two
> memories, verbal and visual, may simultaneously be taken in, stored and
> made ready for retrieval. (p. 104)

Terr argues that the visual memory remains true to the traumatic event which precipitated it, whilst the verbal memory is prone to elaboration and distortion. We must be careful here. The problem with this argument is that whilst the visual memory may be truthfully retained, its source (such as a dream) may be misperceived (Belli & Loftus, 1994).

What we arrive at is the implication that early trauma may create a deeply 'burned in' unconscious schema, with powerful conditioned affective responses, which continually organises later experience; however, it may not be possible ever to locate or recall consciously and accurately what that trauma was.

LEARNING NOT TO REMEMBER

Summarising our current knowledge of response to trauma, van der Kolk (1994) comments:

> a vast literature . . . has shown that the trauma response is bimodal: hypermnesia, hyperreactivity to stimuli and traumatic re-experiencing coexist with psychic numbing, avoidance, amnesia and anhedonia. These responses to extreme experiences are so consistent across the different forms of traumatic stimuli that this bimodal reaction appears to be the normative response to any overwhelming and uncontrollable experience. (p. 254)

The point which is crucial to the present discussion is that amnesia and hypermnesia, not remembering and remembering too much, are both responses to trauma. It is a matter of everyday clinical experience that patients who have been abused in childhood will describe active attempts not to think about, or to underplay the significance of, their painful early experiences; on the other hand, when the person does begin to think more about their childhood, perhaps in the context of therapy, then he/she feels overwhelmed with remembering too much too intensely.

Terr has studied traumatised children over many years. She finds that recall for single blow traumas in an otherwise trauma-free environment, which she calls Type 1 traumas, are usually recalled with startling precision and detail. By contrast, Type II traumas which involve repeated brutalisation are processed very differently. She writes (1991) 'The defenses and coping operations used in the Type II disorders of childhood – massive denial, repression, dissociation, self-anaesthesia, self-hypnosis, identification with aggressor, and aggression turned against the self – often lead to profound character changes . . . Children who experience Type II traumas often forget. They may forget whole segments of childhood . . . Repeatedly brutalised, benumbed children employ massive denial . . .' (pp. 15–16). What Terr describes is not really surprising if we consider that the child who is repeatedly abused will have the opportunity to learn ways of reducing their states of being overwhelmed by making use of a variety of mechanisms of defence.

My own impression is that the fundamental mental defence against overwhelming trauma is dissociation. The child flips into a state of autohypnosis, as if thinking 'I am not here – this is not happening to me, etc.' A patient who came to see me specifically claiming a history of perverse ritual abuse could hardly get any words out in our first meeting. Eventually she gasped falteringly 'It's difficult to speak because I'm not here'. When she did in later sessions talk of early experiences of extreme horror, she would refer to her child self in the third person as 'she'. On one occasion after giving me a very fragmented and incoherent account of an experience of a mock operation in which she had been told that 'eyes and ears' with special powers had been placed inside her so that the abusers would always know what she was thinking, saying or doing (a commonly reported experience amongst survivors of cults), she repeatedly muttered the words 'eyes no body'. It took some minutes for me to grasp that she was telling me that she had gone into a state of dissociation in which she experienced herself as just two eyes without a body. She was gradually able to explain that she had learnt from an early age to get out of her body when she was subjected to extreme pain; in her imagination she would, for example, escape into a crack in the ceiling, or into a lightbulb – clearly using some kind of spontaneous form of autohypnosis. Often she would tell me of some early experience of abuse and trauma and subsequently have no apparent memory of having told me, although she would acknowledge a memory of the events she had described.

This material gives just a hint of the ways in which the consciousness and memory of a cult-abused victim may be scrambled, with the deliberate intention of creating maximal difficulty in remembering, in telling and in being believed. If we add to this the possibilities of abuse before language is acquired, the confusions induced by the use of drugs administered by abusers, and the natural intermingling of reality, dreams and fantasy in the child part of the mind, as well as the unconscious use of images as metaphors, then we can see what a devil of a job we have in sorting out what really went on!

A patient pointed out to me that it is relatively easy to persuade a survivor of childhood trauma that their memories are false because these may be encoded in a dissociated state – so that the main personality does not recognise them as her own. If we try to imagine the experience of a fragmented dissociative personality, it is like having other people living inside one's body, who claim to have certain memories, but having no way of knowing whether they are true. Moreover, the narrative of abuse may be presented by the patient in a frightened, confused and childlike state of mind – dissociated from the adult state of mind – so that no rational and adult discussion with the 'narrator' is possible.

TRAUMA, ABUSE AND THE SENSE OF REALITY

A phenomenon I have observed with a number of patients is that where a person appears to have been repeatedly traumatised in childhood, he/she often is left with an unreliable sense of reality. If asked, the person may acknowledge that he/she sometimes has difficulty distinguishing whether something really happened or whether it was a dream. Over time, their account of 'memories' of childhood events may vary – perhaps with a recurring theme but with details and persons involved changing; details of one scene of abuse seem to be transposed and remixed to form new scenes, making identification of the true original scene extremely difficult. It is as if repeated childhood trauma may lead not just to repression or other forms of motivated amnesia, as is sometimes suggested, but also to an even more *unreliable* memory and sense of reality.

Why might this be? One possibility is that if autohypnotic dissociation is a primary defensive response to repeated trauma, a person might then become prone to enter hypnoid states of mind in which judgement of reality is impaired. In such a state a person could be autohypnotically generating false memory narratives which mixed elements of truth and confabulation, just as may happen in 'memory' recall in induced hypnosis.

A further possibility is suggested by a bit of Lacanian theory. With regard to the relationship of the mind to the outer world, Lacan (1977) postulates three orders or dimensions: the Real, the Imaginary and the Symbolic. The Real is essentially unknowable; for example a biological need can only be known through an image or a word, but not directly. The Imaginary is the realm of images, fantasies and wish-fulfilments – the world of the dream which follows the primary process forms of thought. The Symbolic order is arrived at through entry into the shared social world of language and culture; no one can avoid this transition from the Imaginary to the Symbolic without being psychotic. Lacan saw this achievement being structured through the Oedipal crisis, through acceptance of the incest taboo and the 'Law of the Father', which forbids both mother and child to repossess each other and which therefore represents a fundamental separation between fantasy and reality. The child's identity and sense of boundaries and reality requires that he/she be excluded from the 'primal scene' of the parental intercourse.

In the light of these Lacanian insights, what happens if there is incest with the father or if the child is included in the primal scene? It would follow that then there can be no proper entry into the Symbolic, since the 'law-giver' is the 'law-breaker'. There will be no clear sense of where the

'Law' is situated. Whilst perhaps escaping full psychosis, the person's sense of reality will be defective. He/she will be immersed in the Imaginary, as if trapped in a dream. The boundary between 'inside' and 'outside' will be unclear. Internal dream and external reality will confusingly intermingle.

Similar problems may arise if there is cult ritual abuse. If we accept the hypothesis that there are indeed perverse religious cults, then some children may be secretly exposed to bizarre activities which could normally only occur in a dream or nightmare, and which are totally outside the shared language and culture of society. Such experiences could not be spoken about and therefore could not be given words and would be foreclosed from consciousness. If primitive fantasy and reality meet up in this way then the outer world becomes identified with an archetype in which the Terrible Mother and the Terrible Father are perceived as real. Again the barrier between fantasy and reality is blown away.

Clinical illustration 4

Some years ago, when I knew nothing about ritual abuse, a patient told me of a strange and horrifying event. No specific 'memory recovery' techniques were used. As far as I am aware the patient did not talk to any other survivors of this kind of abuse, nor read about it. The account that emerged was a surprise and a profound shock which left me bewildered and confused.

Helen was 40 years old – a schoolteacher of French origin; she was in once per week psychoanalytic therapy. From the beginning she had presented extensive material relating to sexual abuse from her father. There was no 'recovered memory' here; she appeared never to have been amnesic for it and even described abuse continuing into her adult life. There were also minor hints of more peculiar elements – e.g. her father's apparent claim to have paranormal powers, her belief that he used to drug her and memories of a period in her childhood when disgusting objects, including animal limbs, were put through the letter box (possibly at a time when her parents, now both dead, were attempting to leave the cult they had been involved with). For a long time these allusions to more bizarre experiences remained obscure.

There were often indications in the transference of early experiences of sadism. She often perceived me as wanting to control her and repeatedly humiliate her. If I seemed to understand her she felt that this was only in order to gain more opportunity to hurt her and to control her mind.

Sometimes she feared that I would somehow be in league with her father. Her experience of the world seemed to be pervaded by cruelty, terror and her own intense rage.

One session she reported a frightening experience. During the week she had been opening a jar of spaghetti sauce in her kitchen and had accidently dropped it; some of the sauce had splashed up the walls. On seeing this, Helen had run out of the kitchen in a state of great terror, feeling that it reminded her of something but not knowing what. Subsequently she had recalled a vivid childhood 'memory' of a terrifying scene in the woods – the details of which need not concern us here, except to say that it was of quite a different order to anything she had described before.

Recovery of memory and blocking of memory

What was I to make of this apparent memory? Whatever the origin of its content, this sudden emergence of detailed imagery and narrative seems typical of flashbacks of RA, which are often preceded by much material regarding sexual abuse; the RA material emerges later, as if from a different layer of mental storage. The flashback is often highly detailed and shocking and its occurrence is in itself traumatic and evokes denial; for example, in the session following this, Helen was preoccupied with a wish not to believe her own account. She experienced urges to punish herself, to slash her wrists, and asked me in a childlike voice whether I now wanted her to kill herself. The power of the processes of scrambling or blocking of memory (if that is what it was) in these cases is illustrated by Helen's account of how she and her sister used to have discussions about whether they should go to the police but they could never remember what it was they were meant to be going to the police about; they knew something had happened but could never remember what. She told me that she felt she had always remembered what had happened but had not before been able to connect the memories with words – which is essentially Freud's theory of repression. Helen described how certain associative cues had in the past triggered terror – e.g. her first church communion and drinking a bowl of lukewarm soup – but had not been able to make the connection consciously.

There were other features of dissociation in her presentation – e.g. she described a split between the one who came to the session and the one who remembered all the horrors when she was alone. Similarly I noticed that on occasion she would talk in a way that gave no hint whatsoever of ritual abuse and strange perversion, and at other times her discourse would be filled with allusions to this.

The dynamics of communicating this material

Did I go in search of this material? Did I expect to find it? No. My response to hearing this and similar material has contained a mixture of shock, disbelief, horror, dread and terror – and confusion – a sense of difficulty in assessing reality. These I suspect are typical countertransference reactions to a communicated experience which is like an assault on one's sense of reality.

I experience the countertransference as one of a split ego state, part of my mind believing the accounts and another part thinking they are preposterous. In this kind of material there often seems to be an intermingling of elements which are shocking and believable, with those which are unbelievable. Some survivors of cults claim that this is a deliberate ploy to undermine credibility of witnesses. Inherent in deep perversion appears to be a delight in confusion and subterfuge, playing tricks with reality and the sense of reality, the interweaving of truth and lies.

I am certain that Helen could not have told me about these things until she felt that I could be receptive to them. Moreover, until she told me she could not tell herself. Her perception of the look of horror on my face when she told me of the events greatly troubled her and she frequently referred to this in the years following. She complained that I looked so shaken that I was of no help to her in coping with her own reactions. She felt that she must protect me from further trauma, fearing that I would not tolerate more revelations, whilst at the same time needing to know that I could be emotionally affected by her experiences. It was important to show her, through interpretation, that I could bear to hear what she needed to tell me and could think about it with her.

Helen made much progress but in the later stages of the therapy was aware of a continuing struggle against forgetting, recognising her own wish to forget. She remained preoccupied with her fear that I might forget – her point being that *somebody* had to remember. She pointed out with great dismay that I did seem to forget some details of the terrible experiences she described – and when I checked my notes I realised that she was correct.

Was it true? Did Helen really witness such serious crimes? Are there perverse cults? How could the account ever be corroborated? How would the therapy have developed if I had disbelieved that there could be literal truth in what she remembered – could she have still got better? I do not know the answer to any of these questions, but I did not disbelieve her – whilst accepting that I could never know objectively the historical truth and that I might be mistaken. On what basis have I believed her account could contain some literal truth, bearing in mind that I have no evidence outside of the consulting room? On what basis do we believe anyone? Could the whole narrative have been a gigantic confabulation? If so what on earth was its source? And what would be the motive behind the production of a narrative which filled the patient with shame and guilt?

EPISTEMOLOGICAL TERROR

I suggest three forms of terror in the consulting room.

We may experience terror as we empathise with the patient in the reliving of early trauma and terror.

We can also experience terror if a part of the patient is identified with the abusers and attempts to terrorise us, a form of projective identification.

I am also familiar with what I will call 'epistemological terror'. This is the anxiety and anguish that can be felt over the inability to know whether something terrible really happened or whether it is a fantasy – and contrary to some traditional psychoanalytic views, it does matter – it does matter to a patient's view of self, family and wider relationships whether her father actually raped her or whether she merely fantasised that he did.

I have a patient whom I have been seeing for some years. Frequently she produces material which seems to relate to ritual abuse, and indeed it seems plausible that she was subjected to this – yet neither of us has ever arrived at any conclusion about this. If we grasp the possibility that something terrible was witnessed or was done to the patient, and if this possibility begins to seem real to both participants, then we face the terror that both patient and therapist might be mistaken, caught up in a folie à deux; or if we face the possibility, on the other hand, that the images of terrible events are like dream images, bearing a metaphorical but not literal truth, then our terror is that we may both be caught in a collusion to avoid the unbearable literal truth. The therapist walks a tightrope. Yet this metaphor is not entirely apt, implying as it does that he/she must stick to the straight and narrow and avoid falling into error. The therapist cannot just stay in some kind of central position of 'neutrality' – to do so is not neutrality but a cop-out – but must help the patient explore the possibilities that are thrown up. Parts of the patient which are in terror may need encouragement to speak, may need indications that they will be heard and believed. An expression of seemingly neutral acceptance which covers private scepticism will be perceived by the patient as indicating not a safe emotional environment. The therapist is in an unenviable position here. If he/she does not believe the apparent recollection of trauma, the child parts of the patient will withdraw. If he/she believes the accounts, there could be accusations of colluding with a 'false memory'. I believe there are ways through this dilemma but it is a difficult journey.

The patient I mentioned who produced images of ritual abuse, without our having arrived at any conclusion about its meaning, watched a recent TV programme about a trial in the USA of a group of people who were accused of ritual abuse of children in their care. The programme clearly implied that the convictions were flawed because the evidence from the children was contaminated by suggestions from the therapists. The jury had apparently found this an exceptionally agonising trial; some had become ill. The patient felt that the accused were guilty but also felt that the evidence was indeed contaminated. We talked about this as a metaphor for our struggle and ordeal in her therapy; within her mind, there was a prosecuting counsel that wanted to expose abuse, there was a defence which wanted to deny the abuse, there were the child witnesses who needed help and encouragement, but whose evidence could then be said to be contaminated by suggestion – and then there was the jury, she and I struggling to make sense of the evidence and the conflicting claims. Our only advantage is that we are not under pressure to arrive at a premature verdict. Truly the tolerance of uncertainty is a most crucial and difficult discipline.

It might be argued that a courtroom is not an appropriate metaphor for the process of psychotherapy. But insofar as a court and a psychoanalysis are both attempting to arrive at the truth, then the analogy is apt, especially when criminal offences are being considered. Children and child parts of the adult patient do need to be helped to tell their story and to be listened to in order to recover – but in providing this help we run the risk of contaminating the evidence. In this and other ways too our work is inherently and unavoidably hazardous. Damned if we listen and damned if we do not, we can only endeavour to keep our minds open and try to hear and continue to think.

Whitfield (1995) provides a good overview of the memory debate and its implications. A substantial multiauthored volume addressing issues in the assessment of allegations of child sexual abuse is edited by Ney (1995).

> *Perhaps therapy can become the place where our pain is truly witnessed and our memories are appreciated, even celebrated, as ongoing, ever-changing interactions between imagination and history.*
>
> (Loftus & Ketcham, 1994)

SUMMARY

One hundred years ago Freud was preoccupied with the problem of distinguishing true and false memories, just as we are today. There are indications that Freud could not assimilate the evidence of sexual and perverse abuse of children. Memory which is processed through the conscious and verbal systems may be unreliable. On the other hand, it is possible that enactive or behavioural memory may be startlingly accurate. Repression of memory of childhood abuse may be a very ordinary process of learning not to think about unpleasant memories, combined with the mechanism of denial. Severe and repeated trauma may be more fundamentally blocked from consciousness through a restriction of processing through the verbal system. People who have been repeatedly traumatised in childhood may be left with a defective sense of reality, which makes the problem of knowing what is a true and what is a pseudo-memory even more difficult. The problems of assessing memory of trauma in clinical practice are immensely complex and confusing.

Chapter 7

MULTIPLE PERSONALITY DISORDER/DISSOCIATIVE IDENTITY DISORDER

I will begin my discussion of multiple personality disorder with a consideration of some clinical phenomena that will be fairly familiar to many British psychoanalytic practitioners. Within the Kleinian tradition there have been a number of accounts of struggles between different parts of the mind that pursue their own agendas and have their own organisation, yet are not reducible to Freudian concepts of the structural divisions of the mind into id, ego and superego. Usually the picture is of a more obvious, relationship-oriented and reality-seeking personality, and a more destructive, psychotic and relationship-opposing personality.

GANGS, MAFIAS AND COHABITEES

Miss S, an unemployed nanny in her early twenties, had been in analytic therapy for a couple of years. She often described a state of considerable anxiety experienced when she came for her sessions, which she termed 'the jitters'. One day she told me that she had been experiencing extreme anxiety for several days, was having nightmares and had recurrent frightening fantasies that someone was after her. She had no idea why she was feeling so anxious. As she continued to talk about this it emerged that she had begun to feel the panic the day before her boyfriend, with whom she lived, was due to return from a two week trip away. She described how she had felt very distraught at his absence for the first week but had then got used to being without him and being alone in the house; she said she had even begun to feel it might be preferable to be alone. I suggested that having got used to her boyfriend's absence she might have then experienced his imminent arrival as an intrusion on her state of isolation, threatening to stir up all her conflicts about neediness. She agreed with this but then reported that she was hearing a kind of voice inside that was telling her not to listen or relate to me. I commented that she seemed to be describing something in her mind that sought to withdraw her from relationships with others, including withdrawing her from me and telling her not to relate to me. In reply she told me that it was this same voice she had listened to when she had decided to leave her boyfriend and live in a flat on her own some months previously, a move which had been very damaging to her relationship and which she had deeply regretted. I emphasised that this showed even more how this part was opposed to relationships. She then said that this perhaps explained why she felt such dread if she ever visited her own flat because she feared she would never get out of it again; she said that she was afraid she would commit suicide if she went back to that flat. She recalled that she had sometimes referred to the atmosphere in the flat as 'evil'. She said that when she had first moved to the flat she had enjoyed the isolation, feeling it was a great relief not having to relate to anyone. I said that it now appeared from what she was saying that this part had managed to seduce her away from relationships and into a cocoon of isolation, which initially had seemed pleasing, but when she had attempted to leave she had discovered she was in prison with a thuggish jailor – the figure that she now felt was after her. This seemed to make sense to her and she added that perhaps this was why she was afraid she would commit suicide if she returned to the flat. I commented that this voice appeared intent not only on taking her away from relationships but also was oriented towards death. She then told me that she felt this voice also generated thoughts in her mind that she was worthless and useless and should die because she felt so wretched about herself. I said that it seemed that this voice endeavoured to undermine her, partly through lies and internal propaganda designed to break her relationships with other people and with reality and to render her vulnerable to its control so that it could imprison or destroy her. She said she could see that this was the case. I added that perhaps this explained something further about the 'jitters' she felt on coming to see me, reflecting her struggle against the destructive voice inside. She agreed, adding that she felt the same 'jitters' when she was attempting to relate to other people.

It had become clear that she was describing a voice in her mind that wanted to lure her away from relationships, imprison her and perhaps kill her. Having succumbed to the seductive pull and propaganda of this destructive-narcissistic part, she experienced great difficulty and anxiety as she attempted to reach out to relate again; it was as if she had become imprisoned in narcissistic isolation and the jailor part of her mind was now threatening and pursuing her as she tried to escape. It was this same destructive-narcissistic part which regularly attacked the object-relating part of herself that wanted to relate to the therapist, resulting in 'the jitters'.

This mental structure is similar to that described by Rosenfeld (1971) in his account of the internal 'mafia gang', the repository of destructive narcissism derived from the death instinct. The 'mafia' aims to imprison and isolate the dependent object-seeking part of the mind, using threats and thuggery to bring about their aims; this situation may be represented in dreams by gangs, criminal organisations and violence. This organisation also has some similarity to Bion's (1967) description of a division into a sane and a psychotic personality, the latter being essentially destructive and opposed to relationships. It may also be likened to the description of 'the indentificate' presented by Sohn (1985) and the 'cohabitee' outlined by M. Sinason (1993).

The destructive personality within the mind tends to be hidden, carrying out its work in relative secrecy. Sinason states: 'Living his whole life out of sight and out of the mind of others, the cohabitee becomes attached to his isolation and hates to be seen he would sooner die than acknowledge that he has any needs to meet . . . his hate and negativism never change . . .' (p. 220). In the case of Miss S described above, her destructive mental part was not experienced overtly as a voice. However, many more ill or unintegrated patients do experience hallucinatory voices. In fact I have the impression that not infrequently psychotherapists mistakenly assume that when their patient refers to a 'voice' in the mind it is a metaphorical reference to a thought; since most therapists do not hallucinate voices it requires an empathic leap to grasp that many patients do.

Working in a general psychiatric service, I see many patients who experience hallucinatory voices. Often they present a diagnostic ambiguity over whether they are best considered to be suffering from schizophrenia or from a dissociative disorder. It is now recognised that there is much overlapping symptomatology. On the whole, it can be assumed that hallucinatory voices experienced as external are indicative of schizophrenia, whilst voices experienced internally are suggestive of a dissociative disorder. What both have in common is that the voices almost always are not neutral in content or intention, but are extremely destructive, often urging the patient to commit suicide or to mutilate their body. These voices can also often be identified as the source of mad delusional ideas. It is as if there is a delusion generator inside the mind, spewing out propaganda designed to undermine the person's relationship with other people and with reality.

One patient, Miss G, pictures an organisation of shadowy figures arranged around the back of her head. She calls them the 'outside people' and reports that they have been there for as long as she can remember. Sometimes Miss G is sane and functioning well, but at other times she is drawn back into psychosis, often if she is under some particular stress at work or in her home life. At these times her mind becomes full of madness, all manner of delusional ideas, both grandiose and self-denigratory. I have learnt to enquire, when she is in these states, whether the mad thoughts and beliefs are being put to her by the 'outside people' and she invariably confesses that they are. It is then necessary to remind her that the messages she is receiving internally are lies, designed to draw her away from relationships and reality. She is sometimes able to understand that 'the outside people' have had a devastating effect on her development but she has difficulty giving up the belief, which they present to her, that she needs them and that they are her reliable source of help. The impression is that when the sane part of her mind is relatively strong and she is managing to function in the world the 'outside people' remain dormant, but when she is under stress then the forces pulling her towards madness become more active.

Destructive internal voices seem to take a particularly ferocious objection to being discovered by the therapist. When being referred to during a therapy session they tend to intensify their activity, telling the patient not to listen to the therapist and perhaps to break off therapy. If the patient discloses some of the destructive activity of the voices, he/she may then feel very frightened at the prospect of retribution when the therapist is not there – rather in the way that a bully may threaten punishment later when the victim has reported the bullying to an authority. Sometimes a destructive voice will engage in a hostile dialogue with the therapist.

What is the source of these destructive entities within the mind, which seem to embody the death instinct, being suffused with cruelty, hatred and envy? Are they a response to trauma or an inherent constitutional part of the mind? Often it is hard to know. What is certain and predictable is that any therapist who discovers and attempts to engage with the problem of these destructive voices is in for a battle. The inner conflict will intensify before it is (if ever) resolved.

Would the patients I have described so far here be considered to have multiple personality disorders? Perhaps not, but there is possibly a continuity between these states of covert 'habitees' and full-blown MPD/DID states. Some years ago I interviewed a 19-year-old female patient, newly admitted to the psychiatric ward. She had been experiencing hallucinatory voices which told her to kill herself and she had indeed made suicide attempts. During the interview I asked the patient, whom I shall call Jane, whether it was possible for me to speak with any of her voices; I had at the time just begun to develop some awareness of dissociative states. To my amazement she moved to another chair and said 'Hello, I'm Libby'. I said I was pleased to meet her and asked her to tell me about herself. She said 'I've got shoulder length red hair'. (Jane had curly blonde hair.) I enquired about her view of Jane. She said 'We hate her and we want her to die, she deserves to be punished.' I asked why Libby hated Jane and she said it was because she had told about being abused by her step-father; Libby said Jane was not supposed to tell about this and that they had screamed at her inside her mind that this was not true – but then added that they were even more angry with Jane for subsequently retracting and saying that her stepfather had not abused her. Libby went on to say that they were determined to make Jane die. I pointed out that there was a problem with this aim. Libby asked what this was. I said the problem was that if Jane died then Libby would die too. Libby looked puzzled and asked why this was so. I replied that it was because she and Jane shared the same body and if the body died Libby would also die. Libby, still looking puzzled, asked if I was sure about this and I assured her that this was true. Libby said she had not thought about that before.

Immediately here we are faced with some typical problems in evaluating dissociative states. The first point is that MPD can seem embarrassing! The theatrical quality of the presentation and the way the interviewer is drawn into the drama do not fit comfortably with a medical setting and the attempt to assign a psychiatric diagnosis. Is the patient having us on? Are we being covertly made fun of? Has the consulting room been turned into a theatre for a ridiculous charade? Faced with this, will we not our-selves appear ridiculous if we describe this to psychiatric colleagues? Moreover, what are we to believe about her experiences? There appears to be considerable internal dispute about the reality of her childhood.

One point which struck me at this time was that this patient was per-forming spontaneously (albeit in response to my initial invitation for a dialogue with a hallucinatory voice) the kind of switching into alternative personalities which is undertaken as a deliberate therapeutic strategy by the contemporary therapy called 'Voice Dialogue' developed by Stone and Winkelman (1987); here the patient is invited to move physical posi-tion and act as if personifying an alter attitude and in this way to drama-tise various sides of an internal conflict in order to facilitate inner dialogue. In this context the approach is unashamedly dramatic, using dissociation deliberately as a means of sorting parts of the personality into clearer elements as a prelude to greater communication and integra-tion. It is perhaps analogous to the way the great spectrum of political opinion amongst a population will sort into a relatively small number of political parties which represent clusterings of opinion and attitude on a range of topics; this sorting allows a more coherent political debate to emerge because people know broadly what a Tory or a Labour supporter believes in.

Jane turned out to have a number of alter personalities, both adult and child, and was, I believe, clearly suffering from a multiple (or dissociative) personality disorder, which was eventually resolved with psychotherapy over a lengthy period. Consider another example. A patient in conventional analytic therapy suddenly got up from the couch, ran across the room and crouched in a corner near me, saying in a child-like voice 'He keeps hitting me. Please make him stop'. She appeared to have switched into the state of mind of a frightened child who was telling me, as mother in the transference, of her physical abuse by a man in whose care she had been left. A dissociative switch, a child alter, a regression in time – but would this patient be described as having a full multiple personality disorder? Probably not, but it is easy to see the continuum as we view a range of examples.

One of the features of the full MPD syndrome is that the person has a variety of alters who serve different functions and who may cooperate or be in competition with each other. For example, Rachel was the main or 'host' personality in a young woman but she also had Rebecca, who was flirtatious and vivacious and had acquired the husband, and Mary who was serious, assertive and went to work in a job carrying much responsibility; there were also a number of child alters. Rachel tended to be depressed and hopeless. At a point in the therapy when the possibility of integration was being talked of, Mary began to object strongly, arguing that *she* should be the main personality and that Rachel should go. Rachel missed an appointment, explaining that she had the wrong date in her diary. During her next session, Rachel was again hopeless, tearful and despairing. Suddenly she switched to Mary, who angrily remarked: 'You see what she's like! Would you want to join up with her?' She then added triumphantly that it was she, Mary, who had altered the date in Rachel's diary in order to sabotage the therapy.

FROM COVERT TO OVERT MULTIPLE PERSONALITY

The underlying structure of MPD/DID often tends to be covert. Patients do not often announce that they are multiple, nor do they disclose, unless asked sympathetically, that they hear voices. However, psychotherapeutic exploration will often result in the covert disorder becoming overt – a process which unfortunately can invite the naïve accusation that the therapist has created the MPD iatrogenically. The simplest instance of this is the way that the personality switching process may be evoked merely by the therapist asking if he or she might speak with one of the patient's voices. For example, Pauline had been seen for two assessment interviews and had presented as depressed and suicidal, with destructive internal voices and a history of sexual abuse. In the third meeting she said she was feeling much better, more cheerful and definitely not suicidal any more; she could offer no reason for this other than simply to say that her mood had changed. On my enquiring more about her mental state, it emerged that she was still experiencing internal voices. I said to her that I had a question that might sound a little strange, but that I was wondering whether any of her voices would be prepared to talk to me more directly. She appeared unfazed by this request, consulted internally for a moment and then replied that their answer was 'no' and that these matters were none of my business. A moment or two later I was startled by her suddenly asking in a slightly different and rather aggressive voice: 'Got any paracetamol?' I replied that I did not have any and asked why she wanted them. She said she wanted to take an overdose and kill herself. I asked what had happened to the person I had just been speaking to who had felt more cheerful. 'She's gone' was the reply.

Mary, a woman in prolonged and profound suicidal despair, told me in our first meeting of a dream she had some years previously which she felt was significant in the onset of her depression. In the dream she goes into a room and sees a woman kneeling over a locked chest; she realises (in the dream) that she is awake at the wrong time, that she is in this woman's time and that the woman is angry to be found. In her thoughts about this dream she felt the chest represented her locked-away memories which the woman was guarding. She also associated this woman with a hostile voice in her mind which told her to kill herself. She felt that this woman was called Hazel. When Mary told me this dream a few years ago I was struck by its strange quality, the way it seemed to portray the dreamer's experience of another inhabitant of the mind who was pursuing her own agenda and who did not want to be discovered. I had little understanding of dissociative processes at the time.

Several years later and at her own initiative, Mary contacted a clinic specialising in the treatment of multiple personality disorder, having read about the clinic in a magazine. Part of the treatment approach employed there was to identify alter personalities and then to eliminate them in a hypnotic fantasy, a strategy that seemed to be considerably successful in some instances. After a visit to this clinic, she returned to see me and spoke in an extremely angry manner, telling me that she was 'Hazel' and that she was damned if she was going to be got rid of. She declared that she had carried all the memories of abuse for years and that she was not now going to be just dispensed with so that Mary could 'walk out like a little princess as though nothing had happened'. She further announced her intention to 'slash the body' so that it would be ruined for Mary. I had not previously spoken to this alter called Hazel (or indeed to any other alter), whose overt appearance seemed to have been provoked by the threat, from this other clinic, to eliminate her. Gradually Mary disclosed many other alter personalities. It was this patient who first taught me something about multiple personality disorder.

So here are some instances of an overt state of MPD emerging in response to an invitation or cue from a therapist. Does that mean that the therapist created the MPD iatrogenically – or is it more a matter of discovering what is there to be observed? Clearly the observer influences what is observed, but this is inevitable in any psychotherapy. In the case of Mary, what appeared initially to be a relatively hidden and internal structure became an outwardly enacted and observable relationship between different parts of herself.

DIAGNOSTIC ASPECTS: CRITICISMS OF THE CONCEPT OF MPD

Although there has been a mushrooming of literature on the subject in recent years, mainly from North America, there have also been persistent severe criticisms of those who perceive, diagnose and treat multiple personality disorder. For example, the five papers on MPD that have appeared in the *British Journal of Psychiatry* since 1989 have all been highly critical and dismissive of the concept and the therapy (Fahy, 1988; Fahy, Abas & Brown, 1989; Merskey, 1992; Piper, 1994; Merskey, 1995). The publishing policy of this, the leading British journal in psychiatry, seems curious. Its readers are subjected to a series of papers attacking a concept that is remote from the consciousness of most British psychiatrists!

Piper

Piper (1994) writes a review article which can be taken as a typical example of the critical position. He begins: 'Several aspects of the diagnosis and treatment of multiple personality disorder (MPD) are disquieting'; he goes on to discuss six concerns: vague and poorly elaborated diagnostic criteria; the recent sharp increase in the number of patients alleged to have the disorder; exposure to malpractice risks; difficulties with the issue of child abuse; encouragement of regressive and non-responsible patient behaviour; moral and legal responsibility of patients with MPD. I will discuss each of Piper's concerns in turn.

Vagueness of diagnostic criteria

Piper criticises the DSM-111-R criteria for MPD, which are as follows:

A. The existence within the person of two or more distinct personalities or personality states (each with its own relatively enduring pattern of perceiving, relating to, and thinking about the environment and the self).

B. At least two of the personalities or personality states recurrently take full control of the person's behaviour.

Piper worries about the distinction between personalities and personality states and whether the definition is satisfied 'if the personality state appears only in the therapist's office . . . or only under hypnosis, or only when the patient is stressed?' He further complains that the terms 'personality' and 'personality state' are inherently ambiguous and he refers to slightly differing emphases amongst MPD theorists in describing alter personalities. He asks 'Where then is the line of demarcation between normal and pathological, between normality and "multiplicity"?'

The problem here is that Piper begs the question of whether there is inherently any clear demarcation between normal and pathological. An assumption that there is such a boundary might characterise psychiatrists preoccupied with classification rather than psychotherapists or psychoanalysts who are used to perceiving a whole range of pathology in an individual patient and to perceiving pathology within normalcy – ever since Freud's *Psychopathology of Everyday Life*. The psychoanalytic clinician can comfortably talk about psychotic or autistic parts of the mind within the neurotic patient, or of psychotic positions in infancy. Conversely it is possible to speak of excessive 'normalcy' as pathological (Bollas, 1987). Many years ago, Fairbairn (1952) pointed out that patients may do the rounds of many different forms of mental pathology and defence mechanisms, presenting as now hysterical, now dissociative, now obsessional, now depressive, etc. From this perspective that does not regard forms of mental pathology as sharply demarcated, the idea of a spectrum of dissociative states does not seem at all surprising. Nor does it seem a matter of great conceptual difficulty that some alters might be described as elaborately developed personalities, whilst others might be thought of as personality 'fragments'.

Putnam (Putnam, Loewenstein, Silberman et al., 1984) argues that MPD could be regarded as a 'superordinate diagnosis' on the grounds that 'amnesia, anxiety, mood changes, hallucinations, somatisation, and anorexic-bulimic symptoms, amongst others, generally can be conceptualised as manifestations of different alternate personalities or of interactions between alternate personality states.' Piper complains that 'It is only a short step from this position to one of considering every patient to have MPD.' Perhaps this provides a clue to the intensity of the hostility here. MPD threatens to offer a new implicit paradigm of mental disorder, based around trauma and dissociation. Certainly it is a matter of everyday clinical observation that patients with strong dissociative tendencies frequently acquire a great many diagnostic labels over the years. An alter who hears hallucinatory voices may be diagnosed as schizophrenic; another may be called depressive; yet another may have an eating disorder; one may be promiscuous; another may avoid sex; an alternation between a depressive alter and a confident outgoing one may lead to a diagnosis of manic depression. It has been noted that MPD patients show even more 'Schneiderian' symptoms (including voices arguing and commenting on one's actions, influences playing on the body, thought withdrawal and insertion, 'made' feelings, impulses and acts) than do schizophrenic patients, even though these are meant to be diagnostic of schizophrenia (Fink & Golinkoff, 1990; Ross et al., 1990). Dissociative processes can lead to much diagnostic confusion. I have known patients admitted to hospital in a very disturbed state, perhaps severely depressed, suicidal, self-harming, or hallucinating, who after a certain time appear 'well' and can be discharged as having made a good recovery when all that has happened is that there has been a personality switch – another alter is 'out'. Many patients in practice are rarely given definite diagnoses, perhaps because most clinicians are aware that diagnostic classifications are embarrassingly imprecise and fluid in psychiatry. In my view, the answer is not to attempt to establish more precise and reliable criteria, but rather to accept that this position reflects something about the nature of mental disorder. After all, the term 'borderline personality disorder' has come into widespread usage and this covers a great multiplicity of symptoms and behaviours; a vast proportion of patients attending a psychiatric service could surely be given this label. Piper concludes his critical discussion of diagnosis with the comment: 'In conclusion, patients diagnosed as having MPD belong to a very heterogeneous group that has poorly demarcated boundaries with many other psychiatric conditions.' Precisely!

The recent sharp increase in alleged MPD patients

Piper is troubled by the explosion in numbers of diagnoses of MPD during the 1980s and 90s. He quotes from a letter by Ross (1990) to the effect that 5 per cent of all psychiatric admissions in Britain or South Africa would meet DSM-111-R criteria for MPD, finding this claim incredible. He points out that Modestin (1992) found in a survey that just three of the psychiatrists in his sample contributed 128 of the 221 MPD cases. He also quotes Thigpen and Checkley (1984), authors of *The Three Faces of Eve*, who argue that in the 30 years that they have had hundreds of referrals of patients thought to have MPD, they have only seen one case other than Eve whom they regarded as having a genuine multiple personality.

Piper lists the factors proposed by Kluft (1987) to account for the increase in numbers of diagnosed cases:

1. more widely disseminated information about MPD;
2. narrowing of the definitions of other conditions such as schizophrenia, with which MPD may be confused;
3. greater scrutiny of cases where there is failure to respond to appropriate treatment for some other condition;
4. increased awareness of the hitherto unacknowledged high prevalence of child abuse and incest.

Piper finds it implausible that these factors alone could account for the increase. He concludes: 'It is difficult to ignore the most parsimonious explanation of this phenomenon: that the DSM criteria are elastic enough to accommodate a very broad group of patients, and that some practitioners have begun to apply them uncritically to their patients.' However, another parsimonious explanation is that the DSM criteria do indeed accommodate a broad spectrum of dissociative conditions and that increased numbers of clinicians have become sensitive to the prevalence of dissociative phenomena amongst psychiatric patients.

Personally I find nothing surprising about this increase in the prevalence of the diagnosis. Ten years ago I did not have a working concept of dissociation. I rarely gave any thought to the concept of multiple personality disorder, which I assumed was extremely rare. I certainly did not consider that I had ever come across such a patient. To be sure, there were patients whom I perceived as very disturbed and whom I did not feel I really understood; but I would have diagnosed these as schizophrenic or borderline, completely missing the dissociative dimensions. The concepts of trauma-dissociation provide a powerful explanatory paradigm which was not available until the MPD literature of the mid-80s onwards; but without familiarity with the phenomena and the concepts, the clinician is unlikely to perceive dissociative pathology.

Malpractice risks

Piper refers to a warning by Hardy, Daghestani and Egan (1988) that clinicians face malpractice litigation if they fail to diagnose MPD in patients with the condition; the argument is that MPD has a good prognosis when properly treated and a poor prognosis when it is not. Here I am entirely in agreement with Piper that an effort to sue a therapist for not diagnosing MPD would be misguided. Let us hope that Britain never mimics the litigation madness of the USA!

Piper cites a paper by Serban (1992) which discusses a case where a patient sued a psychiatrist for incorrectly diagnosing her as having MPD. The patient had demonstrated behaviours considered typical of MPD but had later claimed she had simulated these to conform to the physician's diagnosis. A number of specialists interviewed the patient and no consensus was reached about the accuracy of the MPD diagnosis.

As Piper comments, it would indeed 'seem unreasonable to sue a clinician for failing to diagnose MPD when it is so difficult to distinguish between real and simulated cases.' Part of the problem here is that MPD inherently involves pretence and simulation; that is what it is about – the defensive use of pretence. A close analogy is with a person under hypnosis who does as the hypnotist commands but later claims that he was deliberately complying with the demands of the situation; whatever the rationalisation, the person *was* responding to the hypnotic commands.

Problems with the issue of child abuse

Piper's argument here is basically that trauma and abuse are widely reported in the backgrounds of people with MPD but there is little independent verification of this abuse. This of course opens into the whole complex debate about the reliability of memories of childhood and the issue of false memory narratives of childhood abuse. The problems of memory are discussed in more detail elsewhere in the book. Piper is surely correct to raise this issue and to point out that in therapy we construct 'narrative truth' (Spence, 1982) rather than literally correct 'historical truth'. However, most clinicians who work with severely disturbed psychiatric patients would probably agree that in many instances such people seem to have had very troubled and disordered childhoods, even if we cannot be sure exactly what happened to them.

Encouragement of regressive and non-responsible behaviour

Piper refers to the recommendations of a number of specialists who advocate various forms of encouraging alter personalities to appear and to communicate – such as calling the alters out by name, engaging in lengthy conversation with individual alters, taking a history from each one, engaging in age-appropriate behaviours with child alters, etc. He comments: 'In addition to whatever else such techniques may do, they must certainly sanction and reinforce the patient's belief in his or her dividedness, and encourage the production of more symptoms.' It is difficult to argue with this; the clinician must always be treading a careful path between the aim of acknowledging and exploring the patient's mental structure, on the one hand, and the danger of fostering increased psychopathology on the other hand.

Piper further comments:

> The literature on treatment of MPD is dominated by those advocating the kind of techniques listed above; this gives the impression that there is only one proper, effective, and orthodox method of treating MPD. However, given the present state of knowledge about treating this disorder, dogmatism about the proper method of treatment is premature.

I could not agree more with this statement. In my view it is wise to be suspicious of any clinician who claims to know for sure how best to treat dissociative states. MPD and related states are deeply confusing and complex; the only appropriate therapeutic stance is one of extreme caution.

Moral and legal responsibility of patients with MPD

Piper refers to Halleck (1988, 1990) who draws attention to the point that the concept of MPD has 'several grave implications for attributing moral and legal responsibility to those with the disorder'. Undoubtedly this is so. The moral and legal philosophical problems are considerable. If a dissociated alter commits a crime, can the host personality be held responsible? Can a collection of personalities make legal choices? If one alter chooses to marry, become pregnant or have an abortion, or enter a legal agreement, what are the implications with regard to the other personalities who may not agree? If a person is 'taken over' by an alter, this is still a situation of a person being taken over by themselves – the plural 'themselves' being curiously apt here. Should this mean then that a patient with MPD can be regarded as responsible for all his/her behaviours?

There are no easy answers to any of these questions. However, the problems are not entirely dissimilar to those encountered with other severe mental states, including psychosis and instances of crimes committed whilst intoxicated with drugs.

Piper concludes his review by arguing that many patients diagnosed with MPD are probably rather suggestible people whose symptoms are created by a combination of role play, shaping and hypnosis. The problem is that even if this were so, it does not explain how these people come to be patients in the first place. If someone is attending a psychiatric clinic and is displaying symptoms of MPD then *something* is wrong with them!

Aldridge-Morris

Another extensive critical review of the concept of MPD is provided in a book by Aldridge-Morris (1989), whose bias is expressed in the title: *Multiple Personality. An Exercise in Deception.* Concluding that MPD is 'a psychological disturbance which is endemic to the United States of America' (p. 108), he considers that the patients in question are suffering from a form of hysterical psychosis combined with the influence of suggestion from the therapist. Unfortunately, Aldridge-Morris's arguments are undermined by occasional misjudged comments. For example, he argues that

> Those practitioners who are so convinced of the reality of this syndrome belong to a professional subculture with some striking hallmarks as common denominators . . . generally favour hypnotherapeutic techniques, are psychoanalytic or neoanalytic in orientation and . . . see their patients over long periods of time . . . might suggest that multiple personality is more in the eye of the psychoanalytically inclined therapist than in the psyche of the analysand. (p. 43)

In fact, most contemporary writers on the treatment of MPD favour techniques derived from cognitive-behavioural approaches, as well as making some use of hypnosis because the patients tend to be in a natural state of hypnosis anyway. The concept of MPD is not part of the psychoanalytic tradition and is not compatible with Freud's theory. Relatively few psychoanalysts make use of the concept of dissociation. Hypnosis is definitely not part of the psychoanalytic tradition since Freud abandoned it 100 years ago. Moreover, the hypothesis of iatrogenesis, often advanced by the MPD-sceptics, has not been supported by any documented case in the literature. An entire issue of the journal *Dissociation* (vol. 11, No. 2, 1989) is devoted to discussion of the iatrogenesis hypothesis. As for the suggestion that dissociation is 'endemic' to the USA, contemporary diagnostic tools reveal that MPD/DID is as common in other parts of the world as it is in the USA (Ensink & Van Otterloo, 1989). In his review of the book, Coons (1990) comments: 'Although some of the arguments by Dr Aldridge-Morris might have been plausible in 1985, they don't hold water in 1990. It will be a great shame indeed if this book results in the continuing underdiagnosis of MPD in the United Kingdom and elsewhere.'

FURTHER DISCUSSION OF DIAGNOSTIC ISSUES. WHERE DOES MPD/DID LIE IN RELATION TO OTHER PSYCHIATRIC DISORDERS?

A more balanced and sympathetic, yet very scholarly and thorough, review of diagnostic issues is provided by North, Ryall, Ricci and Wetzel (1993) in their book *Multiple Personalities, Multiple Disorders*. Discussing the problems faced by dissociation theorists, they comment:

> Recent proponents of MPD have met resistance at practically every turn in mainstream psychiatry. Neither of the two dominant schools of psychiatry in America fully accepts MPD as a disorder. The basic concept of MPD does not harmonize with established concepts of traditional psychoanalysis. Biological psychiatry, on the other hand, cannot assimilate MPD into its demands for rigourous scientific proof because relevant data on MPD are not currently available and not easily obtained . . . Perhaps no other psychiatric disorder has aroused as much passion within the psychiatric community as MPD. (p. 23)

North et al. emphasise the diagnostic overlap between MPD and borderline personality disorder, antisocial personality disorder and particularly somatisation disorder (Briquet's syndrome). In surveying 22 published popular personal accounts of MPD they conclude that all the individuals displayed prominent somatoform, sociopathic and borderline features, in addition to the dissociative disorder that was emphasised. As they point out, the severity and degree of disability associated with MPD argues against the iatrogenesis of the condition; whilst it is conceivable that the form of the disorder could be to some extent shaped by the treating clinician, the reality that most MPD patients are severely disturbed or damaged, by any criteria, cannot itself be an artifact. The startling phenomena of MPD can distract from the recognition that even if the dissociative symptoms were removed, a person with a number of severe psychiatric disorders would still be left.

This is quite a crucial point. MPD is usually associated with a history of severe abuse or neglect. It is well known that severe trauma gives rise to a number of post-traumatic symptoms, of which dissociation is only one. Therefore it would be most surprising if there existed a post-traumatic syndrome in which the only symptom was a highly developed system of dissociation. North et al. compared 10 published studies of samples of

MPD patients. They found that: (a) there was a predominance of females, ranging from 73–100 per cent; (b) the mean number of alters ranged between 6.3 and 15.7; (c) the prevalence of physical abuse was between 40 and 89 per cent, and sexual abuse between 60 and 90 per cent; (d) the occurrence of rape or sexual assault in adult life was 24–67 per cent; (e) the rate of attempted suicide was 60–81 per cent. Clearly MPD is part of a broad grouping of trauma-based psychiatric disorders. North et al. describe it as a 'polysymptomatic, polysyndromic disorder', emphasising particularly the comorbidity with Briquet's syndrome. This raises the question of whether MPD should be regarded as a *superordinate* diagnosis (as argued by those such as Putnam, 1989, and Ross, 1989), or as a *coordinate* diagnosis, or as a *subordinate* diagnosis.

Why should MPD be singled out as the crucial feature of these traumatised patients? As Tozman and Pablis (1989) comment: 'If PTSD does cause MPD, why is not PTSD emphasised inasmuch as this is a more significant, ubiquitous, and often unrecognized condition' (p. 708). It is possible to argue that MPD could be regarded as a coordinate diagnosis, existing alongside a number of other diagnoses within the same patient. The clinical implication of this position would be that each of the patient's problems, such as multiple personalities, borderline personality disorder, anxiety, depression, somatoform disorder, etc., should be considered in their own right and treated accordingly. Another position is to argue that MPD should be considered as a subordinate diagnosis, a symptom complex accompanying another superordinate disorder such as Briquet's syndrome or borderline personality disorder. This view is taken by Fahy (1988). North et al. summarise the known comorbidity patterns of five related conditions: MPD; somatisation disorder; antisocial personality disorder; borderline personality disorder; and conversion disorder. They find that the overlap with MPD of the other conditions is extensive. Moreover, they point out that other features regarded as characteristic of patients with MPD, such as a female preponderance, a history of childhood abuse, and suicide attempts, have also been described as characteristic of patients with Briquet's syndrome, borderline personality disorder and antisocial personality disorder. This high comorbidity with other disorders has been used to argue that MPD should be regarded as a marker of severity rather than a disorder in its own right.

Clearly the relationship between MPD/DID and other diagnostic groups is complex. Personally I often find myself writing diagnoses such as 'severe trauma-based borderline personality disorder with marked dissociative features'. However, there does appear to be a group of patients for whom the dissociative tendencies are so marked that, once detected, these appear as the most striking features of their disorder. Moreover, in these patients the whole survival strategy appears to have been built around the development of a highly complex system of elaborate alter personalities. The 'success' of the dissociative strategy is such that alters may be available who appear well-functioning and pass as normal; the severity of disturbance may be hidden from many in the patient's life, in a way that would not occur with a person with borderline personality disorder without an elaborate system of dissociation. In fact there are some data from psychological tests that indicate that patients with MPD often have a unique form of personality organisation based on dissociative and post-traumatic factors, which is not reducible to a borderline or psychotic character structure (Armstrong & Loewenstein, 1990).

A SUPERORDINATE DIAGNOSIS?

A diagnosis could qualify as superordinate if it accommodated a number of other diagnostic features in a particular patient. For example, a diagnosis of MPD may bring coherence and order into the otherwise puzzling situation of a patient having received a number of different diagnoses at different times; different alters may present with seemingly quite different problems. Diagnosis of MPD may be a parsimonious explanation for the existence of a variety of seemingly unrelated symptoms. Another way in which MPD may be seen as a superordinate diagnosis is if it reveals a hidden structure and order behind the surface heterogeneity of symptoms, or if the diagnostic assessment can detect hidden symptoms which appear primary. Drawing upon research with the Structured Clinical Interview for DSM-IV Dissociative Disorders (SCID-D), Steinberg concludes that the five symptoms of amnesia, depersonalisation, derealisation, identity confusion and identity alteration are the primary dissociative symptoms carrying diagnostic significance; these are however seldom revealed to the interviewer who does not enquire about them. Steinberg (1993a) recommends that evaluation of these five dissociative symptoms should routinely be incorporated into diagnostic evaluations of patients with histories of trauma.

FORMAL ASSESSMENT OF MPD/DID

There are now several formal interview tools for assessing MPD/DID: The Dissociative Disorders Interview Schedule (Ross, 1989); Structured Clinical Interview for DSM-IV Dissociative Disorders – SCID-D (Steinberg, 1993a); Loewenstein's 'office mental status examination for chronic complex dissociative symptoms and dissociative identity disorder (Loewenstein, 1991).

A useful screening instrument that may help in picking up those patients who should be further assessed for dissociative disorders is the Dissociative Experiences Scale (DES) which is a 28 item self-report questionnaire (Bernstein & Putnam, 1986). This takes only a few minutes to complete. There is evidence that it is both reliable and valid (Frischholz et al., 1990; Putnam, 1991). A similar but more recent screening tool is the Dissociation Questionnaire (DIS-Q) developed in the Netherlands (Vanderlinden et al., 1993); this sorts into four subscales: identity confusion, loss of control, amnesia, and absorption.

SUMMARY

There are some phenomena familiar to British psychoanalysts which have something in common with MPD/DID; these include notions of coexistence of sane and psychotic personalities, internal 'gangs and mafias', cohabitees. There are a number of trauma-driven disturbances of development and personality which are varieties of long-term post-traumatic stress disorder – a kind of characterological PTSD, which has much overlap with borderline personality disorder. Some degree of dissociative phenomena is usual in PTSD, along with a range of other symptoms, including mood and arousal disturbances, hypervigilance, anxiety, self-harm, and hallucinatory and flashback imagery. Often the dissociative phenomena are rather hidden, revealed only by careful assessment. In some patients the dissociation is so extensive and elaborate that it can be regarded as the primary, albeit covert, symptom. The advanced dissociation of a full-blown MPD/DID state can make possible a higher level of functioning (apparent or actual) than would otherwise be expected in view of the extent of childhood trauma or neglect. There are now several good interview schedules and screening instruments for assessing dissociative disorders.

Chapter 8

WHAT IS GOING ON IN MULTIPLE PERSONALITY DISORDER/ DISSOCIATIVE IDENTITY DISORDER?

PRETENDING

On a clinical and descriptive level, MPD is, intrinsically, no more than a brutalised child's whimpering in the night and wishing with desperate earnestness that he or she were someone else, somewhere else, and that what had befallen him or her had befallen someone else. Most parsimoniously put, MPD appears to be a dissociative condition of childhood onset.

(Kluft, 1994a, p. 16)

MPD is a little girl imagining that the abuse is happening to someone else . . . The imagining is so intense, subjectively compelling, and adaptive, that the abused child experiences dissociated aspects of herself as other people . . .

(Ross, 1989, p. 55)

Thus Kluft and Ross make clear the point that MPD is about pretence and denial in the face of unbearable reality. The person with a severe dissociative disorder lives in a world of pretence. Imagination is used to protect against and compensate for experience which has to be denied because it is too terrible to bear and because there is no one to help the child to bear it. As Freyd argues (1993) in her 'betrayal-trauma' theory, perception of severe abuse by a caregiver may be blocked from processing into consciousness because it conflicts with a more primary need to retain attachment to the caregiver. Typically, as one gradually is told the historical narrative behind a patient's dissociative pathology, the impression is that dissociation was inevitable; that the environment was so full of contradictions, denials and repudiation of extreme cruelty that these could only be mirrored in the dissociative structure of the developing child's mind. For example, one might hear that a father would regularly abuse the child during the night but would never refer to this at other times and the nocturnal monster would appear completely incongruent with the seemingly loving father of the daytime; or a father might appear as a pillar of the community and the church in public, whilst presenting a very different face to the child in private. The child might be bound to a malevolent secret, under threat from the abuser or from fear of being condemned him/herself. If the abuse occurs outside the family, the child may feel the secret has to be kept from the parents; very often the child may feel responsible because the abuser may have groomed the child, one subtle step at a time, sometimes over a period of years, perhaps including fostering a relationship of trust with the parents – so that the child feels thoroughly corrupted and implicated and condemned to shameful silence. If the abuse occurs within the family, by father, mother, stepfather, brother, uncle, grandparent, etc., the secret may be kept from the non-abusing parent, but this requires continual monitoring of communications, with intense conflicts between the wish to let the cat out of the bag and the fearful attempts to keep it in. If abuse, especially severe sadistic abuse, comes from both parents, the resulting dissociation seems to be particularly profound; the child has no escape from the irreconcilable juxtaposition of abuse and source of protection – no escape other than mutilation of his/her own mind. Moreover, the child will conclude that since something bad is being done to them, it must mean they are being punished; since they are being punished, it must mean they are very bad. The abused child feels condemned forever, mired in secret guilt and shame which can never be put right. Lacking resources in the environment which could provide soothing, acceptance and reassurance, and also not having the cognitive resources available to an adult, the child may be driven to resort to denial, pretence and dissociation. Spontaneous self-hypnosis and trance-logic are used to create a more tolerable world of pretence.

MPD/DID is a personality structured around pretence. Little wonder then that some will argue that such a patient is 'pretending' to be multiple. Of course the patient is pretending – that is what a multiple patient is, a person who is pretending to be multiple. Then can the patient simply give up the pretence and become 'cured'? No, the surrendering of the pretence is extremely difficult and hazardous because the personality has been structured by the pretence. One part of the mind knows that experience A is so, whilst another part pretends that experience B is so instead. If B is given up then A may have to be experienced in its full terror and pain, with no escape.

The examination of MPD/DID as a pathology of pretence raises the question of its affinity with other pretence-based personality disorders, including such striking examples as Munchausen's and 'Munchausen's by proxy' (Goodwin, 1988). It can readily be seen that there are a number of states of mind and personality which involve invented identities. Martin (1994) has explored the notion of the 'fictive personality', which he sees as a dimension of narcissistic disorder which is inherent in a wide range of mental life: 'the capacity of people, chameleon-like to use or be used by fictions, and to take on the costumes and shapes and colours of the psychic environment in which they operate' (p. 126). Another psychoanalytic diagnosis left relatively unexplored for several decades, but recently revived by Sherwood and Cohen (1994), is that originally proposed by Helene Deutsch (1942) in her concept of the 'as-if' personality. By this term she meant patients who present a form of pseudo-relatedness, adapting chameleon-like to their surroundings, and lacking any firm and consistent identity. These are patients who appear relatively normal but who are not what they seem, but this may not become apparent for some time into the therapy. They are pretending. As Sherwood and Cohen comment: 'therapists may find themselves thinking that these patients are just going through the motions. This is correct; they are behaving as if they were patients' (p. 13). These authors see as-if pathology as involving a 'severe identity disturbance . . . built around primitive types of identification, including imitation . . . [which] prevents a sense of continuity with self across time' (p. 56).

Sherwood and Cohen (1994) see the aetiology of the as-if personality as having roots in a particular kind of breakdown in mother–infant mirroring. The balance may become tipped so that the child mirrors the mother (who may be depressed) and does not receive mirroring of his/her own aliveness. However they hint at more of a trauma-based aetiology in some instances: 'In a few cases we have (eventually) discovered alcoholism and sexual abuse in our patients' families, but even when these clearly pathogenic factors are present we have been surprised that this information was, first, presented relatively late in treatment and, second, that it was presented in a flat, matter-of-fact manner with no evident affect' (p. 78). They comment further on the dissociation manifest in these patients' narratives: 'They sound almost as though they were talking about someone else's family – they are that uninvested emotionally . . . Patients sound as if they are outside the family and watching it all from a distance' (p. 79).

It seems feasible to consider MPD/DID patients as part of a broader family of patients with pretend identities – all of which tend to cause disquiet amongst therapists, analysts and psychiatrists. These are people who are not what they seem, who use pretence, imitation and illusion in order to survive in a world which has not provided support for living authentically. Clinicians or nurses who sense the pretence often feel angry with the patient, registering a danger of being 'taken in' or fooled. Consider how much pain and complex pathology can be dismissed by a label such as 'gross hysteric'; such a term can be applied as if no further understanding is then required. If there is pretence in the pathology then the patient is not really a patient, is the implicit reasoning.

Sherwood and Cohen (1994) consider the as-if personality to be a form of 'quiet borderline' disorder, which they contrast with the more recognisable 'noisy borderline'. The quiet borderline is a covert disorder, like many forms of MPD. We might think in terms of quiet and noisy MPD/DID. The quiet forms of MPD seem to have a background in childhood loneliness and the development of imaginary companions. Both noisy and quiet forms may involve hypervigilance to others' moods, desires and expectations; the former in order to avoid trauma, the latter in order to maintain contact with a caregiver. The quiet MPD patient may selectively present personalities which are judged to interest the therapist or conform to his/her expectations – and may experience anxiety when the therapist does not offer a role or any clear clue as to what is required. Alter personalities may be presented which are like personified manic defences, defending against a state of depression or emptiness, especially if it is feared that the therapist would not be tolerant of, or interested in, the depression.

Most commentary on MPD/DID assumes that the cause always lies predominantly in severe childhood trauma – with some exceptions such as those who argue for an iatrogenic origin (e.g. Aldridge-Morris, 1989), and those who emphasise a more complex relationship between trauma and MPD (e.g. Tillman, Nash & Lerner, 1994). However, my own impression is that exogenous trauma may not always be the crucial driving factor. Loneliness and childhood depression can lead to the development of a complex compensatory world of imagination which may result in MPD. Another possibility is that innate sensitivities stemming from an autistic or schizophrenic vulnerability may mean that the sensory and human world is inherently traumatising.

The latter process is described by Donna Williams (1992) in her autobiographical book *Nobody Nowhere*. Williams suffered from autism and she tells very vividly of the terrifying impingement of the world, the sheer sensory overload which for her was inherent in being alive. She described how she developed a number of dissociative alter personalities to cope with this traumatically overstimulating world. She writes:

> People were forever saying that I had no friends. In fact my world was full of them. They were far more magical, reliable, predictable and real than other children, and they came with guarantees. It was a world of my own creation where I didn't need to control myself or the objects, or the animals and nature which were simply being in my presence. I had two other friends who did not belong to this physical world: the wisps and a pair of green eyes which hid under my bed, named Willie. (p. 8)

Willie was initially experienced as a protector against intruders in the night. She continues:

> I was frightened of him, but so I thought were they; and so come hell or high water, I sided with this character . . . I took to sleeping under the bed and I became Willie. Willie became the self I directed at the outside world, complete with hateful glaring eyes . . . By now I was interacting with the world as Willie. The name was probably derived from my own surname, and some of my behaviour was certainly modelled upon and in response to my violator, my mother. (p. 10)

She was three years old at the time of the emergence of Willie. Donna developed a number of other alter personalities. What is of particular interest here is that Donna did not regard her mother as the cause of her difficulties. Indeed she found her mother's failure of empathy and her violence to be her saving grace. 'My problems thrived on violence which told me I was safe and no one could get close to me' (p. 195). 'Had my mother been kind and loving, trying to involve or reach me, I'm sure I would never have had the freedom to find emotionally detached corners of the world from which to study and teach myself things . . . Thank God my mother was a "bad" mother' (p. 180). This example is of interest because it shows how the trauma which may lead to dissociation may involve an interplay between external and internal factors. For some vulnerable children, love itself may be experienced as overwhelming.

Clinical illustration

The case of Angie illustrates how a dissociative disorder may arise out of a matrix of childhood depression and lack of affective attunement from caregivers, combined with contradictory emotional communications.

Angie, a moderately successful young artist, presented initially with anxiety, panic attacks, low self-esteem, an anorexic eating disorder, and disturbed interpersonal relationships. On being taken into therapy it rapidly became apparent that dissociative processes pervaded her life. For example, she lived with one man, whilst having a relationship with another man, neither of these men knowing about the other. With the man she lived with she was quiet and sexually inhibited, whilst she would also, unbeknown to him, lead another life in which she was a sexual 'femme fatale', very lively, wearing different clothes, speaking with a different voice and relating to a quite separate group of friends. When asked if she felt guilty, in relation to her cohabiting partner, regarding her relationship with the other man, she explained that she did not, because when she was with her partner the other relationship seemed like something another person was doing. One problem she encountered was that the act of talking to the therapist about these dissociated parts of her life resulted in the dissociation beginning to break down. This was very painful for her. She remarked: 'When I hear what I am saying I hate myself.' She began to feel more depressed.

A recurrent feature of the therapist's experience was of being bombarded by a contradictory and confusing array of beliefs, attitudes and arguments which showed no regard for logic. She would for example speak ragefully of her parents' behaviour towards her, whilst at the same arguing that they were absolutely correct. Any line of interpretation which the therapist attempted to explore would be met with a barrage of confusing disputation which would leave him feeling helpless and enraged. Gradually it became clearer that she was conveying something of her own experience of the confusing and contradictory behaviour of her mother – and also that she was giving expression to a very sadistic part of herself that continually condemned her. We began to understand that her MPD was based partly upon her experience of the multiplicity of her mother. It seemed that her mother would express contradictory attitudes at different times, and would implicitly forbid her to point these out.

After a couple of years of therapy, Angie's underlying depression became a recurrent theme. She would often describe what she called 'the panics' on coming to her session. Gradually we understood that this panic reflected her fear of showing her true state of depression and inner loneliness, a fear that I would find this boring and would therefore abandon her. It became possible to reconstruct a possible picture of her as having been a temperamentally (biologically) depressed child who would cry a great deal, and with whom her parents were not adequately attuned. This experience seemed to be represented by a recurrent dream in which she is a small child screaming at her mother who is not hearing her. She began to realise that she had developed a variety of alter personalities in order to escape from the depression and to preserve a bond with her parents. She had become a clown performer who would entertain. She had also developed a number of other personalities that would perform various social functions. At one point she described how she had been watching some old family cine films and, whilst the other family members who were viewing were laughing in delight, she was feeling extremely upset, because she knew that behind the cheery face of the little girl on the screen was the depressed and lonely child she had been. In short, her various alter personalities were a variety of personified manic defences against a depression with which she had received no help as a child. As this emerged into the transference she experienced a dread that her depression and despair would not be tolerated by the therapist – but gradually she gave up her alter states in relation to the therapist and became more able to be whatever her authentic mood happened to be. Interestingly she described her abandoned alter personalities now as like dreams.

Angie had created pretend versions of herself in an attempt to preserve a bond with her parents. This elaborate pretence left the more authentic and depressive part of herself isolated from human mirroring and attunement.

WHAT ARE ALTER PERSONALITIES?

Superficially, perhaps the most striking feature of MPD/DID is the existence of alter (alternate) personalities. The same body may appear to be inhabited by different people, using different names, expressing different attitudes, displaying different behaviours, having different knowledge and appearing to have had different life histories. Occasionally one might encounter different personalities which appear to be unaware of the existence of each other, as if having the illusion of being the sole personality in the body. More commonly, the alters appear to have some knowledge of each other, but some have a more complex awareness of the dissociative system than do others.

Another feature that may initially be startling to the clinician faced with their first MPD patient is that some alters may be of an opposite sex to the biological gender of the patient's body. This is not really very puzzling so long as it is remembered that the alter is a pretence, an illusion which is believed. In the world of alters, anything is possible. This is because alters are partly based upon make-believe, and the underlying reasoning is not derived from normal linear logic but consists of 'trance logic', the toleration of completely unrealistic and contradictory ideas which might be found in a state of hypnosis. The very notion that different 'individuals' can exist within the same body is in itself a form of trance logic, as is the assumption, often expressed, that one alter could kill off another personality through inducing suicide and then continue to live in the body. MPD is not a condition in which different people exist within the same body, but a state in which a person has been driven by trauma or overwhelming conflict to escape into the pretence that they consist of a number of different individuals. A patient with MPD is a person pretending to have a multiple personality. This pretence has, however, structured their experience of self over many years and cannot easily be undone. Moreover, it is pretence that is experienced not 'as-if' but concretely.

To an extent, we might draw an analogy between alters and dream figures. Both dreams and alters rely on non-realistic dream-logic or trance-logic, or to use the original psychoanalytic term, primary process thinking – and both are a pretence without an 'as-if' quality (Franklin, 1990). Roth (1992) argues that trauma is common to the aetiology of both dreams and MPD, every dream being a potential nightmare as the ego struggles to deal with forbidden impulses and disturbing meanings of 'day residues'. He comments: 'The dissociated experiences, symbolised by alters, howl about the multiple personality like mysterious family ghosts, seeking a proper transference figure to bring surcease through revenge and grief. Alters, like dream symbols, disguise unbearable affects' (p. 113). Fairbairn was an analyst who wrote about dissociation and multiple personality at a time when most of his colleagues did not, and he even wrote a master's thesis on the distinction between dissociation and repression (Birtles & Sharff, 1994). He was possibly the first analyst to recognise that the various figures in a dream may represent different parts of the self (Fairbairn, 1944).

Alters come in many shapes, sizes and functions. The only limits are those of imagination itself. Some alters carry out adult coping functions; for example, one may go to work, another may deal with social functions, yet another may have a sexual relationship, etc. Others may contain particular affects; for example, one may be a repository of depression and may complain bitterly that the others leave her with all the despair. Almost always one finds that another important group are the traumatised child alters; these may contain memories of abuse – sometimes there appears to be a different child alter for each episode or variety of abuse. There may be child alters of different ages covering the whole range of childhood. Another group of alters are the persecutory or malevolent ones, usually seeming to be based upon an identification with the original abuser(s); these may be extremely dangerous, often urging other personalities towards suicide and generally fostering terror in the system.

There may be alters who have an overseeing function, able to be aware of much of the system of personalities, and sometimes having a gatekeeping function in terms of who is allowed access to the various personalities. Often a therapist will need to work through the gatekeeper. A related function taken on by a particular alter is that of 'internal helper'; usually this is an alter with a good grasp of the overall system and who offers help and guidance to the therapist.

Usually it is only a relatively few alters who take full control of behaviour and who 'come out' and interact with other people. Many remain hidden from external view, exerting their influence from inside, perhaps in the form of internal 'hallucinatory' voices. Sometimes an inner voice can be prompted to come out by the simple act of the therapist asking to speak to this alter.

Numbers of alters seem to vary enormously. In their comparison of ten studies of samples of MPD patients, North et al. (1993) found the mean numbers of alters varied between 6.3 and 15.7. However, there are reports of very large numbers of alters. One patient would make references to 'the assembly' which would debate and vote on certain decisions – giving the impression of an enormous, quasi-political arena. In some patients the system of alters appears to be very complex indeed. The therapist's experience can be rather like exploring underground caves; just as one thinks the cave has been mapped out, another opening is discovered, leading to further caves and so on. The organisation of alters is genuinely systemic, with hierarchies of controls, boundary and gatekeeping functions, and management of the interface with the external world.

The system of alters seems to be most complex in those patients who appear to have had a background of severely perverse, sadistic or cultic ritual abuse. These also seem to have the greatest number of alters and the most virulent of the malevolent alters. Such patients pose the greatest difficulties and challenges in treatment.

Do the alter personalities exist prior to the therapist discovering them? This is a variant on the iatrogenesis hypothesis. Of course it is impossible to know for sure, unless there is corroboration by someone who knew the patient well prior to therapy; on the other hand, the absence of prior observation of alters does not preclude their existence. Some clinical phenomena strongly suggest that the system of alters was not created iatrogenically. For example, the host personality of a patient whom I had been seeing for some time did not know that there were alters, and nor did I. At a certain point, to my initial astonishment, various alters began to present themselves to me. The host apparently remained unaware of these. One of the alters, with something of an inner helper function, began to try to communicate to the host the fact that the patient had a dissociative identity disorder. She began to write notes to the host explaining this. The host told me that she had found notes in her handbag which were extremely puzzling to her. On the advice of this inner helper alter I tried to speak to the host about her multiplicity. She was disbelieving. Although she was aware that there were periods of time which she could not account for, she could not accept the explanation of a dissociative disorder with alters. Eventually I mentioned the names of some of these alters. The host expressed bewilderment and demanded to know how I knew these names. She protested that although she was familiar with the names as having an internal significance, these were just names in her mind, aspects of her inner imagination, that only she knew about. She insisted that there was no possibility that these 'names' would come out and take over her behaviour. Nevertheless, she had to acknowledge that the fact that I, an external person, knew these names did provide some evidence to support the proposition that she had a multiple personality.

In many cases, the complex and bewildering nature of the dissociative system of alters argues against the possibility of iatrogenesis through suggestion or demand characteristics; the phenomena are often not what the therapist expects. Although the existence of a particular alter prior to its discovery by the therapist may not be possible to prove, what can be ascertained with reasonable certainty are the general dissociative phenomena, such as amnesia, depersonalisation, derealisation, experience of identity confusion and identity alteration, as assessed for example using Steinberg's SCID-D standardised interview.

Are alters true personalities? This is another question that often preoccupies those who are relatively unfamiliar with dissociative disorders. Of course any particular alter will not have the range of life experience and complexity of emotional life that a non-dissociative personality will have. An alter is, by definition, a part personality; the complete personality clearly is the total of all the alter personalities. However, some alters are more developed and have a more complex range of experience and emotion than do others. Many alters are developed for specific functions only, some are the containers of specific memories, and some were developed to cope with specific experiences or abusive tasks. Some alters remain as young children in their imaginative identity. Others may have developed at a much later stage and may claim to have no experience of trauma; this is often the case when there is an alter who presents a surprisingly high level of functioning and seeming lack of disturbance in a circumscribed area of life. There is great variability amongst alters and amongst MPD/DID patients. It really does not matter too much whether an alter is thought of as a 'personality' or a 'personality fragment'.

Putnam (1989) succinctly describes alters as: 'highly discrete states of consciousness organized around a prevailing affect, sense of self (including body image), with a limited repertoire of behaviours and a set of state-dependent memories' (p. 103). A little later (Putnam, 1992) he conceptualises an alter as a 'behavioural state'. He writes:

> Behavioural states are specific patterns of psychological and physiological variables that occur together and repeat themselves, often in highly predictable sequences, and that are relatively stable and enduring over time . . . Variables that define a discrete behavioural state include: affect, arousal and energy level, motor activity, posture and mannerisms, speech, cognitive processing, access to knowledge and autobiographical memory, and sense of self. (pp. 96 & 97)

In the changes in behavioural state of a patient with MPD/DID, there may be shifts in all these variables. However, switching of consciousness and behavioural state are a normal feature of life from birth onwards, as Wolff (1987) has described in his studies of infants – who show, for example, variations between alert inactivity, waking activity, crying, regular sleep and paradoxical sleep. These states are normally mediated via a complex and subtle system of infant–parent coordination, in which each affects the other's behavioural state – processes which have been studied by contemporary infant-researchers such as Stern (1986), as well as older analysts such as Winnicott (1960). Bach (1994) suggests that the parents have three tasks in relation to these developments and management of behavioural states:

1. To facilitate the development of a variety of differentiated waking and sleeping states.
2. To encourage self-regulation of these states so that they are stable and context appropriate.
3. To encourage the integration of these states so that the transitions between them are relatively smooth and the sense of self remains relatively stable throughout.

Putnam (1992) makes a similar point that the parents' task is to help the child to recover from disruptions of state and to maintain a sense of self across states. In many respects this function is that described by the psychoanalytic self psychologists (Kohut, 1971, 1977) as lying in the domain of the 'selfobject' – those empathic activities by the caregiver that are necessary for maintaining the cohesion of the self.

It is understandable that if the parents expose the child to, or fail to protect the child from, severe and repeated trauma, and if they behave in very different ways at different times, and if they fail to provide appropriate soothing when the child is distressed, then these functions described by Bach will be abrogated. The child may be driven to employ radical switching and dissociation in an attempt to manage states of overwhelming affect – or sometimes cast into a frantic search for stimulation, perhaps self-abusive, in order to escape from painful states of underarousal. Some patients will on occasion request large doses of tranquillising medication to knock them out when they are unable to bring about a switch of state any other way.

The transition between behavioural states, or alters, is usually termed 'switching'. This may be fairly obvious, accompanied by clear changes of body posture, general demeanour, bodily shudder or convulsion-like movement, a twitch of the face, or roll of the eyes (Putnam, 1994) – or there may be no easily observed clue that switching has occurred.

Sometimes one has to infer a switch because the patient is suddenly expressing an attitude quite different from a moment before, with a different affect and a different attitude towards the therapist; checking with the patient will usually provide corroboration as to whether or not there has been a switch. Switching is often accompanied by what Putnam (1989) has called 'grounding' behaviour. This seems to be to do with orienting the new alter or behavioural state. The patient may look around the room, as if processing information about their location; this may especially be the case if the particular alter has not emerged in the consulting room before. Related grounding behaviour may involve touching the chair, wall, or part of the body such as the face. Bach (1994) draws attention to research examining the behaviour of therapists just prior to making transference interpretations or other significant dynamic formulations to the patient. Typically the therapist would make some characteristic movement, such as a foot kick, shift of body posture, or some kind of self-touching. Bach (1994) suggests that changes in behavioural states or in states of consciousness, whether of an MPD or more normal variety, are usually accompanied by switching and grounding behaviour of some kind. Through considering the wider field of shifts in behavioural and consciousness states, it is possible to see that MPD/DID alter and switching phenomena represent a further development of processes that occur normally.

A rather startling dimension to the psychophysiological reality of dissociation is the existence of biological differences across alters. There has been a large amount of research looking at this, beginning with Morton Prince (Prince & Peterson, 1908). In a review, Coons (1988) comments: 'To date, studies have been conducted to investigate changes across personalities in virtually every organ system of the body.' Some differences between alters are certainly thought-provoking, such as differences in visual acuity and spectacle prescription amongst alters within the same patient (e.g. Shephard & Braun, 1985) and differential response to medication (e.g. Putnam et al., 1984). To some extent these differences may be similar to changes that can be achieved under hypnosis, consistent with the view of MPD/DID as a disorder of self-hypnosis.

Another aspect of alters, as Smith (1989) points out, is that they can also be regarded as varieties of false self. Winnicott (1960) describes the development of the false self on the basis of compliance with a caregiving environment that does not adapt sufficiently to the infant. The primary purpose of the false self is the protection of the true self from annihilation. This clearly is part of the purpose of alters, but the alters of the MPD patient function in addition to protect the true self from unbearable assaultive pain and unbearable knowledge. What we find here are complex linkages and layerings of false selves.

Finally a few comments are necessary concerning the relationship between alters and possession phenomena. Some alters claim to be, or are said by other alters to be, of non-human origin. Not infrequently there are alters that behave like traditional descriptions of demons. Originally MPD/DID was considered to be a state of demonic possession, one of the first descriptions being the biblical account of Legion 'for we are many' (Matthew 5). This idea emerges again in some more contemporary studies of MPD/DID; e.g. Allison (1980); Crabtree (1985); Friesen (1991); Scott Peck (1988). Certainly there are serious theological studies of possession phenomena (e.g. Koch, 1972; Perry, 1987). Moreover, the contemporary New Age 'spiritual' practices of 'channelling' raise many puzzling questions about the possibilities of possession by discarnate entities (Klimo, 1991). These channelling phenomena, somewhat similar to mediumistic activity, usually occur after the prolonged practice of meditation and involve the experience of a non-human entity entering the mind, becoming a kind of internal 'guide', and often presenting extensive metaphysical teaching. The recipients of this guidance may report profound changes in their experience and general outlook on life. In some channelling practices there is a deliberate invitation to 'spirits' to enter the mind. Whether such activities and experiences are mere foolishness, self-hypnotic trickery, or genuine metaphysical phenomena, and whether they are benign or dangerous, there are some remarkable parallels with the dissociative phenomena of MPD/DID, not least in the *idea* that non-human entities may inhabit the mind. Is a demonic alter simply an alter that believes itself to be a demon, or could there actually be demons in addition to dissociative alters? An internal helper in one patient, with a strongly Christian belief, told me that people with MPD are easy targets for demonic possession because the demons can insinuate themselves in amongst the alters, entering through the 'cracks' in the personality and intruding their voices amongst the many other dissociative voices; this alter also informed me that MPD patients were particularly vulnerable to demonic entry at the time of switching. Thus the patient herself believed there was a difference between alters, that in principle can be integrated, and demons, which inherently could not be integrated. There is no easy way to test this hypothesis, but it can not be entirely ruled out except on the basis of an a priori dismissal of the possibility of any metaphysical realm. The presence of 'demonic' parts of the mind seems most pronounced in those patients who appear to have been subject to severe abuse with occult overtones. This could simply reflect an internalisation and personification of experiences of extreme malevolence from which all 'humanity' has been excluded. However, in these patients other paranormal phenomena are also presented which are difficult to understand. Ross (1994) suggests that trauma 'opens a window to the paranormal' resulting in psychic and ESP phenomena; he notes that individuals reporting psychic capacities tend to be highly dissociative and to score highly on the Dissociative Experiences Scale, as do traumatised people who develop MPD/DID. These are not easy matters to address, but not to mention them would be merely to avoid an intellectually and emotionally troubling dimension that nevertheless crops up with a number of patients. However, it is not uncommon to hear reports of patients who have suffered through being told their alters were demons and being subjected to deliverance ministries within church fellowships. Psychoanalytic conceptualisations of the demonic are offered by Grotstein (1979) and Eigen (1993).

DEEP DISSOCIATION

I have not seen this phenomenon described before. It may be rare, but is sufficiently interesting to be worth considering in terms of what it suggests regarding the nature of dissociation.

There appear to be differing degrees and levels of dissociation. Some dissociative processes seem little more than elaborations on normal shifts in attention, arousal, mood and consciousness. Others seem of quite a different order. There are instances in which the dissociation is not merely a recategorisation of experience as belonging to someone else, the formation of an alter, but involves a deeper kind of escape from severely traumatic experience. The following example illustrates this.

A patient stopped attending her sessions for a number of weeks. I was then contacted by another of her alters, Wendy, who explained that Gillian, whom the alters regarded as the patient and as the main personality, had gone 'very far out' in response to some recent abusive experience. Wendy was worried that Gillian would not return and that she, Wendy, could not hold the fort indefinitely; she described how she was having to cover for Gillian and was leaving notes in Gillian's handbag regarding important events that had taken place in the previous few weeks. Wendy thought that a much longer than normal session would be required for Gillian to return. After much consideration and discussion this was arranged, along with a nurse cotherapist.

Wendy explained that Gillian would be able to make a partial return, sufficient to talk about her situation but not sufficient to function in the world; if she attempted a full return she would have to progress through a number of stages, which would include travel down a 'tunnel' and a stage of not understanding language. Wendy called internally for Gillian, who, as predicted, did return sufficiently for a preliminary discussion. She was severely disoriented in time and place. On demanding to know the date she was disbelieving, insisting it was a couple of months prior to the date she was told; this would have been the time of her escape into deep dissociation. She was shown a newspaper with the date, which she had to accept but still remained puzzled. She argued that she did not wish to return because then she would be faced with the pain she had escaped from. After some discussion of the difficulties Wendy was experiencing, Gillian agreed to attempt to return. She then curled up on the floor and began to stimulate herself by violently pinching her hand and rocking. She remarked that she was 'very far out' because she could not find the 'shadow'. After some minutes of strenuous activity she gasped that she had grasped the shadow. She then indicated that she had to progress along a 'tunnel', a stage which she had previously predicted, having described the tunnel as consisting of some kind of swirling patterns. Grasping the hand of the nurse, she was helped to 'progress' through the tunnel. She then entered a stage in which she appeared as a very young and terrified child who had no access to, or understanding of, words. On being given paper and pencil she drew crude drawings representing scenes of sadistic abuse.

Gillian did not manage to return from her deep dissociation in this session, which took most of a day, and which in terms of its agreed purpose was a failure. Some months later Gillian again reappeared to a partial extent during a session. The last time she had appeared had been during the height of summer. Now it was the depths of winter with thick snow all around. She looked out of the window in amazement, since subjectively for her summer had instantly changed to winter. Gillian's full return from deep dissociation took many more months, eventually occurring spontaneously.

The phenomena described here are very strange. In trying to respond to the problems such a patient presents one is drawn into a mysterious and complex subjective world, an alien inner landscape. How are we to understand this? A kind of dream state? An elaborate process of self-hypnosis? If so, who is the author and programmer of the trance fantasy? And how can we best help someone in that state? I do not know. What I feel certain of is that unmodified analytic therapy cannot address what is going on. Part of the reason analytic therapy cannot accommodate some of these states of mind is because the patient is in the grip of pretence, but it is pretence from which illusion is foreclosed. The pretence is made concrete and felt to be real. At this level, an analytic interpretation is useless.

HOW CAN WE MODEL WHAT IS HAPPENING IN A SEVERE DISSOCIATIVE DISORDER? COMPETITION FOR MENTAL SPACE – THE GLOBAL WORKSPACE MODEL

Consider an analogy with an ordinary PC computer. After writing an account of an experience, I have various options about how to record it, what file name to use and what directory to file it under. I could file it under self, or I could use a directory called 'not self', or one called Bill, or Fred, or Jane or 'nothing whatsoever to do with me'.

Normally a computer can display only one file on the screen at once. However, supposing we had a malfunctioning computer, such that several files were competing for the screen at the same time. We might see a rapid alternation of different files from different directories, or we might have a very confusing display of information on the screen. This is something like the experience of some, but not all, people with dissociative disorders. On occasion the person with MPD may feel confused and disoriented as a number of alters attempt to speak or take control at once, internally shouting a cacophony of incompatible demands and opinions. Another analogy would be with a competition for access to a microphone or some other broadcasting system.

Bernard Baars (1988) has offered a cognitive theory of consciousness based on the idea of a Global Workspace. This is an information exchange that allows different processors within the mind to interact and communicate with each other. Consciousness is like a blackboard or bulletin board, on which different information processors within the mind can communicate or 'broadcast' to each other. In a severe dissociative disorder, it is as if different parts of the mind take over the broadcasting centre at different times and prevent others from having access. Therapy with dissociative patients usually involves some form of bringing about communication between the dissociated parts. For a time the therapist him/herself might function as the Global Workspace, the bulletin board, since it is the therapist who hears from all the alter personalities. I have one patient who spontaneously began to use writing as a means of inter-alter communication. She writes extensive accounts of her thoughts and attitudes and gives them to me; these involve a multiplicity of handwriting styles and points of view. It is a disconcerting experience for the therapist to realise the multiple diverse transference relationships occurring simultaneously – to realise that while responding to one personality there are many others observing with quite different attitudes and agendas.

COMPREHENSIVE THEORIES OF THE ORIGIN AND FUNCTION OF MPD/DID

Theories of MPD/DID prior to about the mid 1980s tended to be very partial and incomplete and generally unsatisfactory. This historical point was also the time when we were beginning to understand something more about post-traumatic stress disorder. It became possible to understand MPD as a complex 'post-traumatic condition of childhood onset' (Kluft, 1994a).

Kluft (1994a) lists a number of earlier unsuccessful 'single factor' theories of MPD: ego weakness; personification of parts of the mind; conflicted identifications; conflicting and unhomogenised introjections; repression; primitive wish fulfilments; use of aspects of self as transitional object or selfobject; splitting; ego state theory; neo-dissociation theory of the hidden observer; sociological theories of role-taking behaviour.

Amongst contemporary single factor theories, he includes: the assumption that MPD is simply the result of child abuse, ignoring the point that not all abused people develop MPD; the hypothesis that MPD is simply the result of the abuse of self-hypnosis – the problem here being that most highly hypnotisable individuals do not develop MPD, and there is no evidence that hypnosis alone can create stable MPD; psychoanalytic concepts of developmental conflicts which ignore the dimension of exogenous trauma. Regarding the latter point, Kluft comments: 'the trauma response stands aside from, although it influences and is influenced by, other developmental lines' (1994a, p. 19).

Kluft argues that more complex polyfactorial approaches are needed to conceptualise MPD/DID. He lists three such current approaches, including his own. One formulation is that of Stern (1984), who provides what he calls a 'paradigmatic description of the etiology of a multiple personality'. This will involve, first, abuse or neglect of the child, with exposure to a caregiver with severe psychopathology; the initial dissociation occurs in childhood in response to sudden trauma caused by at least one other person; the splits in the personality may not become obvious until years later; the environment may include strict religious beliefs; there may be confusing messages about identity; intelligence will be average or high; the function of alters may change over time but the primary task is to protect the main personality from others or from internal conflict.

A second polyfactorial approach is that of Braun and Sachs (1985), who present their 'Three-P theory' of MPD. The three P's are the Precipitating, Predisposing and Perpetuating factors. Predisposing factors include (1) an inborn capacity to dissociate; (2) exposure to severe and overwhelming trauma. The precipitating factors are to do with the formation of an alter when a series of fragmented episodes linked by a common affective state take on a life of their own. Regarding perpetuating factors, dissociation may become self-reinforcing, subsequent life events and family patterns may further reinforce dissociation, and, through stimulus generalisation or transference, other people will tend to be reacted to as those who caused the original trauma.

Kluft's own four-factor theory involves the following:

1. A capacity for dissociation.
2. Life experiences that traumatically overwhelm the non-dissociative defensive/adaptive capacities of the child's ego.
3. Dissociative defences make use of the available substrates for dividedness; substrates may include factors such as state and mood-dependent memory, contradictory parental demands, double binds, identification with a parent's multiple personality, and the use of autohypnosis.
4. The child is not provided with adequate protection (stimulus barrier) against further overwhelming experiences, appropriate soothing, and opportunities to express and process their pain.

Kluft's theory seems able to account for many aspects of MPD/DID. It is worth noting that, according to this model, the trauma does not have to be abuse, not does it have to be external in origin. The model is compatible with Donna Williams' (1992) account of the development of her alter personalities as a result of her autistic sensitivity which rendered the world intrinsically traumatising.

The emphasis upon the absence of soothing is in my view very important. Probably a child can cope with most kinds of trauma, providing there is someone available who can hear about it, be empathic, and can sooth and reassure (van der Kolk & Fisler, 1994). This is the realm of the 'selfobject' described by Kohut and the psychoanalytic 'self psychologists', that aspect of the child's relationship with the parents that is to do with the provision of empathy, and which is necessary for the maintenance of the coherence of the child's self structure. Although writing about narcissistic personalities rather than MPD, Kohut (1971) described vertical splits in the psyche resulting from failures in this selfobject function, as opposed to the horizontal splits of repression; the concept of a vertical split certainly has some similarity to the concept of dissociation.

As the MPD/DID patient gradually allows the therapist access to the pain that made the alters necessary, we find the immense unbearable loneliness of the child who had no one to tell, no one to provide empathy and no one to counter the distorted thinking which assumes the child is to blame and will be condemned. Out of this unbearable loneliness are created the imaginary friends, in addition to those alters whose function is to experience the pain and spare the host. Often the impression is that the child lived in what was, subjectively and possibly objectively, an utterly malevolent world in which no one external could be trusted. Sometimes the account suggests that the abuser(s) deliberately sought to create that impression in the child so that he/she would not attempt to disclose what was going on. For example, an abusing father may tell the child that the mother knows all about what is done and approves of it; or a network of perverts may tell the child that all kinds of people are involved in the abuse, such as police, doctors, teachers, etc., with the result that the child distrusts any authority he/she might otherwise consider confiding in. In this way the child is given the idea that there is no alternative to the world of endlessly repeating abuse.

SUMMARY

In addition to being constructed out of the primary defence of dissociation, MPD/DID is characterised by alters which are imaginative creations developed through pretence. In the case of traumatised children who develop MPD/DID, the original pretence is that he/she is not present or not in the body when the trauma or abuse is taking place. Alters have various functions, such as being a repository for memories of trauma, a location for particular affects and impulses (homicidal or suicidal), a vehicle for restitutive fantasies, the preservation of islands of good functioning, and a number of other survival functions. Simple single factor theories of the development of MPD/DID are not adequate. There are several more complex, polyfactorial models, which better accommodate the clinical and research observations. The lack of availability of adults who can provide soothing to the traumatised child may be a crucial factor in whether or not he/she has to resort to desperate defences of dissociation and alter development. Exogenous trauma may not always be a clear factor in the development of MPD/DID; intense loneliness or depression in childhood, or unusual sensitivity may also contribute to the creation of imaginary friends who offer comfort.

Chapter 9

THERAPEUTIC CONSIDERATIONS WITH MPD/DID

The first point I would like to make here is that I do not know how best to treat patients with severe dissociative disorders. Part of the reason for this is that although MPD/DID patients have much in common with each other, they are also each quite idiosyncratic, with their own complex internal structures and nuances of inner experience. The idea of a standardised therapy for patients with MPD/DID seems a contradiction in terms. Nowhere is the stance of 'learning from the patient' (Casement, 1985) more necessary than in work with MPD/DID.

MPD/DID patients are extremely vulnerable. They may have been severely traumatised in childhood and the potential exists for them to be traumatised again in therapy. Their sense of reality and perception of reality may have been undermined in childhood and the danger is that it could be again in therapy. The therapist must stay in the position of not knowing what went on in the patient's childhood – because he/she was not there. This is important not only because it is true that the therapist does not know objectively the historical situation, but also because the patient's own account may vary, and different parts of the patient may present differing accounts; it is not uncommon for one alter to describe an experience of abuse and for another alter to deny it and accuse the first one of lying.

The person who was abused or traumatised in childhood often has a very fragile sense of autonomy. False compliance with a therapist's view is always a danger – which may be followed ultimately by a violent repudiation of the therapy. Another danger is that of the patient being overwhelmed by reconnecting with warded off experiences of trauma. Through listening to my patients I have learnt to tread very carefully, gently and often slowly when facing experiences of trauma. I do not hold the view that it is always necessary or appropriate for childhood trauma to be faced fully and in detail; nor do I assume that I can know that it is better for a person with MPD to become integrated in any particular case. I do not assume that I know how best to treat dissociative disorders.

LIMITATIONS OF THERAPY

The patient with MPD/DID is very frightened. Their inner state of multiplicity is usually concealed, the outward display of differing alters being just the tip of the iceberg; most of the dissociative system is covert, actively concealed from the 'public'. Revealing the system of alters to a therapist can feel like surrendering the security that has been depended upon throughout life so far, and can seem to raise the threat of annihilation. The therapist may be the only person who knows the system of alters. Even a spouse may know just one or two alters. No person other than the therapist may engage so many alters. This makes the therapist seem a very dangerous figure. The dependence upon the therapist can seem terrifying. Premature talk of integration may evoke terror amongst the alters, threatening the surrender of separate existence, and stirring intense inter-alter rivalry. In this context the therapist may be regarded as a potential murderer.

Therapy may not be possible in a particular case for any of the following reasons:

1. Some alters may be too hostile and destructive. Because of their antagonism to the therapy, the cure may be more life threatening than the illness.

2. The childhood trauma may be too severe to face. Attempts to address the trauma leave the patient overwhelmed. The patient gets worse and does not get better.

3. A setting for therapy which is both secure and understanding is not available. It is necessary to keep the patient alive and to protect him/her against intensely self-destructive impulses. At the same time, the staff of a unit need to have some understanding of the problems of MPD/DID and some sympathy and empathy with the patient.

4. The system of alters is too complex, with much layering, and including alters that are beyond integration, such as dedicated perverse 'satanic' alters.

5. The severity of the trauma, deprivation and distortion of the normal expectable environment may be so extreme, as in some perverse ritual abuse settings.

The fact that a patient has dissociated into neatly demarcated personalities does not mean that undoing the dissociation will result in a healthy personality, especially if the early environment has been very largely malevolent. Indeed, undoing the dissociation may leave the patient even more resourceless than before. In working with dissociation, it is always advisable to proceed with extreme caution.

For most people the natural state is to experience self as more or less a multifaceted unity. By contrast, for the MPD/DID patient, the 'natural' state is to experience self as a multiplicity of dissociated parts. For the therapist to push for integration when the patient is not willing is to attempt to impose an alien organisation. Therapeutic ambition often needs to be curbed. It is not for the therapist to know what is best or what is possible for the patient. Sometimes a partial treatment compromise is the best that can be achieved, an improved democracy amongst the alters. Sometimes continuing psychiatric care, with symptom alleviation through major tranquillisers and potent antidepressants must be settled for. Occasionally, and seemingly against all the odds, patients find the resources to recover.

HOW TO MINIMISE THE DANGER OF RETRAUMATISATION IN THERAPY

The MPD/DID patient's dissociative disturbance began in trauma. Therapy that attempts to facilitate genuine recovery is likely to involve revisiting that trauma. Not surprisingly, therefore, therapy with patients who have been traumatised in childhood is usually stormy, difficult and frightening. A crucial concern in the therapy must always be to minimise the danger of the patient becoming again overwhelmed with unbearable affect, including terror. The therapist must aim to support the patient's sense of safety and mastery.

The MPD/DID patient will have a defective sense of autonomy. He/she will have had experiences of being dominated, manipulated and abused by others. Fears of these experiences being repeated will naturally be greatly fuelled in the transference to the therapist. The patient may appear to need to control the therapist. Therapists with particular narcissistic sensitivities to being controlled may have difficulties with these patients. Whilst it is important not to let the patient invade the therapist's own boundaries, it is necessary that the patient should have their own appropriate sphere of autonomy and control over the therapeutic process, including the speed of movement of the process. For example, if the patient wishes to avoid the couch, restrict the length of sessions, miss sessions, sit near the door, remain silent, etc., these should be accepted and the need for control should be explicitly acknowledged and affirmed, although the particular meanings of these actions should be explored as far as possible. It is crucially important to allow the patient to resist, to withdraw, to 'not communicate' and 'not relate' – and the therapist just has to tolerate the boredom of these phases.

Most MPD/DID patients, and indeed most patients who have been severely traumatised in childhood, will at times generate what Langs (1978) calls a Type C communicative field. Whereas a Type A field is rich in symbolic metaphoric communication, and a Type B field involves communication through interactional pressures (of projective identification), the Type C field is essentially devoid of commmunication. The function of Type C is not to communicate, to ward off and keep at bay the threatening mental contents. In a Type C field of a traumatised patient, there may be long silences, seemingly empty of affect, verbal narratives may fail to develop and cohere so as to reveal underlying dynamic tensions and meanings as they would in a Type A field, and the therapist may have difficulty staying awake. Such metaphoric images as do emerge may inherently connote the concealment of disturbing meaning: for example, an image of a sealed box, a toxic or nuclear core encased in protective material, an astronomical 'black hole' (from which no information can escape), or a dream scene of a figure guarding a locked chest. There is nothing for it but to sit out these periods and wait for dynamic meaning to emerge. Sometimes it is important to convey explicitly to the patient that these empty periods of therapy are acceptable and tolerable to the therapist.

One point that must always be kept in mind in working with patients who may have been severely traumatised in childhood is the importance of trying to ensure that the patient does not leave the session in a frightened child alter. Analytic therapists are used to thinking in terms of the child or infant within the adult, and to addressing interpretations partly to infantile parts of the mind. However, it is not always understood that the dissociative patient may switch *completely* into the state of mind of a confused and traumatised child. The danger then is that a disoriented child has left the consulting room, albeit in an adult's body. I find it is best if this problem is discussed openly with the patient and strategies agreed upon for managing the transition back to the outside world. These might involve certain alters agreeing to take over at the session end, or the therapist asking for an adult part to appear as the session draws to a close.

If the patient *is* in a crisis, particularly if this involves suicidal or parasuicidal impulses, then relieving the tension of this state of mind and helping the patient to cope with their affects, impulses and inner images becomes the main focus. As Horevitz and Loewenstein (1994) comment: 'Failure to maintain self-control never warrants further "depth" exploration of the historical reasons for this failure, but instead mandates close attention to the immediate precipitants of the problem and the failure to cope in every-day life' (p. 299). A patient was due to attend a job interview and the anticipated encounter with a rather bullying male authority was stirring up considerable anxiety which was threatening to overwhelm her. She felt that her anxiety was probably heralding the emergence of a flashback of trauma involving her tyrannical and perverse father. These thoughts about the flashback emerged towards the end of the session. It was not appropriate to attempt to explore the content of the memories/fantasies at this point. Instead, the therapist emphasised that what they could be sure about was that her anxiety had its source in something other than the job interview itself and that it was important for her to try to remember that whatever had terrified her in the past was not happening in the present. The patient felt calmed and 'held' by this comment from the therapist, which was literally 'stating the obvious', but in her traumatised state of mind, in which the past was invading the perception of the present, this distinction was in danger of being lost.

A valuable collection of writings from the patients' own perspectives is the book entitled *Multiple Personality Disorder From The Inside Out* (Cohen, Giller & Lynn, 1991). Some of the points that are emphasised are: the need for the state of multiplicity to be accepted – trying to suppress the patient's dissociative manifestations is not helpful; the need for therapists to be both knowledgeable and humble in working with MPD; the centrality of the issue of trust – the need for the therapist to be trustworthy, and the patient's inability to trust because of their early experiences; the need for the therapist to be reliable and available; the terror evoked by the therapist's holiday breaks; the terror inherent in the whole state of MPD; the importance of the patient's being in control of the pacing of the therapy and of decisions involving the therapy.

GENERAL PRINCIPLES OF TREATMENT

Useful general guidelines for treatment of MPD/DID are provided by a committee of the International Society for the Study of Dissociation (Barach et al., 1994). These represent a current consensus about good practice. What I advocate here is broadly consistent with these guidelines.

The present consensus view is that the aim of the early stages of treatment should be to help the patient stabilise and feel safe. Interventions should be explanatory and supportive. Premature interpretations and/or exploration of trauma will destabilise the patient and lead to dangerous crises. Uncovering and mapping out the system of alters should proceed at the patient's own pace. A clear structure for the therapy should be established and agreed with the patient.

Kluft (1992) has elaborated some clinically derived rules for psychotherapy of MPD/DID, based upon an understanding of what causes the disorder. These rules are summarised as follows:

1. Because MPD/DID originates in violated boundaries, therapy should provide a secure treatment frame.

2. In MPD/DID the person feels a lack of control; therefore the therapy must facilitate the patient's sense of mastery and active participation.

3. The MPD/DID patient has been an involuntary participant in abusive activities; therefore the establishment of a therapeutic alliance is crucial.

4. Inherent in MPD/DID is the hiding away of what has been unbearable; this must in time be uncovered and the emotion abreacted.

5. Conflict amongst alters is often inherent in MPD/DID; therefore collaboration and inter-alter empathy should be encouraged.

6. The person with MPD/DID has often been subjected to extremely confusing and misleading communications; therefore the therapist's communications must be clear and of a kind the patient can understand.

7. The child who develops MPD/DID has often been subjected to extremely inconsistent behaviours from caregivers; therefore the therapist should be consistent.

8. Hope has often been nearly destroyed in these patients; the therapist should endeavour to restore realistic hope.

9. MPD/DID usually results from experiences which have been overwhelming (and therefore traumatic); pacing of the therapy is essential.

10. The early 'caregivers' have usually not demonstrated consistent and responsible care of the child who develops MPD/DID; therefore the therapist should be very responsible and moreover must expect responsibility from the patient, calling him/her to account for lapses in responsibility.

11. Much of the patient's early experience has been characterised by abandonment, neglect and lack of protection, as well as abuse; therefore, silence, inappropriate 'neutrality' and affective blandness will be perceived as rejecting and uncaring, repeating aspects of the early environment.

12. The thinking of many of the patient's alters will be distorted, showing, for example, the self-blaming assumptions of the abused child; these cognitive errors must be identified and addressed.

These guidelines have an obvious validity stemming from the inherent nature and logic of MPD/DID. However, the psychoanalytic clinician will wonder whether these do not amount to an advocacy of a 'corrective emotional experience', the somewhat notorious concept first proposed by Alexander and French (1946). It is generally felt that this represents an essentially non-analytic and manipulative stance. I do not think that Kluft's guidelines have to be understood in this way. Mostly they state only what should be expected in any good psychotherapy, in terms of the realistic, empathic, reliable and benign stance of the therapist. The therapist will inevitably fall short of the ideals portrayed in the guidelines. What is important it seems to me is that the therapist should recognise the impact of these failings and be able to interpret them to the patient.

Clearly one of the aims of most therapies for MPD/DID is to bring about greater communication between the alters, possibly leading to integration. Exceptions to this principle are those therapies which aim at a hypnotic elimination of the alters in order to release the untraumatised original personality; this approach goes against the consensus and further research is required to assess its efficacy. The process of internal communication is illuminated by the model of the Global Workspace (Baars, 1988) which suggests that the function of consciousness is to provide a forum in which mental processors can 'broadcast' to each other, allowing exchange of information and cognition of a kind not available when processors remain non-conscious. Prior to treatment, the MPD/DID patient has a severely deformed Global Workspace – like a broadcasting station that is repeatedly hijacked by different groups of dissidents as well as by forces of the establishment. Inter-alter communication may be very limited, although it may take place in circumscribed ways; for example, one patient referred to 'the assembly', an image which inherently suggests some kind of internal debating chamber. Inter-alter empathy may be even more limited. For a long time the therapist's mind may have to function as the Global Workspace, since it is he/she who hears the communications of a variety of alters, who may not hear each other. The general aim of therapy with MPD/DID – and perhaps the aim of any analytic therapy – is ultimately to expand the patient's Global Workspace, so that internal communication and internal freedom are enhanced.

Entering into therapy inevitably evokes extreme anxiety since a complex system that has allowed a certain kind of survival for many years is under threat. The very fact that the system is being revealed is a considerable threat, since part of the 'raison d'être' of the dissociative system is concealment. As a result of this disclosure the patient as a whole feels intensely vulnerable. The emerging inter-alter awareness may evoke a painful consciousness, located *somewhere* in the system of consciousnesses, that there is no core to the personality, no coherent and central sense of 'I' – and an equally painful awareness that it is not like this for everyone.

RELATING TO THE ALTERS

How are the alters to be found? Sometimes an alter will spontaneously appear, with startling effect upon a therapist who may not have suspected the presence of alters. Usually this would be an alter in quite a key position. Alters are more likely to appear if given an invitation. By this I do not mean suggesting the presence of alters in patients who show no signs of having alters. The clinician will first have ascertained through appropriate assessment that the patient does have a dissociative disorder (e.g. Steinberg, 1993b). In the course of this the patient may disclose the internal experience of identity confusion, or of internal voices. It may then be possible simply to ask if the therapist might talk with one of the voices, or to ask if there is any other person inside who would like to talk. The sceptic might say that this would lead to an iatrogenic creation of alters where none existed independently of the therapist's suggestion. My reply to this is that if these gentle enquiries are put to a neurotic non-dissociative patient, alters do *not* emerge (although I am not speaking here of the kind of aggressive therapeutic regimes, sometimes described, which may themselves have a cult-like character).

What is often found is that as some alters begin to emerge and speak directly to the therapist, more and more become apparent, eager to speak and to be known. It is like a group of prisoners who have been kept in semi-solitary confinement, suddenly realising that there is someone they can talk to. Competition for the internal Global Workspace also becomes apparent, perhaps indicated by rapidly changing facial expressions and looks of confusion, reflecting a multitude of inner voices all talking at once. Child alters may wish to come forward, only to be blocked by other alters who function as 'protectors' guarding against the danger of retraumatisation.

There may, however, be much ambivalence amongst the alters about being known by the therapist, this being both desired and feared. For example, in the early stages of therapy, a patient feared that the therapist was in a powerful and dangerous position because she was given access to knowledge of the alters. Gradually the patient realised with a mixture of disappointment and relief that the therapist could not easily distinguish and identify the alters and had only a limited grasp of the complexity of the internal system. The therapist was not then seen so much as either an omnipotent rescuer or a potential destroyer.

For much of the time the therapist's task will be to listen respectfully and to get to know the alters. The work can be essentially analytic, being non-directive, non-manipulative, attentive to transference, and characterised by the stance of 'sustained empathic enquiry' (Stolorow, Brandchaft & Atwood, 1987). Many alters will prove willing to disclose their particular attitudes, life histories, function within the system and their view of the therapy. Since the alters do experience themselves as different individuals, it is important to respect this subjective sense of difference, at the same time as indicating an awareness that they are all parts of one person. If the subjective experience of separateness is not acknowledged by the therapist – for example, in refusing to acknowledge different names of alters – then the alter system may retreat to a more covert position, but it will not go away. Some MPD/DID patients who have been in previously unsuccessful therapy, with therapists who did not accept their alterity, describe how they complied with the therapist's requirements by developing an alter specifically for the therapy, the rest of the system remaining hidden.

The suggestion of integration may provoke intense rivalry and even warfare amongst the alters, as some struggle for dominance. Often a particular alter will assert that he/she should be the main personality and will talk disparagingly of the others. Chaos may break out, with rapid and disorganised switching between personalities. It is necessary to reassure the system of alters as a whole that no 'political solution' will be imposed on them from outside and that internal agreement must be reached.

At some point traumatised child alters may appear, either spontaneously or with the agreement of a gatekeeping personality and the therapist. The child alter will appear to have the emotions and the cognitions of a child. Through the child alters, the trauma remains alive in the present. It is as though no time has past, as if the child has remained permanently in a state of trauma. When speaking of trauma or abuse, the child will use the present tense. The child may be fearful of telling of abuse, perhaps because of threats made by the abuser. He/she is also likely to be self-blaming, as abused children usually are. It is necessary for the therapist to enter into the 'trance logic' of the child alter and respond to the fears, the shame and the guilt, at the level that the child experiences them. At these times, although the therapist is in the room with another adult body, he/she is talking to a frightened child. The distorted thinking of the child alter, especially the attribution of blame to the self, needs to be addressed, just as would be the case with a child patient. Sometimes it may be necessary to enter into the 'trance scene' of the abuse and introduce changes to modify the trauma; for example, the therapist may say to the child alter that the abuse should not be taking place and that if the abuser approaches the child again, he/she can tell the therapist. How can such an intervention be psychoanalytic? The point is that this is the kind of thing one would say to a child who is being abused; the concrete logic of the alter state of mind means that one *is* talking to an abused child. An adult alter can understand a psychoanalytic interpretation; for the child the language must be simple and concrete.

Much of the time the therapist will be conversing with one alter at a time, perhaps with some (but not all) of the others listening and observing. Sometimes, especially in crises, it will be important to address the group as a whole. This can be done quite simply by stating that one has a message for the whole group. Such communications are helpful not only in terms of the particular group message but also in so far as the act of addressing the whole indicates that all the personalities are to be taken into account. Examples of whole-group communications are: statements about the ground-rules of therapy; clarifications of the therapist's stance; reassurance that no 'solution' will be imposed; evocation of collective responsibility for checking the activity of a suicidal alter – and so on. A therapist's experience in family and group work will often be found relevant here. (For an elaborated view from a family therapist's perspective, see Goulding and Schwartz (1995).)

QUESTIONS OF MEMORY AND TRUTH

The hearing of narratives of abuse and trauma from child alters raises the question of the veridicality of these narratives – a matter of much current debate. Of course it cannot be assumed that what an alter reports is completely true, or partly true, or even metaphorically true. It is quite possible that it contains no truth at all. On the other hand, the account may be true to the child's experience. The therapist is unlikely to be in a position to know. Uncertainty is inherent in the structure of MPD/DID, indicated by the way in which one alter may describe a situation which another alter will repudiate; a position not unlike that played out in the wider social field by the various lobbying groups which argue from conflicting and totally incompatible positions regarding memories of abuse.

Ross (1994) describes a patient called Pam, who during the course of treatment, reported news that her mother had committed suicide. Over the next two months she engaged in a substantial and painful process of mourning. She became upset at further news that her father was already living with another woman. Moreover, her father's new fiancée sent her a card signed 'Mom', a gesture which seemed astonishingly insensitive. However, a male alter was contacted who admitted to having planted this completely false information; her mother was not dead. This alter explained that his motivation had been to assist Pam who had been worried about the state of her parents' marriage; he had reasoned that if he persuaded her that her mother was dead she could be relieved of this worry. On the basis of this false information, Pam had engaged in a perfectly plausible process of mourning. As Ross comments: 'The only difference between such false memories and real memories is the fact that the events never happened' (1994, p. 65).

Gannaway (1989) argues for the unreliability of the MPD/DID patient's memories through reference to Spiegel's (1974) concept of the 'Grade Five Syndrome'. This concerns the characteristics of the most hypnotisable people, those scoring 5 on a scale of 0–5, which is less than 5 per cent of the population. These characteristics include the following: a posture of trust; tendency to suspend critical judgement; use of 'trance logic'; a capacity for focused attention; excellent memory; affiliation with new events; a fixed personality core underneath the malleable overlay. Gannaway reported that in a sample of MPD patients, all met the criteria for Spiegal's Grade Five.

Moreover, Spiegal (1974) described a 'compulsive triad' amongst Grade Five people. This consists of: compulsive compliance; source amnesia; rationalisation. According to Gannaway's line of argument, if MPD/DID patients tend to be Grade Fives, then they are likely to comply compulsively with perceived expectations, forget where an image or narrative comes from (i.e. whether it is from a memory or a suggestion from another person), and fill in the gaps with spurious explanations. On this basis, Gannaway concludes, the MPD/DID patient may be at high risk of developing pseudo-memories.

MPD/DID may be rooted in trauma, but it is also rooted in fantasy. If alters are developed in early childhood, they emerge from a matrix of pre-operational thinking (in terms of the Piagetian stages), when magical and dreamlike thinking is normal (Franklin, 1990). Gannaway comments: 'Within the world of trance logic, the uniqueness and vastness of the internal system is limited only by the creativity and psychodynamic needs of the constructor' (p. 209).

In endeavouring to reconstruct what may have taken place in childhood, the therapist would do well to attend to what is repeated in the transference, in the here-and-now of the consulting room, at least as much as what is reported by alters as memory narratives.

TRANSFERENCE AND COUNTERTRANSFERENCE

The therapist must ultimately settle into him or herself as the final common trans-
ferential pathway for the patient's blending together an amalgam of alters
(Roth, 1992, p. 116)

With MPD/DID patients there will be a multiplicity of transferences. It can be disconcerting to discover that one is being watched and listened to by a multitude of personalities, with a wide spectrum of attitudes and agendas.

Neutrality is always considered important in analytic work, in the sense of not favouring any particular part of the mind; the therapist should maintain a position 'equidistant' (Anna Freud, 1936) from the various conflicting parts of the mind. The importance of this becomes vividly apparent with MPD/DID patients, in whom the conflicting parts of the mind are personified as characters who will come right out and complain in no uncertain terms. It can be tempting subtly to side with the point of view of a seemingly more 'healthy' alter and collude in criticism of a more 'sick' alter. There might be an alter who is regarded by the others as the designated patient. Other alters might be bemused at the suggestion that they too are involved in the therapy, perhaps protesting that they come only to help the sick one – rather like a husband who agrees to attend marital sessions in order help his 'sick' wife, disregarding his own contribution to their problems. Like groups and other 'people systems', there are processes of projection, disavowal and scapegoating amongst the alters. There may be attempts by some to form collusive alliances with the therapist, whilst others may hold back in aloof contempt for the therapy, whilst yet others may be actively hostile and sabotaging to the therapy. Then there may be the child alters, eager to reach out and be accepted and listened to, yet also fearful of further trauma. There may be many others – and in the more complex cases, layer upon layer of systems of alters.

Of course the transferences of each patient will be determined by their idiosyncratic childhood experiences and inner structures of fantasy, desire and terror. However, there are certain common constellations, particularly the perceptions of the therapist as abuser and as colluder with abuse.

In the abusive transference position, the therapist is perceived as power-ful, malevolent, controlling, manipulative, deceptive, potentially murderous, etc. These qualities can be woven into the experience of the therapist in his/her therapeutic work. For example, he/she may be feared as someone who would 'murder' some of the alters, or impose an alien therapeutic solution, or retraumatise the patient through premature abreaction. More rarely the therapist is perceived as potentially and literally a rapist, sometimes even in league with the original abuser(s). The therapist's countertransference may be of guilt and a sense of damaging the patient.

Some alters may also take up the position of abuser, with the therapist and other alters in the victim position. Thus the therapist may be exposed to sadistic activity by an alter, perhaps being forced to witness the patient's body being cut, being subject to scornful contempt for the therapist's endeavours, gleeful accounts of destructive activity that is being planned for later, or finding the patient has come to the session having taken an overdose. In this position the therapist may experience intense yet impotent rage, just as the child victim would have done originally.

In the collusive abandoner or neglector position, the therapist is perceived as like a mother (or other caregiver) who turns a blind eye, or cannot bear to know about the abuse. In so far as the therapist fails to grasp clues to abuse and trauma, or forgets something that has been communicated, then he/she is felt to be like a mother who ignored or rebutted the child's attempts to tell about what was going on. Laub and Auerhahn (1993) suggest that in trauma or abuse there is always felt unconsciously to be an absence of a protective mothering function, so that the internal mother is felt to be colluding or standing by uncaring, whatever the behaviour of the actual mother.

Parts of the patient may also enact the neglector position. Thus some alters may appear very dismissive of the anguish of other alters, or may accuse others of lying or exaggerating or being 'hysterical', or of 'making it all up to get attention'.

Another transference variant, peculiar to traumatised/abused people, including those with MPD/DID is that of 'traumatic transference'. This is described by Kluft (1992) as follows:

> For the person who has experienced real trauma, the 'as if' or ludic conception of the transference experience fails to hold. Here-and-now and there-and-then often become blurred, in the absence of psychosis. The patient may come to experience within the transference a revivification of a past trauma, either misperceiving the therapist as an actual figure from the past or continuing to perceive the therapist as the therapist, but nevertheless unconsciously perceiving him/her as if he/she were that other figure. (p. 156)

This is a kind of temporary transference psychosis, where there is specifically a disorientation with regard to present reality, a failure to differentiate past and present. The past invades the present; the patient fails to recognise that he/she is experiencing a memory and not a piece of present reality. At these times it is the therapist's task to help restore the distinction. Apparent transference phenomena may not be based so much on internal models of relationship (the usual view of transference) but on a kind of flashback of a sequence of events, misperceived as taking place in the here-and-now with the therapist. This is similar to Blank's (1985) notion of 'unconscious flashback', described in connection with Vietnam war veterans who may relive a past traumatic event, in terms of the accompanying emotional reactions, without realising this is happening.

A further transference dimension is that of the 'selfobject', a concept first described by Kohut (1971) and subsequently developed by many others in the 'self psychology' tradition (see Mollon, 1993). This refers to those aspects of the responsiveness of others – especially empathy and recognition – that are sought because they are necessary to the cohesion and sense of aliveness of the self. Typically the MPD/DID patient will have been grossly deprived of these selfobject functions in childhood. Once the system of alters gets the idea that the therapist offers him/herself as a selfobject, then there may be no stopping them, as more and more clamour for attention and recognition. Offering oneself as a selfobject does not mean adopting an artificial or non-analytic stance; the provision of selfobject functions arises naturally out of the stance of analytic empathy. The selfobject dimension of transference may be distinguished to an extent from the historical and projective dimensions. In reaching out to the selfobject the patient is seeking new experience, development-enhancing functions which have not been found before. The traumatised child alters need the provision of empathic understanding in order to work through their trauma. This would correspond to factor four of Kluft's four-factor theory of MPD/DID.

At the same time as the alters reach out to the therapist for selfobject experience, many of them will be watching him/her like a hawk, looking for signs of reliability, trustworthiness, honesty, etc. The therapist's body language and tone of voice will be scrutinised for what they may reveal and for indications of congruence, or lack of it, with what is being said. Reaching out to a selfobject involves great vulnerability and a scanning for signs of emotional danger. If danger is perceived there will be withdrawal. The anticipated selfobject danger (in terms of being misunderstood, greeted without empathy, or not recognised, for example) will be based upon historical experiences of selfobject trauma.

There may come a point when the patient enters what I call the 'crisis of trust'. As a result of the therapy there may be a lessening of the capacity to dissociate, but the dissociation was set up to cope with an unbearable situation. Therefore the patient feels threatened by traumatic memories from within and an unsafe situation from without. On the basis of historical transference perceptions the therapist is perceived as dangerous. Nowhere feels safe. There is no going back to the previous degree of dissociation, but the therapy is now felt to be a terrible mistake. Secrets of the dissociative structure have been revealed to the therapist. One patient commented: 'We can't pretend with you. Do you know how frightening that is for us? A life-time's work and effort nullified as soon as we see you.'

At these times the therapist too may feel a sense of crisis and disorientation. Was it a mistake to embark on the therapy? Lyon (1992), commenting on her experience with her first MPD patient, remarked: 'In the mirror of her shattered personality, I could never see a reflection of myself as a good enough therapist. The only cohesive element was an identification with her pain, which allowed me to patch together in my mind the confusing bits and pieces of her experience' (p. 94). The therapist who wishes to feel comfortable, secure and free of guilt in his/her work is well advised to avoid taking on patients with MPD/DID!

An extensive discussion of countertransference in the treatment of MPD is provided by Kluft (1994b), whilst Pearlman and Saakvitne (1995) present a comprehensive account of countertransference and vicarious traumatisation in work with incest survivors in general.

ADJUNCTIVE THERAPIES: HYPNOSIS, GUIDED IMAGERY, EMDR, COGNITIVE RESTRUCTURING, PHARMACOTHERAPY

Since patients with MPD/DID are inherently in varying states of hypnosis – spontaneously slipping in and out of trance, undergoing age regression, experiencing hallucinations, misperceiving present reality, and employing 'trance logic' – the use of hypnosis and related processes follows rather naturally. Indeed one could argue that it is impossible to avoid working with hypnosis with these patients regardless of whether a formal induction is used. If a child alter spontaneously appears in the consulting room and begins describing and reliving a trauma, originating in the past, but experienced in the present, and if the therapist enters into conversational contact with the 'child', then a hypnotic state is being worked with. If a frightened child alter protests that it is not safe to tell the therapist about the abuse because the abuser has said the child will be killed if the secret is revealed, and if the therapist enters this drama by telling the child he/she will not let this happen, then the therapist is engaging with the trance logic of the alter – the telescoping of times and places, and the assumption that the therapist can enter a scene that exists only in the patient's memory, rather like an idea of walking into a cinema screen and changing the film script as it is happening.

Most literature on technique with MPD/DID advocates some use of hypnosis. My own preference is for making use of hypnotic phenomena as they arise spontaneously, but generally avoiding deliberately inducing hypnosis. This reflects the importance I place upon protecting the patient's autonomy. Although hypnosis does not necessarily involve any compromise of the patient's autonomy, it always carries the potential for being perceived as intrusive, controlling, manipulative and so on, and thereby grossly distorting the transference relationship. I would caution against the use of hypnosis for penetrative exploration of the patient's mind and certainly it is unwise to use hypnosis for uncovering repressed memories because of the danger of creating pseudo-memories. Any technique which aims to override a patient's natural resistance to uncovering traumatic material may, I suggest, lead to trouble. Nevertheless, sometimes during crises hypnotically based relaxation techniques may be a helpful adjunct in restoring a sense of safety and reducing anxiety. The 'authoritarian' connotations of hypnosis can be eliminated by enabling the patient to select and create the images and sequences to be employed.

Another point when some deliberate, albeit perhaps minimal, use of hypnosis may be appropriate is at moments of integration and fusion of alters. This process of integration can often be quite simple, occurring naturally when dissociation is no longer required – the personalities growing together until differentiation becomes imperceptible. Often, however, the self-hypnotic dissociation which underlies the MPD/DID state may need to be undone through making use of the hypnotic imagery and the trance logic of this state. At an appropriate time, certain personalities may be asked if they are ready to join with each other; if in agreement, it might be suggested that they embrace each other and blend together. This can often be a deeply emotionally moving moment, like the joyful and tearful reunion of long lost friends or relatives – a fact which attests to the profound psychic reality of the self-hypnosis and trance logic of the dissociative state. Usually the sequence of integration would reflect natural links – such as child alters being reunited with each other and then with a mother alter.

This engaging with the hypnotic world of the MPD/DID patient may cause some unease for therapists trained in a psychoanalytic tradition.

The analyst Nancy Williams (1994) describes how she 'came to hypnosis kicking and screaming' and refers to the 'If-it-wasn't-good-enough-for-Freud-it-isn't-good-enough-for-me!' reaction. However, she comments: 'Since dissociative people go into trance states spontaneously all the time, it is not possible to work with them *without* hypnosis – either they are doing it alone, or you and they are doing it cooperatively.' Needless to add, the therapist should be constantly monitoring the conscious and unconscious implications of *any* therapeutic intervention, whether traditionally analytic or extra-analytic.

A recently developed (and rather strange) procedure for treating all kinds of states of psychological trauma is that of Eye Movement Desensitisation and Reprocessing (EMDR), as developed by Francine Shapiro (see Shapiro, 1995). This makes use of the discovery that the repeated movement of the eyes, following the rhythmic motion of a finger or pencil a few inches from the face, whilst thinking of the traumatic event, can lead to a rapid processing of the traumatic experience. The reason why this is effective is not known, although there are a number of hypotheses. Since it has been found that auditory stimulation, through rhythmic side-to-side taps, can also result in the same effect, my own guess is that it is something to do with promoting interhemispheric communication, with enhanced linking of verbal and nonverbal representations of the experience. Whatever the mechanism of this process, what is clear is that it is astonishingly helpful in some instances. A great many research studies have already been published in the few years since its development.

Is this technique applicable to dissociative disorders? Shapiro (1995) cautions that it should only be used in this context when accompanied by specialised knowledge of these disorders. In some earlier reports MPD/DID has been regarded as possibly a contraindication for EMDR. My own limited experience in using EMDR with patients who have suffered extensive and repeated trauma in childhood (as opposed to more limited trauma) is that the danger is of the patient becoming overwhelmed, flooded with painful affect and memories. The technique is certainly effective in abreacting trauma, but too much may be released to be dealt with at the time. Even if a particular trauma is processed adequately during a session of EMDR, the patient may shortly afterwards find that they are flooded with memories of other trauma. Moreover, in the case of patients who experience hostile internal voices, it is often found that these become ferociously assaultive in response to the incursion into trauma territory. Nevertheless, there are some reports of the value of EMDR in some instances of dissociative disorder (Tudor, 1994; Paulsen, in press; Young, 1994). Further research and case studies are needed before this technique can be generally recommended for use with patients who have been repeatedly traumatised in childhood, especially those with dissociative disorders. Obviously an in-patient hospital setting is safest if EMDR, or any other abreactive technique, is to be used. Recently the EMDR Institute produced an 'EMDR Dissociative Disorder Task Force Position Paper' (Fine et al., n.d.) whose recommendations are broadly consistent with the cautions expressed here.

Addressing the cognitive distortions of the alters, especially those of the traumatised children, and challenging the trance logic – such as the assumption that the alters are separate people – should be a central part of any work with MPD/DID. This may be woven into an analytically oriented approach rather than conceptualised as a separate technique. However, there may be occasions when specific procedures derived from cognitive therapy may be appropriate (Fine, 1992). Some of the recent applications of cognitive therapy to personality disorders (Linehan, 1993; Beck & Freeman, 1990), to traumatised personalities (Briere, 1989) and to schizophrenic states (Kingdon & Turkington, 1994) have relevance here.

Whilst pharmacotherapy is not a primary treatment for dissociative disorders, medication does have a role to play in managing severe symptoms in some patients. In addition to the use of antidepressants and anxiolytics, neuroleptics are often prescribed. The latter may be prescribed sometimes as a result of misdiagnosing the patient as schizophrenic. Putnam (1989) advises against the use of neuroleptics with this group, whilst Ross (1994) argues 'The widespread idea that MPD does not respond to antipsychotic medication has no scientific basis' (p. 163). Ross suggests that whilst some MPD/DID patients do well in intensive psychotherapy, others may be best with high doses of antipsychotics and supportive psychotherapy.

AFTER INTEGRATION

Achieving integration is not the end of the therapy. The patient faces the task of living without dissociation. This is no simple matter for a person who has relied upon such a radical defensive alteration of mental state for most of his/her life. New strategies for coping with the difficulties and pains of living have to be developed. The idea of coping with anxiety or anger, for example, without resorting to switching personality, will seem novel and daunting. Moreover, the newly integrated personality will feel raw and vulnerable, prone to new forms and intensities of feeling – and still there are the memories of childhood trauma to be lived with. All of this takes some managing.

Another painful aspect of life which the patient has to face is that of loneliness. While he or she was dissociative and regularly hearing the voices of other alters, loneliness was not an emotion commonly felt by the MPD/DID patient. The internal multiplicity tends to crowd out any potential experience of loneliness. When the voices have gone, it can feel very quiet inside. Sometimes patients will admit to missing their voices. One person experiencing a temporary respite from the relentless onslaught of her very hostile voices remarked that the voices had 'abandoned' her; her use of this word revealed her attachment to these bad internal objects.

OUTCOME RESEARCH DATA

Reviewing outcome data on MPD/DID, Kluft (1994a) states that 'Follow up studies . . . indicate that when highly motivated patients enter treatment with a therapist who is experienced in the treatment of MPD, the vast majority do well' (p. 44). A study of 52 patients followed up after achieving 'fusion criteria' for a minimum of 27 months, found that 94.2 per cent showed clear evidence of improved functioning and had not relapsed into manifest MPD; 78.8 per cent had not suffered continuing or recurrent difficulties in any form. Good psychotherapeutic outcome is also reported by Coons (1986).

There are no doubt many patients, however, whose motivation is challenged by the severity of their disturbance and by the hostility towards therapy of some of their alters. These people are unable to sustain psychotherapy long enough, and have not the resources to weather the crises generated by therapy, and therefore cannot pursue this stormy work to its conclusion. For them, support, pharmacotherapy and a more limited outcome are what can realistically be striven for.

SUMMARY

Patients with dissociative disorders are very diverse and the therapy must be adapted to the needs of the individual. Such people are vulnerable, often with a fragile sense of autonomy, which must be protected in the therapy. The danger of retraumatising the patient in the process of therapy is ever present. Because of this, there are limits on what can be achieved in therapy; in some cases a partial resolution is what can realistically be aimed for. It is possible to derive general principles of treatment, derived from an understanding of the nature and origin of MPD/DID (as

Kluft has done). One general aim is to increase inter–alter communication. The model of the Global Workspace provides a useful metaphor. A variety of adjunctive therapies may play a role in the work. Because the patient with MPD/DID is naturally and spontaneously moving in and out of a variety of self-induced hypnotic states, it is impossible for the therapist not to be working with hypnosis even if no formal induction is used. Outcome data suggests good results can often be achieved when certain principles are followed.

Chapter 10

ILLUSTRATION OF THERAPY WITH MPD/DID

The following is a composite fictitious case drawn from characteristics of a number of patients with severe dissociative disorders.

A COMPOSITE FICTITIOUS CASE

Alison, a 25-year-old married woman, was brought into hospital after a number of recent episodes of self-harm, including overdosing on paracetamol and self-cutting. Her husband reported a worsening mental state since a recent visit by her parents. They had been married for just one year. In her general psychiatric assessment she disclosed internal voices telling her she must harm herself. She also described experiences of her thoughts being interfered with and at times appeared very frightened like a small child, begging the doctor not to let 'them' get her. In addition she described occasional hallucinations of large spiders. A tentative diagnosis of schizophrenia was given and she was prescribed neuroleptic medication. On the ward the nursing staff noted that she sometimes appeared very well, cheerful and cooperative, and at other times very withdrawn and frightened. Since she continued to attempt self-harm, often quite unpredictably, she was placed on special observation.

Since Alison responded only moderately to medication, and since she continued to cause considerable anxiety amongst the staff because of her tendency to self-harm, she was referred to a psychologist-psychotherapist for further assessment. The DES was given as a preliminary screening instrument; she produced a score of 40, high enough to suggest a severe dissociative disorder. On interview she disclosed frequent amnesia for periods of time and said that her husband had sometimes told her she had been missing for several hours without her being aware of what she had been doing. She also reported that she occasionally found sexy clothes in her wardrobe which were not the kind she would normally wear and which she did not remember buying. When asked about depersonalisation she acknowledged that she did sometimes experience herself as outside her body, as if looking on at herself from above; sometimes she worried about how to get back into her body when she was in this state. At these times she might occasionally resort to cutting herself, which she found provided relief and a sense of being home in her body. She also described a confused sense of her own identity, as if feeling and behaving like different people at different times, and an experience as if there was an internal war between different parts of herself; she said that friends seemed to find her very puzzling and that her husband complained that sometimes she seemed quite different from the woman he had married.

The therapist enquired about the internal voices. She said there seemed to be several, some female and some male. Some voices appeared clear, instructing her to harm herself and to leave her husband; others seemed experientially further away, as if like whispers that she could not make out; there was also a sound like a whimpering child in the distance – she found this sound to be very eerie and distressing. The therapist asked if it would be possible for him to speak to any of these voices. Immediately Alison shifted posture, holding her head more confidently, but with a more open and relaxed facial expression. She announced that 'she' was Jenny, adding that she had long blonde hair 'like a princess'; Alison in fact had short brown hair. Jenny said that Alison had been abused for many years by her stepfather, but that Alison herself did not know this because Alison wished to see her stepfather as a good man. She said that she, Jenny, had not been abused and that she was beautiful and 'clean', unlike Alison, whom she regarded as dirty. The therapist asked how Jenny knew that Alison had been abused by her stepfather. She said that she had frequently observed this but had looked on from a distance. In describing the stepfather, Jenny said he could appear very different at different times; often during the day he could seem very friendly and caring, but at night when he came into Alison's bedroom, or when he was alone with her at other times during the day, his manner would switch, he would appear menacing and would abuse her. Jenny said she did not watch everything Alison's stepfather did, especially the worst things, but she knew that often he would tie her down to the bed and then assault her in a variety of ways.

The therapist thanked Jenny for speaking to him and asked if there were any other voices who would talk to him. Suddenly the patient leaned forward in an aggressive manner and said that 'he' was fed up of hearing all these lies about Alison's stepfather, whom he declared to be 'an innocent man'. Revealing his name to be Jack, he claimed that both Alison and Jenny were highly manipulative and advised the therapist not to believe a word either of them said. Adopting a confidential tone, he explained that

Jenny had told other lies in the past, such as alleging that her paternal grandfather had abused her. Jack said that Alison should die as a punishment for telling lies. He declared his intention to make her kill herself. The therapist remarked that surely Jack would die too if Alison killed herself. Jack retorted that this was not the case at all – he would simply go and live in someone else. At that point Jack disappeared, leaving Jenny in the consciousness seat. The therapist asked to go back to Alison, who duly returned. On being asked what she recalled of the conversation of the previous few minutes. Alison said she did not recall any of it, she felt she had been asleep, although she thought she had experienced some 'whispers'.

In a further session, the therapist's conversation with Alison was suddenly interrupted by the emergence of another alter, who introduced herself as the 'Overseer'. She explained that since the therapist had been asking Alison about the overall system of alters, it was probably time he met the one who had an overview of it all. The therapist invited the Overseer to tell him whatever she wished to about the alter system. Overseer said that it was not permitted to tell him all, but that she could reveal that there were Jenny and Jack, whom he had met, and also Alicia, who was really the one the husband had married, although he did not know this. She described Alicia as vivacious and funny, an exciting and carefree woman who liked to flirt; she had been created in the late teenage years in order to attract the opposite sex. Overseer said there were also a number of children who had suffered abuse, but that these were guarded by Bill and Jane who were the 'protectors'. She then added that there was one called Linda, whom the therapist should be very careful with. She said they all worried about Linda because she was so dangerous, completely suicidal and held back only because the others managed to keep a check on her and prevent her getting 'out'.

As if on cue, there was another switch of posture and manner, followed by much talk of despair and hopelessness, with what seemed to be a total conviction that nothing could make life worthwhile or even bearable. The therapist asked if this was Linda and she confirmed that she was. She complained that all the others left her with the despair and she was not prepared to tolerate these feelings any longer, adding that she was intending to kill herself as soon as the opportunity arose. The impression was that Linda was used by the rest of the system of alters as a receptacle for the projection of unbearable feelings of depression – a way of 'managing' unwanted feelings which clearly led to a dangerously unstable system, with the very real threat of suicide if Linda ever took executive control. The therapist commented that although Linda wished to die, the others within the system did not, but they too would be destroyed if Linda ended the body's life. Linda retorted that the others should have thought about that before they chose to dump all the bad feelings with her; she said she was quite unable to be other than intent on suicide since that was her nature. As the end of the session approached, the therapist asked if there was another adult personality that could take over in order to leave the consulting room; it was clearly very dangerous for Linda to be in the executive position when the patient left the session. Linda replied angrily that she was not going and that she was fed up of people trying to shove her out of the way. Realising that, through the request for another alter, he was essentially trying to suppress this part of the patient that contained unadulterated despair, the therapist spoke empathically of Linda's need to let him know just how utterly hopeless she felt. Linda replied that there was no point in letting anyone know how she felt because they always tried to talk her out of it. She then said: 'Imagine if you had a precious china doll and it got smashed into tiny pieces and scattered – imagine attempting to put it back together – and then perhaps you can imagine how I feel – and why I think it is pointless talking to you.' The therapist responded by saying that she had communicated very vividly her hopelessness about healing the damage, represented by this image of the scattered fragments; he added that perhaps what she did need of him was to be able to communicate her despair and for him to tolerate this without trying to talk her out of it, without trying to make her feel better. She smiled in response and appeared very thoughtful; she said 'Yes I think that's right.' She added reassuringly that she would let someone else take over when she had left the room.

Over the next few months, many other alters emerged during the sessions. It was as if the system as a whole had begun to recognise that the therapist was prepared to listen to the various alters and to try to understand their experiences and points of view. What was on offer was an empathy and attentiveness never before experienced by most of the alters. Hungrily they surged forward, sometimes fighting with each other for control of communication. There would be moments when the patient appeared confused and distracted, apparently listening to a cacophony of internal voices struggling with each other for executive control. There would also be times when no particular personality appeared to be in control – a state of mind that the patient sometimes termed 'Nobody'. This state seemed analogous to that of a TV set on 'standby' waiting to be tuned to a particular channel. Another analogy which the patient herself provided for this state was the position of an aircraft circling an airport waiting to land (into a personality).

At times there was talk, from an unidentified part of the patient, of the collective sense of having no core identity. She said there was a realisation that all the alters, apart from the children, were adaptations to different circumstances, that the whole personality system was built out of pretence, and that she did not know who she really was; she indicated that this perception was extremely distressing. She said that this had become apparent partly because the various alters had no clear role in relation to the therapist; in most situations involving other people, it was apparent what was wanted, but in relation to the therapist there was no clear cue as to the role required. The implicit invitation 'to be yourself' was profoundly paradoxical to a personality system based upon the assumption of roles perceived to be required by others. Thus the patient seemed to be saying that the dissociative system of multiplicity broke down in the therapy for two reasons: first because unlike most people who would encounter only one alter, the therapist got to know of various alters and to be aware of the existence of the system of alters (they collectively and humorously termed him 'the system networker'); secondly because the basis of the alters-of-adaptation, which consisted of responding to the role cues offered by a situation, could not work in the analytic situation where the therapist waited to be responsive to the patient. This seemed to highlight one of the dangers in certain ways of working with MPD/DID; if the therapist had offered more structure, or had entered into more explicitly 'MPD therapy', using a variety of extra-analytic techniques much of the time, then it is quite possible that there would have been adaptation to this which would have consisted of further pretence based on role-responsiveness (a view of MPD/DID proposed by sociocognitive theorists such as Spanos and Burgess, 1994).

The alter personalities that did not seem to be based upon adaptation to role expectations were the children. Mostly these appeared to be traumatised children who contained memories of abuse and neglect. They appeared to live in the continual present of the abusive past. Often there were allusions from the adult alters of the need for the therapist to contact the children, and indeed child alters sometimes spontaneously attempted to come forward. These were often blocked, however, by the alters who called themselves 'protectors'. It would sometimes happen that a child would briefly emerge (indicated by childlike posture, facial expression and tone of voice) and seem about to converse with the therapist but would then appear to be pushed abruptly out of the way by a protector who would aggressively warn off the therapist. The protectors perceived the therapist extremely negatively, viewing him as highly dangerous, a potential abuser who would aim to impose his will on the group and who would damage the children even further. Disregarding for a moment the multiple personality form of the presentation, the dynamic situation here was not dissimilar to ones which are familiar to many British psychoanalysts, as described, for example, by Rosenfeld (1971): there is a needy child part of the personality who endeavours to reach out to the therapist; countering this is an organisation of thuggish parts of the personality which are opposed to relationships of dependency. It was eventually explained by the Overseer that the protectors were concerned above all to protect the undamaged child – that the greatest threat was of this preserved area of health reaching out and it too being abused – then all would be lost. In this way the internal situation began to sound reminiscent of Winnicott's (1960) description of the false self which organises around the 'true self' to hide and protect the latter.

There were many conflicts and struggles to be addressed before it was possible for the child alters to reach the therapist and tell their stories. Alongside the work that went on actually in the sessions, there appeared to be continual internal debate taking place amongst the system of alters; this in itself seemed to be a consequence of the therapy which steadily was facilitating inter-alter communication. Eventually the Overseer announced to the therapist that it had been decided that the children would be allowed to tell their stories to the therapist. In fact, all the child (and adolescent) alters told the same story, which was of sexual abuse by a stepfather, but experienced at different ages. The youngest alter was said to be age five years and the eldest was sixteen. Details of the abuse described by the alters are not relevant to this account, except to say that it included violence and the use of spiders to terrify her, and that the stepfather behaved quite differently at other times and especially when in the presence of other people, as if being a loving father; he told her (according to the alters) that if she spoke about the abuse to anyone, he would kill her by burying her in a box with spiders. As the therapist listened to these accounts from the alters, he was left with the sense, common in working with MPD/DID patients, that the only way this child could have survived without becoming completely psychotic was by becoming multiply dissociative; this is not to say that the impression was objectively true, but that it was part of the experience evoked in the therapist by the patient's communications.

Alison, who remained the main 'host' personality – the one that most of the other alters regarded as the designated patient whom the therapy was intended to help – did not initially 'hear' the stories of the child alters. She reported only a sensation of faint whispering when asked what she had heard during the accounts. When asked if she would like to know what was said, she replied that she did not want to know. She seemed to have a vague sense that the material would be disturbing for her and felt that she would not be able to cope with it. At one point Alison and the therapist reached an agreement to end the therapy, at least for the time being, since Alison was adamant that further communications from other alters were not acceptable to her; the Overseer also felt at this stage that to inform Alison, against her wishes, of the content of the children's communications might dangerously destabilise the whole system. Alison wanted to leave hospital and try to take up her life again, knowing that the work done had been very partial. However, Alison soon needed to return to hospital since she was again experiencing voices condemning her and seeing visions of spiders.

Alison was not the only one to object to what the child alters had claimed. Jack repeatedly and aggressively emerged and asserted that the tales of abuse were all lies. He claimed that Alison's stepfather was 'an innocent man' and that the children should be punished for telling wicked lies. He argued that the children had made up these stories in order to get attention. At one point the therapist asked Jack why, if Alison had not been abused as a child, did she have a multiple personality disorder. Jack replied that she did not have a multiple personality. The therapist asked why, if that was the case, was somebody called Jack speaking from the body of a woman called Alison. Jack said he was confused and disappeared. On another occasion, Jack produced the following series of arguments, all within the same session: Alison was not abused by her stepfather; even if she was abused, she deserved to be abused; in any case, it was an act of love; all fathers abuse their daughters; no abuse ever takes place anywhere in the world!

One day Alison reported a dream. In the dream she had seen all her child personalities in a room and she had told them she was coming to take them home. She told the therapist she was ready to hear the children's stories. She said the Overseer had already given her some idea of what she would hear and now she was prepared to know the details. A spokesperson for the children, a 'teenage' alter called Jerry, agreed that information would be transferred to Alison, rather in the way that material can be transferred from one file to another on a computer, or from one computer to another – i.e. almost instantaneously. Alison now reported that she had all the children's memories in her own awareness. The therapist spoke to both the children and to Alison about whether they wished to be reunited. They did. It was suggested that Alison could embrace the children one by one and let them merge back into her. This was done, orchestrated by Jerry, and was experienced by both Alison and the children as a tearful and joyful reunion, which was also very moving for the therapist to witness.

There remained a number of non-child alters. Some, including Jack and the protectors, agreed to give up their separate life and said they would donate their strength and assertiveness to Alison, who did begin to assume a tougher manner. Jenny and Alicia said they felt there was less need for them now, but preferred to retain their separate identities for the time being. The Overseer argued that she should remain, on the grounds that she was not so much a personality as a personified and necessary function – and that she was most useful to Alison in this personified form. Linda proved unamenable to integration. She insisted that she had no interest in the therapeutic ambitions of the others because her intention was still to die and she said that nothing could dissuade her from this. However, she considered that the united mass of the integrated others was impossible for her to overthrow and so she offered to 'go to sleep' for an indefinite period, which she said would be like a kind of internal 'suicide'. With some considerable reservations, this offer was accepted by Alison and the Overseer.

Alison left the hospital, maintaining regular appointments with the therapist. She had during all this period also retained regular contact with her parents, which had been a focus of much conflict for her, and also great fear if ever she was alone with her stepfather. She appeared to be afraid that he could abuse her again at will. One day she told the therapist that all of her accounts of abuse by her stepfather had been lies and that he was completely innocent of all her accusations against him. The therapist asked if she meant she had been knowingly lying, and if so, why she had done so. Alison said she thought she had believed the child alter's accounts at the time but she had realised after a recent conversation with her stepfather that the stories had been lies. The therapist asked if she had any idea why she had lied. She said she did not know. Shortly after-. wards, Alison decided to stop her therapy. She maintained some general psychiatric support and a certain amount of medication, both neuroleptic and antidepressant.

Two years later, Alison asked to see the therapist again. She reported a hostile internal voice again. On enquiry this was identified as Jack. He readily spoke to the therapist, saying he was very angry with Alison for 'letting all this abuse go on and then covering it up'. Alison indicated that she once again accepted the accounts previously given by her child alters. She said she had denied the reports before because they had been too painful and also because she had wanted to maintain good relations with her parents, on whom she had felt very dependent, especially when there had been a deterioration in her marriage and the threat of her husband leaving.

There followed a long period in which Alison was quite severely depressed. She often contemplated suicide, but she did not hear voices any more and did not actually make any suicide attempt. She was full of despair, feeling that her childhood had been saturated with abuse and devoid of love, the present was lonely and miserable, and the future was hopeless. After two more years, Alison suddenly declared that she had decided to put the past behind her and get on with her life. She said she had realised that her stepfather need no longer have any power over her. Following this she obtained a job in a cattery and kennels which, by all accounts, she loved. At the time of writing, Alison has continued in this state, fairly happy and hopeful, yet still fragile and vulnerable and prone to crises when under stress. She is still married and retains a tentative hope that one day she might feel strong enough to have her own children; however, she fears, perhaps realistically, that having a baby might stir up her own early experiences in a way that would be destabilising to her. On the whole she does not hear voices any more.

DISCUSSION

Did Alison's stepfather abuse her? The therapist puzzled long and hard about this (as did Alison). On hearing the narratives of abuse he felt greatly moved with sympathy for the child victim; but also, on hearing the recanting, he was very aware of having no basis for assuming Alison had been abused, other than her claim that she had been – a claim which she was now retracting. At every stage the therapist struggled to avoid imposing his own constructions on what was communicated, trying instead to facilitate the patient's internal debate. Who knows whether Alison was abused? It could be that nobody knows. Alison herself does not seem sure; at present she believes she was abused, but it is not inconceivable that she may change her mind again. The therapist does not know. Surely one person who would know is the stepfather? Even this is not certain. Just as victims of abuse may dissociate and become multiple, so too the perpetrators of abuse can be dissociative, not knowing in one state of mind what they have done in another state.

Was this analytic work? In my view it remained essentially so. The only deviation from the usual method lay in the acceptance of the dissociative structure of the patient's mind, and the necessity therefore of talking to the alter personalities at the level of their experience – e.g. as children for whom the traumatic past was forever present. As in any analytic work, the focus was upon intrapsychic conflict, but personified as a community of alters. Transference was as always a central theme, both historical transference of repetition (e.g. the therapist as abuser), and selfobject transference involving the search for a new development enhancing response (Mollon, 1993) – the seeking of empathy and understanding which might make the unbearable become bearable and knowable. The third major theme was that of trauma inflicted by a caregiver, and the ego's attempts at surviving this through the use of dissociation and identification with the aggressor. The patient's painful struggles, involving defensive mental contortions, to retain a relationship with the abuser were readily apparent.

A crucial part of the therapist's stance was neutrality. It was important not to side with one particular alter – to resist the temptation to establish a 'cosy' relationship of collusion with one alter against others. Even more than is the case in analytic work with non-multiple patients, it was necessary not to have favourites amongst the group of mental characters. Another dimension of neutrality was in relation to the accounts of abuse by the stepfather. It was important to keep the mental space (the global workspace) open to both the view that the stepfather had abused her and the view that he had not – and to convey to the patient that both views, and any other views, were acceptable to the therapist as thoughts to consider. In any analytic therapy it is necessary for the therapist initially to have a larger global workspace than the patient in order to encompass a range of conflictual points of view; initially the patient can allow only certain views or pieces of information in the workspace at any one time. Thus in this therapy, the therapist needed to hear all the accounts of abuse, and also the retractions, but keep in mind that he did not know, and could never know, the truth about Alison's childhood. Alison chose to continue regular contact with her mother and stepfather, a position which the therapist neither encouraged nor discouraged. It was recognised that although Alison found her interactions with her parents to be excruciatingly painful and conflictual, she felt very isolated without them, especially with the lack of support from her husband.

How good was the outcome? The therapy covered several years. From an initial state of severe Dissociative Identity Disorder, with hostile internal voices, serious self-harm and a very chaotic level of functioning, Alison moved to a relatively integrated state, mostly without hearing internal voices, but somewhat depressed and continuing to be rather vulnerable and fragile and in need of continuing support from psychiatric services. Her unsatisfactory marriage has meant that she does not always experience support at home, although her husband may be willing to enter marital therapy with her – certainly he seems to have become more understanding and accepting of Alison as a result of meetings with a community psychiatric nurse who discussed the nature of DID with him. The degree of integration of the alter personalities is only partial, but this may be the best that can be aimed for realistically, given the limits on both internal and external resources to support further extensive and intensive therapy. She continues to benefit from antidepressant medication.

Chapter 11

REFLECTIONS ON EVIL. THE MYSTERY OF DEEP PERVERSION

In her book 'Too Scared to Cry', Lenore Terr (1990) relates the following case. Two infants, a boy and a girl, traumatised at ages 7 months and 15 months, repeatedly played a 'game'. Kathryn would sit on Sasha's head again and again, whenever possible. The little boy silently let her do so without protest. What was this repetitive traumatic play all about, what was it a behavioural enactment of? A babysitter wrote a letter to the infants' mothers confessing that they had been abused by a satanic cult. The infants had been 'squatted upon, urinated upon, and defecated upon by adults with whom the babysitter had joined in satanic rites.' Apparently Sasha's penis had been cut with a ritual knife – a cut which Terr saw and described as 'straight and clean' (p. 246).

What had been done to these children, and why? What was the nature of the gratification, or compulsion which the abusers experienced? After all, to urinate and defecate on a child's head and cut an infant boy's penis with a knife seems a rather odd thing to do! Even to confabulate or fantasise such things seems a little weird! On overcoming one's initial horror, it becomes possible to be curious.

Here is another puzzling example.

A woman consulted a therapist because of problems in her current relationship; she loved her partner but experienced anxieties especially in relation to sex. She conveyed in her initial questionnaire responses, even before seeing the therapist, that her mother had made her engage in some kind of sexual activities with her in early childhood, and also that she had been sexually abused by another relative. She had not sought help with these problems before.

In the interview she told the therapist more about these experiences with her mother, referring also to pornographic photographs which her mother would show her. She was anxious and distressed as she spoke about these. One comment the therapist made was that her description of the photographs, which did appear to be deeply pornographic, raised the question of where her mother obtained them. She said her mother got them from another woman and she then added that her mother would sometimes take her to visit this other woman and a man. She added that there was often another girl there as well. In a frightened and childlike voice she spoke of how the children would be made to 'lick' the grown-ups, who would also 'hurt' the children. As she recounted this, she repeatedly interrupted her own account with comments like: 'She was my mother! She shouldn't have done that!'

A further assessment interview revealed that she experienced many symptoms of dissociative disorder, with depersonalisation, derealisation, amnesia and a sense of confusion about her own identity. She did not, however, appear to have a full-blown Dissociative Identity Disorder.

In the next session she again began to refer to abusive experiences with her mother and other people. She appeared very childlike as she was mumbling. She began to talk in the present tense and kept saying 'go away'; she appeared to be struggling with being in the grip of a flashback reliving of some childhood horror, and the therapist's impression was that she was trying to tell the images to 'go away'. She continued to give a graphic present tense account, as if she were a frightened small child describing deeply perverse abuse as it was happening. When she had finished, and appeared to resume an adult posture, the therapist asked if she was ever troubled by any other images like those. She replied 'only in dreams' and she then proceeded to tell what she described as a 'very strange dream'. In the dream she enters a house which looks large from the outside but inside seems smaller, and the inside is like a church. She is sitting next to someone who may be another child. She says she wants to go home but she cannot. She notices that all the people are wearing white robes and then sees that she too is wearing a white robe. At the front is a man who gives people a pill and a drink in front of an altar. She does not want to have these but feels helpless. Towards the back is the 'god' who is a naked man. She knows that after the pill and the drink she will be told to go and 'love the god'; she will have to kiss the man 'to make him bigger, and make him happy'. After telling this she added emphatically 'it's only a dream'.

Following this the therapist found a message on her home answering machine, a frightened childlike voice saying 'I'm so frightened – they're coming to get me'. The next time the therapist saw her she said she found herself increasingly entering very frightened states of mind but did not know why. Rapidly, before the therapist's eyes, she assumed the posture of a frightened child, curled up on the chair. She said 'I'm so frightened – they're coming to get me' and then talked of hiding in a wardrobe. She then recounted the same events described the previous week in her dream, but this time it was not described as a dream but as a real event. There were further details, for example, of witnessing a man lying on top of a boy and 'hurting' him; speaking in the present tense, she agitatedly told the child not to scream because this would make them hurt him more. She also described a sudden bright light, which she then thought was a camera flash. When the therapist commented that what she had described was like the dream she had reported the session before, she asked 'What dream?' The therapist noticed that several times as the end of the session approached she remarked 'I'll be alright – it'll be over soon'. On enquiring about this phrase she explained that it was something she had learned to say to herself for reassurance.

To date there have been several more sessions of this kind, with further strange and disturbing material, including references to threats of being killed if she reveals certain things to the therapist, such as the name of the 'god'. On being asked why these people would have behaved in this odd way she replied that it was because the 'god' required it. There is also congruent material in the transference. In her childlike voice, she has protested that she should not talk to the therapist because she would laugh at her and enjoy seeing her in pain and would think it was 'all a good laugh'. When asked why on earth the therapist would enjoy seeing her in pain and want to laugh at her, she replied that everyone else did.

So what is this all about? Let me say first of all that I do not know. What we *can* know is the following: a patient with superficially quite a high level of functioning, who might be regarded as happy and normal by many who encounter her, reveals on assessment considerable symptoms of dissociative disorder; she describes, even before coming to see the therapist, some rather odd sexual abuse from her mother; the more she tells the more strange and disturbing it sounds; increasingly she slips spontaneously into a regressed traumatised child state and describes strange scenes of ritual abuse; there are references to pornography and to a camera; she describes a 'dream' which has overt ritual abuse content; later she describes the same content but presents it not as a dream; in the transference she sometimes perceives the therapist as sadistic and wanting to laugh at her; she appears extremely frightened. As far as the therapist is aware she has not had contact with other patients, with 'survivor groups' or reading material which might have contributed to the content she presents.

Is the patient reporting memories, fantasies, hallucinations or what? Diagnostically, it is possible to describe her as suffering from a dissociative disorder; whether or not the events she describes are literally true is irrelevant to that diagnosis. Nevertheless, her mental state would be congruent with her having experienced severe childhood trauma of some variety. Moreover, her protests of bewilderment and outrage – 'she was my mother!' – suggest that *something* foul impinged on her that did not come from her own inner world.

I do not know whether satanists or similar groups of cultists exist and carry out rituals involving abuse of children. I have never stumbled across such a group in the course of their activities. An official report (La Fontaine, 1994) concludes there is no evidence of such groups and activities. However, there are a great many personal accounts (provided in: Boyd, 1991; Harper, 1990; Ireland & Ireland, 1994; Ryder, 1992; Spencer, 1989; Stone & Stone, 1992 – to name just a few); none of these can be taken as proof, but collectively they describe a consistent pattern. A Massachusetts study of abused boys in a protection service found that 17 per cent had been ritually abused (Ramsey-Klawsnik, 1990). In Finkelhor, Williams and Burns' (1988) study of abuse in day-care centres in the USA, 13 per cent involved reports of ritualistic abuse. Kelley (1995) reports a study of 134 abused children from 16 day-care centres in 12 different states; those reporting ritual abuse were much more severely disturbed than those reporting non-ritualistic sexual abuse. Similar findings were reported by Waterman, Kelly, McCord and Oliveri (1990). Some police officers appear sceptical, others much less so. Kenneth Lanning, the FBI investigator, cautions about the lack of evidence to support many allegations, but he does state (1992) 'I believe that the vast majority of victims alleging "ritualistic" abuse are in fact victims of some form of abuse or trauma' (p. 135). It is not uncommonly said that occult/satanic dimensions of severe childhood abuse are kept out of prosecutions because they undermine the credibility of the case in the perception of jurors. Nevertheless, Rockwell (1994) lists 14 cases of successful prosecutions in cases involving ritual abuse with occult overtones (mainly in the USA). At present DoH-funded research into ritual abuse in Britain is being carried out at the Portman Clinic in London. We must await the accumulation of evidence over a number of years before coming to any firm conclusions about the existence or nature of ritual abuse.

Recently I had a conversation with an open-minded academic psychologist after we had both heard a presentation at a conference which alluded to ritual abuse. He expressed continuing incredulity at the idea. I asked if he found it believable that there were perverted people who felt compelled to abuse children? Yes, he had no problem accepting that. Could he believe that some of these people might conspire together with like-minded folk in order to abuse children? Yes, that was perfectly believable. Was it possible that some perverse people might be drawn towards perverse religions? Yes, quite possible he thought. Might not some groups of perverts be drawn to embrace satanism since this would appear to be the ultimate perversion, in which bad is claimed to be good? Quite conceivable, he agreed. And is it not likely that some of these groups of perverts might involve children in their sexual and religious perversions? Certainly this seems possible, he acknowledged. I asked him what then was implausible about the possibility of ritual abuse with perverse religious overtones. He said the problem was the number of murders that were reported.

Certainly there are sometimes allusions to murder in material to do with ritual abuse. It is difficult to know whether this refers to aborted fetuses, or vagrants, or runaways, or whether the allusion is to trickery, simulation of murder, threats of murder, perverse theatre, fantasy, or metaphors of the 'murder' of infant parts of the self. Certainly any child who grows up amongst dedicated perverts will feel that his/her childhood has been murdered. Maybe sometimes the imagery of the satanic is an apt means of representing the travesty of childhood, the mockery of trust and the substitution of malevolence for nurture, that the children of perverts have experienced.

What we do know is that pornography exists. We know this because pornography is, in its nature, a record – evidence that something perverse has taken place. We also know that child pornography exists. Consider the following account by investigative journalist Tim Tate (Tate, 1990) and juxtapose this to the case described above of the patient abused by her mother and others.

Tate is describing a film called *Child Love:*

> in it a blonde pre-pubescent girl – probably around eight years old – is molested by what appears to be her mother and father. She is laid on top of the man – whose face is hidden beneath a blanket, while her mother rubs his penis between the young girl's vaginal lips. The girl is required both to force a smile (patently false) and to run her tongue around her lips in a display of apparent sexual excitement. At the same time her mother licks her daughter's vagina and masturbates the man against her anus. In the rest of the film the youngster is variously required to fellate the man; to masturbate him while urinating in a bucket and to lick his testicles while her mother fellates him. After ten minutes the man ejaculates over the girl's face and chest. (pp. 46–47)

Tate refers to other films in the same series which 'appear to show evidence that the children were either drugged, beaten or both prior to being abused on camera' (p. 47).

There also exists pornography showing children being tortured, mutilated and killed. Some of this may be simulated but much appears not to be.

If the pornography exists, then children must have been subjected to these horrors.

In 1975, twenty mutilated bodies were found stuffed into plastic bin bags on the roadsides of four counties in Southern California. The victims were all boys who had been sodomised, mutilated, and in some cases dismembered, before being shot in the back of the skull. Detectives believed some victims were imported from poor or Third World countries, hidden in the floors of trucks (Tate, 1990, p. 175).

The pornography exists. Sometimes the evidence of perverse murder is found. Occasionally people are prosecuted – an early and most notorious case being that of Ian Brady and Myra Hindley. Presumably there is a significant market for this pornography. Therefore there must be people who are profoundly captivated (or captured) by deeply perverse activities involving intensely sadistic abuse of children. If they are drawn to this in fantasy and in visual pornography, then some of them will surely cross that boundary into grossly perverse activity.

Actually we do not need to rely only on contemporary pornography for depictions of deeply perverse and sadistic activity with children. Goodwin (1994) singles out 15 of the 600 sadistic practices described in de Sade's (1789) *120 Days of Sodom*, which she argues correspond exactly to practices described in contemporary ritual abuse. She lists these as:

> locking in cages, threatening with death, burying in coffins, holding under water, threatening with weapons, drugging and bleeding, tying upside down and burning, wearing of robes and costumes, staging of mock marriages, defecating and urinating on victims, killing of animals, having victims witness torture, having them witness homicides, pouring or drinking of blood, and taking victims to churches and cemeteries. (pp. 483–484)

What kind of religion would the deeply perverse person be drawn to? Clearly it would be a perverse one! Moreover, a religion which advocated the pursuit of 'instinctual' gratification, which idealised pain and the infliction of pain, mocked love and humility, and glorified power, would be highly appealing to the sadistic pervert. The perversion could be justified as congruent with a higher 'good'. What would we expect to be the religion of a Nazi? What would we expect to be the sexual preferences of a Nazi?

Those who claim to have grown up within families pervaded by deep perversion often describe links with the industries of pornography, arms and warfare. What truth there is in these anecdotal reports I do not know. They do suggest the existence of a broad attitude of mind which is dedicated to evil.

THE NATURE OF EVIL

When I have previously spoken and written about deeply perverse and sadistic ritual abuse (Mollon, 1994), some have criticised my use of the concept of 'evil', believing this to be a pre-psychological and inappropriate term; others were relieved and pleased that I had called a spade a spade. I shall continue without apology to speak of evil.

What is it? Meltzer (1973) defines perversion as follows:

> the essence of the perverse impulse is to alter good into bad while preserving the appearance of the good . . . To this end it utilises every means at its disposal: seduction, threat, coercion, confusion, intolerance of the good parts to depressive pain, to separation, to jealousy, etc. It seeks to pervert and addict. And these are separate steps in a process extrapolating toward insanity and death. (p. 113)

I believe this is a description of evil. Meltzer seems to be saying that the aim of the perverse part of the mind is to destroy goodness, truth and trust. Indeed perverse child abuse appears to involve a 'murder' of childhood, a metaphorical murder and in some instances an actual murder. I propose that an evil person is someone who pretends to be good whilst secretly intending bad.

This goes beyond certain other views which regard evil as consisting of the absence of some mental quality that would normally be present. For example, Lifton (1971) focuses on the numbing of the perpetrator and the dehumanisation of the enemy – the absence of empathy – that allows evil actions to be carried out. Midgley (1984) argues that evil involves the nurturing of natural hostilities to the extent that they become obsessions, allowed to flourish through a narrowing of other desires. Scott Peck (1983), in a thoughtful and perceptive discussion, seems to feel that evil people are those who do harm whilst steadfastly denying their sense of guilt, and who continually project blame and inadequacy onto others; such people are in dread of becoming conscious of their guilt. He comments:

> Regardless of how well they attempt to appear calm and collected in their daily dealings, the evil live their lives in fear. It is a terror – and a suffering – so chronic, so interwoven into the fabric of their being, that they may not even feel it as such. (p. 141)

Scott Peck takes us part of the way. His analysis explains why some evil people appear so vehemently, self-righteously convinced of their innocence – and are therefore so *convincing*. However, the phenomena of deeply perverse pornography and ritual abuse suggest there are people who are *knowingly* evil, for whom evil has become 'good', or even 'god'. These are people who are not just a bit bad, not just having bad impulses, or bad parts of the mind, but who have idealised badness and have become dedicated to it. Most of us can acknowledge the existence of cruel, selfish and enviously destructive parts of our personality, but the idea of a dedication to evil involves a quantum leap of the imagination for all those who have not thrown their natural loves and passions into reverse gear. The dedicatedly evil person will glory in a deceptive presentation of goodness and respectability. Gelinas (1993) finds idealised presentations of self by a suspected abuser to be strongly indicative of a malevolent home environment.

Goodwin (1994) comments on the sadistic pleasure of successful lying: 'To completely confuse the victim, to make him doubt his own perceptions and memories creates emotional pain and also contributes to the illusion of absolute control and domination that the sadist needs . . .' (p. 489).

Bollas (1995) outlines a specific structure of evil, which involves deception, betrayal and 'murder'. He indicates the following steps in the process. First the evil one presents him/herself to the victim as good; the recipient perceives the evil one as offering to meet a need or a desire, thereby creating 'a false potential space'; in taking up the offer, the victim becomes dependent on the evil one – a 'malignant dependence', since the aim is not to nurture but to destroy; the evil one suddenly and violently changes the presentation from good to malevolent; with the collapse of trust, the victim becomes childlike; the victim experiences the 'murder of being'.

This account is consistent with the evidence of pornography that the aim of perverse abuse is the destruction of innocence, trust and hope. The victim, the perpetrator and the viewer are taught that love does not exist, but only power and cruelty. Life itself is mocked.

In Chasseguet-Smirgel's *Creativity and Perversion* (1985), she suggests that perversion is actually equivalent to devil worship, in that both these attempt to reverse laws, limits and restrictions. She refers to perversion as: 'a universal human temptation going beyond the limits of sexual deviation . . . the pervert attempts to take the Father/Creator's plan in order to make a new universe from chaos . . . a universe where anything becomes possible' (p. 13).

For describing the deeply perverse state of mind, I find it helpful to have a concept of 'the satanic'. By this I mean a constellation of mental attitudes characterised by extreme destructiveness, the pursuit of power, an envious hatred of life and love, a gross narcissism that opposes concern for others, a hatred of vulnerability and weakness, extreme pride and arrogance, and above all *a devotion to lies and confusion* as opposed to truth. As the Kleinian analyst, John Steiner, has often remarked, all perversion is essentially perversion of the truth.

This concept of 'the satanic' is consistent with biblical descriptions of the mythic figure of Satan as 'the father of lies' and 'a murderer'.

What is the source of this state of mind? We are not talking here about a specific sexual fetish, or a deviation in the aim or object of sexual desire; this is not 'paedophilia', but a pervasively malevolent state which is beyond the reach of most people's capacity for empathy. A partial explanation is to point to ways in which the pervert is re-enacting in active form a trauma which was first suffered passively – and that the sadist is projecting his/her victimised self into the child victim, and that the perverse and sadistic acts are a continual repetition of the murder of the perpetrator's own childhood trust. We can understand that the child victims of extreme perversion will almost certainly become deeply dissociative and may grow up to become adults with perversely abusive alters who go on to perpetuate the abuse through the generations. We can also point to ways in which the perversion will be addictive, the manic triumphant exhilaration giving way to depression and potential persecutory guilt, requiring further perverse intoxication to escape this pain – and steadily the need for stronger and more intense 'doses' of perversion. However, this does not explain all. On reading personal accounts of people who have descended into the depths of depravity including involvement in perverse religions (before eventually escaping), the unmistakable impression is of an active process of deception, whereby they are led, one step at a time, through the presentation of false solutions to the problems of life, into increasing evil from which it seems ever more impossible to extricate themselves. Evil seems not passive, not merely an absence of good, but an active and intelligent aspect of mental life.

It is possible to understand how perverse abuse can be transmitted through the generations, in the way that the bullied may grow up to be a bully. However, the unasked and unanswered question remains: who started it – and why? In the end we can neither explain nor understand nor eradicate evil. The truth may be that the manifestations of evil, in pornography, in bizarre and sadistic abuse of children, and in perverse religion, all emanate from the same elusive source – a source which is of unfathomable depth and obscurity and beyond the grasp of psychology.

BEYOND THE PSYCHOLOGICAL

In working with patients presenting with backgrounds seemingly of perverse abuse with occult overtones, one gets used to hearing about paranormal phenomena. For example, one patient reported poltergeist activity in her flat, short periods of time when there would be a frenzy of pictures falling off the wall, doors slamming, the television switching itself on and off, etc. More common are accounts of strange activity *within* the mind. For example, patients describe instructions appearing in their mind, telling them to go to a certain place at a particular time, where a meeting would be held. Or the person might feel compelled to get in their car and drive, not knowing consciously where they were going, but finding people waiting for them on arriving at a certain place, perhaps outdoors. Telekinesis is not uncommonly reported, as is levitation – either of the self, or witnessing others in this state. Whether these are genuinely paranormal phenomena, or reflect some aspect of dissociative functioning, or are the result of hallucination, or drug intoxication, is difficult to know. They seem to be reported almost exclusively by people who have had some kind of occult involvement.

I once had a patient who was perversely abused as a child, but with no occult aspects to this. As an adult, however, she had a brief involvement with a group of satanists. They gave her drugs and took her to some of their meetings. The effect on her mental state resulting from this very limited contact was horrifying. She began to experience an internal hallucination of chanting in her mind, similar to that which she had heard at the meetings. The chanting would be accompanied by an overwhelming compulsion to go to a certain place at a certain time, 'knowing' that there she would meet someone from the group. Her dreams would also be full of scenes of intense perversion, again accompanied by the chanting. She awoke one morning in a churchyard to find herself full of semen in various orifices and communion wafers placed around and inside her. In addition she increasingly expressed 'satanic' attitudes, talking of her delight in painful and perverse sex, proclaiming her view that Satan ruled the world and her wish to align herself with this figure and thereby gain power. This alternated with her expressing anguished feelings of helplessness about her sense of entrapment with this evil group. She eventually did extricate herself and become free of the effects on her mind, but the process was slow and painful, with the 'satanic' dreams continuing for some months.

It is hard to know what to make of this kind of reported experience. Presumably people are attracted to perverse religions not only because these reflect their perverse state of mind, but also because they believe they do indeed give them access to paranormal powers.

THE EXPERIENCE OF WORKING WITH PERVERSELY ABUSED PATIENTS

Over the last few years I have encountered several patients whose background appears to have been one of severe abuse, with perverse religious aspects. I have not sought them out. I do not seek to 'specialise' in such work. My heart has sunk as the communications of deep perversion and the destruction of childhood have emerged. Each patient has been deeply dissociative, highly disturbed, full of terror and rage, and generally extremely worrying in a variety of ways. None have wanted to display their perverse background openly, their communications being hesitant, obscure and elliptical, inhibited by intense anxiety and shame.

My experience is of feeling burdened – by communications of bewilderingly bizarre evil, the truth of which I have no way of knowing. To speak of perverse ritual abuse, of satanism, is to invite ridicule and sometimes intense hostility. The common impulse is to shoot the messenger who speaks of what people cannot bear to hear. The existence of false allegations of abuse and of failed prosecutions offers ready support for those who wish to believe ritual abuse is merely a contemporary myth. The scenarios offered by some proponents of the false memory position are superficially plausible, especially to those who are not clinicians. Those of us with the misfortune to encounter ritual abuse material in our clinical practice know that these matters are not so simple.

Another aspect of the countertransference is the experience of confusion and feeling 'filled with the bizarre'. The therapist is assaulted with communications of horror which are profoundly disorienting, bursting whatever frameworks of understanding are normally used. These narratives of the uncanny must be borne in mind, often with no means of knowing what is literally true and what is not.

Here is an example of a woman I attempted to work with a few years ago. The experience was shocking and haunting.

Clinical illustration: Vivienne

Vivienne was a very disturbed hospitalised woman, highly prone to self-harm, whom I saw for about six years – the frequency of session varying at different phases of the therapy. The various psychiatrists she saw generally regarded her as having a severe personality disorder; she was never diagnosed as schizophrenic. At the time of my working with her she was in her forties, an only child, her parents both dead. She made clear from the beginning that she had been severely abused in every way as a child and described in the first interview some extremely perverse and sadistic activity involving her parents. This was congruent with her transference to the institution; she felt that the staff prevented her suicides and kept her alive solely in order to torment her sadistically.

She often seemed to struggle with a wish to disclose more about her early experiences. Gradually it became clear that a part of her wished to communicate with me, whilst other parts of her mind aggressively warned her against doing so, employing threats, lies and propaganda; these voices in her mind would tell her that I had evil intentions towards her and also mock her and laugh sadistically and tell her that she could never be free of them. The result of my recognising the existence of these voices and communicating this awareness to her, was that the vicious activity of the malevolent mental organisation increased. She would be instructed to attack me, which she did not do, and would be compelled to damage herself. She handed me a note which said that I did not understand how dangerous all this was and that the family secrets must not be revealed. She would be subject to an increased barrage of mad voices; she felt they wanted to drive her completely insane, to kill her or to have her locked away for ever. At times they appeared to attempt to confuse and disorient her totally by making her doubt every aspect of reality, such as time and place, in order to make her doubt her own memories. The voices would go wild if she attempted to speak to me. After just a few minutes with me she might, for example, begin pounding the double-glazed windows with an armchair and then be placed in a seclusion room where she could be observed pounding her head with her shoes, screaming that the voices had driven her completely mad – and indeed she would look like an old drawing of a crazed inmate of Bedlam. They would tell her that I would die as a result of her disclosures. They once told her that they had caused, through supernatural means, a baby to die in the neighbouring Maternity Unit, as a punishment for telling me secrets and that if she revealed any more they would kill another one. At one point they stopped her eating for several weeks, telling her that something terrible would happen to her or to someone else if she ate, and that this was a punishment for telling. I had never before thought of a patient as being in the grip of evil, but this was how I began to view her – and at this stage I knew nothing about perverse ritual abuse. The tyrannical organisation in her mind appeared not only evil but intelligently so; it would vary its tactics in its attempts to shut her up. It appeared to be provoked by the sheer fact that I had detected it. When this kind of activity was at its peak her sessions could last as little as five minutes. This was all that was tolerable or safe for either of us; any longer and she would be overwhelmed with the compulsion to attack either me or herself. My own experience in the session when she was in these states was of intense oppression, mental and physical, of nausea and headache – this experience of mine appearing to coincide precisely with her periods of visual and auditory hallucination.

Eventually material emerged regarding the perverse ritual content of her early abuse. The voices in her head then told her (a) that it was not true and that she had wickedly made it all up; (b) that I did not believe her; (c) that she would be even more severely punished if she revealed any more. As she was recounting events to me she would interrupt with angry shouts of 'I'm not lying' – her attempts to counter the heckling of the voices. Once she handed me something she had written:

> Vivienne you are dead and you know why. Keep your mouth shut. Whatever you do or say we will never leave you alone. You have nowhere to run child. You will never know security so why don't you give in and turn to us. You belong to us – you are one of us – admit it. Join us child – we will take care of you – you know the rules child.

It also contained the scrawled words 'Death, Destroy, Distrust, Devil'. (The words are quoted here verbatim, but for clarity I have inserted punctuation.)

Then as more was revealed she began to hallucinate visually what she referred to as 'the woman in blue'. This sinister figure, whom she identified with some kind of priestess at the rituals of her childhood, would always appear to her during her sessions whenever anything related to her voices or her memories was touched upon. It became quite obvious to me when she had flipped into this visual hallucinatory mode, because her facial expression would suddenly change and she would stare at a particular chair where she experienced this figure as being; I would experience at these moments the familiar, albeit subtle sense of oppression. Rarely did Vivienne let me know the content of what was communicated by this figure, but what was clear was that it was highly malevolent. Often, apparently the woman in blue would order her to attack me. During some of these sessions, Vivienne would sit silent and still, giving me the impression she was struggling against overwhelming urges to assault me – I would feel considerable anxiety and took to ensuring there were no heavy objects within her reach; we would negotiate how she would leave my room, the danger being that if unescorted she would run away and attempt to kill herself, but if I walked with her to the ward she would attack me – often we arranged that a female nurse would come to collect her. When Vivienne succumbed to this figure's instructions to harm or kill herself, the woman in blue would become her friend, speaking to her gently and seeming caring. On at least two occasions Vivienne made very serious attempts to kill herself whilst under the spell of this and other internal parts; once she jumped off a very high bridge and on another occasion swam out to sea to drown herself, feeling compelled to follow a 'blue light' – both survivals seemed little short of miraculous.

Once she gave me a note which she said was from the woman in blue. It read:

> Leave Vivienne alone. We have her almost. She belongs to us. She will join us. She wants some peace and having me will give her that. You don't know all about us because we won't let Vivienne tell you. We need Vivienne. She is the chosen one. She will, and has almost given herself to us. But you will have to go because you are trying stop Vivienne joining us. (Verbatim with some inserted punctuation.)

One event which Vivienne alleged was an occasion in her adolescence occurred when she was pregnant and was dragged from her bed and taken to woods where, during a ritual, her baby was aborted and she was made to watch as it was thrown on a fire; she recalled the smell of burning flesh; she was made to eat some of the placenta; she was surrounded by hooded figures chanting. In art therapy she endlessly painted this scene, repeatedly painting in and painting out certain details, including the woman in blue. She told me of two recurrent dreams. In one she is in the centre of a circle of hooded figures chanting; her child tries to break through to get to her; he then attacks her with a carving knife. In the second she gives birth to a baby which is placed on her chest; it turns into a monster which begins clawing at her.

Many times I felt that the prudent course would be to withdraw from this work, giving up in the face of such a malevolent internal world. What prevented my doing so was that she begged me not to and communicated that there was a terrified and tormented child inside her, struggling to let me know of her experiences (whether these were literally true or not). There were broadly two stages to this therapy; first her struggle over remembering, and then her struggle over whether she could tell what she remembered. For a long time it appeared that she had overcome her amnesia, but was terrified to tell me of her memories. Eventually, after a break in our work, and when we agreed that it would be our last session because she was leaving the hospital and moving away, she did tell me – on condition that I promised never to tell anyone what she said. I have kept this promise – but I can say that what she told me was entirely consistent with other accounts of perverse cult activities. Her eventual disclosure was stark, succinct and very moving.

I am sometimes asked if I 'believe' in the existence of satanist ritual abuse. Always my answer is that I do not know whether it exists. I do know what I have experienced in the consulting room, that I have been subject to narratives of extremely perverse abuse, allegedly involving groups. Are these literally true, or are they representations of 'bizarre objects' (Bion, 1957) formed through the interplay of destructive infantile fantasy and malevolent environment? I do not know. One thing is for sure; whatever can arise in perverse fantasy, someone somewhere may be driven to enact.

Perhaps the Marquis de Sade, most wretched of perverts, can provide the final comment on the descent into limitless evil:

> Once a man has degraded himself, debased himself through excesses, he has imparted something of a vicious cast to his soul, and nothing can rectify that situation. In any other case, shame would act as a deterrent . . . but here that possibility has been eliminated altogether . . . All that before affected one disagreeably, now encountering an otherwise prepared soul, is metamorphosed into pleasure . . . [T]hat heart which of old contained some virtues, no longer recognizes a single one. (*The 120 Days of Sodom*, 1789/1990, pp. 495–496)

SUMMARY

Accounts of ritual abuse suggest profoundly perverse activity. The question of the existence of cults which abuse children is controversial. What is less in doubt is the existence of pornography depicting deeply perverse abuse of children, including murder. The phenomena of deep perversion suggests the possibility of a state of mind which is dedicated to evil and to a perversion of normal values. Evil appears to be an active component of mental life and not merely an absence of good. The source of evil is obscure.

EPILOGUE

Dissociative disorders are works of trauma and fantasy. A simplistic theory that emphasises only trauma or only fantasy will be misleading and may result in an unbalanced view of development and an ineffectual or damaging mode of treatment. Whilst it is always the *interplay* between inner fantasy and traumatising reality that is important with any patient, for the seriously traumatised, the trauma is primary. The trauma structures the fantasy, which either represents the trauma or is compensatory to the trauma. Our rapidly accumulating knowledge and understanding of the psychological and biological impact of trauma, and the long-term characterological effects of childhood trauma, mean that trauma must again assume a central place in psychoanalytic theorising if it is to reflect current knowledge.

In working with the dissociative personality, we encounter defence and transference as well as trauma and fantasy, dimensions which are all within the domain of psychoanalysis. Yet, as we have seen, the very nature of dissociation strikes at the roots of psychoanalysis, at least in its Freudian origins. Taking the dissociative patient seriously means being led into forms and styles of work which superficially do not appear analytic – for example the need to talk to child alters. An unmodified analytic approach, which does not take account of the dissociative structure of the patient's mind, which insists on relating to the patient as if he/she were divided only by splitting or repression, can offer a kind of reassurance in its consistency, but can hardly be expected to address the core issues.

Couch (1995), in describing Anna Freud's classical view of the limited scope of analysis, comments:

> In her . . . paper on changes in psychoanalytic technique, Anna Freud wrote along these lines: our psychoanalytic understanding of . . . severe disorders has far outstripped our capacity to help them by analytic therapy. What the child's ego has done to itself during development can be undone by the ego in analysis – but what has been done to the ego by early deprivation or trauma, can only be healed through a modified 'ego building' approach.

> Naturally she believed that analysts should try to help such patients but that standard analytic technique should be modified with them. (p. 165)

In this respect, Anna Freud reflected the sober awareness of the limits of analysis which characterised her father's views. This was in contrast with others, most notably Melanie Klein, who felt that analysis could be applied unmodified to any mental disturbance including psychotic states.

The approach outlined in this book is in the spirit of Anna Freud's view that, with those who have been environmentally damaged, an analytically informed approach is appropriate, but not an unadapted analytic technique. We must provide a setting in which the patient can, when the time is right, relinquish dissociative defences. Through consistency of approach and through interpretation we must help the patient to establish a sense of safety in the therapeutic setting. In addition we must provide *functions* that have not been available before. The therapist's own mind, which is part of the therapeutic setting, provides an enlarged 'global workspace' within which various dissociated parts of the patient's mind can communicate; the therapist hears and gathers thoughtfully the various conflicting communications before any part of the patient's mind can do so. The patient gradually discovers that the therapist's mind is not dissociative. It may be some time before the patient can draw upon this enhanced global workspace and make it his/her own.

The second function the therapist offers is that of empathy, particularly for the traumatised child alters; this may have been grossly lacking in the patient's childhood. It seems to be the absence of an empathic and reliable caregiver which makes trauma impossible to cope with (van der Kolk & Fisler, 1994). These development-enhancing functions of the provision of empathy and the global workspace, which temporarily compensate for what is missing in the patient's own mental capacities, can (in the terms of Kohutian self-psychology) be regarded as lying in the selfobject dimension of the transference – the search for new experience, as opposed to the repetition of what has been experienced in childhood (Mollon, 1993).

Both these functions can also be related to Grotstein's (1981) concept of the 'background object of primary identification'. This is formed out of the experience of feeling 'backed', or supported, or held. It provides a framework of background experience that organises and holds coherently the potentially dissociated parts of the mind. For the traumatised or abused patient this background experience of consistent support has been missing. The consistency and reliability of the therapy setting provides a backdrop against which the patient can begin to organise their experience.

There are no quick fixes for the patient severely traumatised in childhood. A patient whom I have seen for a number of years has recently made significant strides towards health, through giving up drugs, alcohol and her manic-chaotic lifestyle. Her background involved perverse sexual abuse and her adult life has been extremely disturbed. In reflecting upon her present determination to take her life in the direction of health, she emphasised to me that, although the therapy had been life-saving, there was absolutely nothing I could have said or done which could have speeded up this process; it had to run its course.

What the patient seems to need is for the therapist to remain interested, thoughtful, hopeful and consistent – as a reliable 'background object' – whilst the stormy battles of dissociated parts are played out. Perhaps understanding the nature and source of dissociative disorders helps us, as therapists, to tolerate and last out the work whilst the healing process runs its course.

APPENDIX: GUIDELINES FOR PATIENTS REGARDING MEMORIES OF CHILDHOOD EVENTS*

In view of the unreliability of memory of childhood events and the dangers of creating false memories, we have prepared these notes so that you can be accurately informed about relevant scientific knowledge regarding memory.

HOW ACCURATE IS OUR MEMORY? IS MEMORY LIKE A VIDEO TAPE MACHINE?

Memory is not like a video tape machine. It does not faithfully record as on a film everything that a person perceives. Memory is partly accurate and partly prone to a great many errors. Our memory for events may bear a rough resemblance to what actually happened, but may also include many inaccuracies. In some ways memory is like telling ourselves a story; each time we tell it, the story may be changed slightly. The adult's memory of childhood events may be particularly prone to error because of the length of time involved.

TO WHAT EXTENT CAN WE BE SURE OF THE SOURCE OF OUR MEMORIES?

Research suggests that under most circumstances people can successfully distinguish events that happened from events that were imagined. However, if there is extensive and repeated thinking about an imagined event, the person can come to believe that the event actually happened.

---

*as used in the author's own department

This kind of false memory could become highly detailed and vivid to the person.

HOW RELIABLE IS RECALL OF EARLY EVENTS?

Nothing can be recalled accurately from before the first birthday and little from before the second. Poor memory from before the fourth is normal.

IS IT POSSIBLE FOR THE MIND DELIBERATELY TO 'FORGET' UNPLEASANT MEMORIES – A PROCESS SOMETIMES CALLED REPRESSION?

The forgetting of certain kinds of painful experiences is often reported – but the precise process involved in the mind is unclear. There is currently much debate about whether this kind of forgetting of trauma takes place, and if so, how common it is. There is no firm research evidence that fully supports the idea of repression of memory. Apparent memories recovered later may in fact be false memories.

IS IT POSSIBLE TO HAVE FALSE BELIEFS ABOUT THE PAST?

There is a great deal of evidence that memories and beliefs about the past can be inaccurate in various ways. To what extent it is possible for a person to arrive at completely false memories that have no basis in fact, is a matter of much current debate.

CAN HYPNOTIC TECHNIQUES HELP IN RECOVERY OF MEMORIES OF CHILDHOOD?

It is possible (but not certain) that hypnosis can help to elicit memories of the past, but the problem is that it can also elicit quite false memories. Memories elicited through hypnosis are extremely unreliable. For this reason we do not recommend hypnosis as a means of recovering memories.

CAN SO-CALLED 'TRUTH DRUGS' ELICIT LOST MEMORIES?

Drug-assisted abreactions (a reliving of frightening events) have a long tradition in psychiatry and were used particularly after the Second World War to treat emotionally traumatised soldiers. However, as with hypnosis, there can be no certainty that events 'recovered' during an abreaction are literally true, especially when these concern childhood events of long ago.

IS IT A GOOD IDEA DELIBERATELY TO SEARCH FOR MEMORIES OF TROUBLING EVENTS IN CHILDHOOD?

There can be two unfortunate consequences of *deliberately* searching for memories of traumatic events: you may be overwhelmed by what you remember; you may produce false memories. It is best to allow your memory to respond naturally.

HOW SHOULD YOU VIEW AN APPARENT MEMORY OF A CHILDHOOD EVENT WHICH SUDDENLY EMERGES IN YOUR MIND?

It is important not to jump to premature conclusions about an apparent memory of childhood. What has come into your mind may be literally true as a memory, or it may derive from fantasy or a dream or from some other source. It is the task of your doctor/psychotherapist/psychologist/counsellor to help you think about these possibilities and for you to arrive at your own conclusions in due course. It would be most unwise for you to take any course of action in relation to particular individuals solely on the basis of a 'memory' recovered during therapy.

We hope you find these guidelines informative and that they help to avoid misunderstandings regarding very complex processes in the mind.

Phil Mollon

REFERENCES

Abraham, H.C. & Freud, E.L. (1965). *A Psychoanalytic Dialogue: The Letters of Sigmund Freud and Karl Abraham*. New York: Basic Books.

Adamec, R.E., Stark-Adamec, C. & Livingston, K.E. (1980). The development of predatory aggression and defence in the domestic cat. *Neural Biology*, **30**, 389–447.

Adult Children Accusing Parents – Newsletter. September/October 1993.

Aldridge-Morris, R. (1989). *Multiple Personality. An Exercise in Deception*. Hove: Erlbaum.

Alexander, F. & French, T.M. (1946). *Psychoanalytic Therapy*. New York: Ronald Press.

Allison, R.B. (1980). *Minds in Many Pieces*. New York: Rawson, Wade.

American Psychiatric Association (1995). *Diagnostic and Statistical Manual of Mental Disorder, 4th edn*. DSM-IV). Washington, DC: American Psychiatric Association.

Armstrong, J.G. & Loewenstein, R.S. (1990). Characteristics of patients with multiple personality and dissociative disorders on testing. *Journal of Nervous and Mental Disorders*, **178**, 448–454.

Baars, B.J. (1988). *A Cognitive Theory of Consciousness*. New York: Cambridge University Press.

Bach, S. (1994). *The Language of Perversion and the Language of Love*. New York: Aronson.

Balint, M. (1969). Trauma and object relationship. *International Journal of Psycho-Analysis*, **50**, 429–435.

Barach, P., Bowman, E., Fine C., Ganaway, G., Goodwin, J., Hill, S., Kluft, R., Loewenstein, R., O'Neill, R., Olsen, J., Parks, J., Peterson, G. & Torem, M. (1994). *ISSD Guidelines for Treating Dissociative Identity Disorder (Multiple Personality Disorder) in Adults*. Skokie, II: ISSD.

Baranger, M., Baranger, W. & Mom, J.M. (1988). The infantile psychic trauma from us to Freud: pure trauma, retroactivity and reconstruction. *International Journal of Psycho-Analysis*, **69**, 113–128.

Bartlett, F. (1932). *Remembering*. Cambridge: Cambridge University Press.

Beck, A.T. (1967). *Depression. Clinical, Experimental and Theoretical Aspects*. New York: Harper & Row.

Beck, A.T., Emery, G. & Greenberg, R.L. (1985). *Anxiety Disorders and Phobias. A Cognitive Perspective*. New York: Basic Books.

Beck, A.T. & Freeman, A. (1990). *Cognitive Therapy of Personality Disorders*. New York: Guilford.

Belli, R.F. & Loftus, E.F. (1994). Recovered memories of childhood abuse: a source monitoring perspective. In S.J. Lynn & J.W. Rhue (eds) *Dissociation. Clinical and Theoretical Perspectives*. New York: Guilford.

Bernstein, E.M. & Putnam, F.W. (1986). Development, reliability and validity of a dissociation scale. *Journal of Nervous and Mental Disease,* **174**, 727–735.

Bion, W.R. (1956). Development of schizophrenic thought. *International Journal of Psycho-Analysis,* **37**, parts 4–5. Also in *Second Thoughts,* 1967.

Bion, W.R. (1957). Differentiation of the psychotic from the non-psychotic personalities. *International Journal of Psycho-Analysis,* **38**, parts 3–4. Also in *Second Thoughts,* 1967.

Bion, W.R. (1967). *Second Thoughts. Selected Papers on Psychoanalysis.* New York: Aronson.

Birtles, E.F. & Scharff, D.E. (1994). *From Instinct to Self. Selected Papers of W.R.D. Fairbairn. Vol 11. Applications and Early Contributions.* New York: Aronson.

Blank, A.S. (1985). The unconscious flashback to the war in Vietnam veterans: clinical mystery, legal defense and community problem. In S.M. Sonnenberg, A.S. Blank & T.A. Talbott (eds), *The Trauma of War: Stress and Recovery in Vietnam War Veterans.* Washington, DC: American Psychiatric Press.

Blass, R.B. & Simon, B. (1994). The value of the historical perspective to contemporary psychoanalysis: Freud's 'seduction hypothesis'. *International Journal of Psycho-Analysis,* **75**, 677–694.

Bleuler, E. (1950). *Dementia Praecox or The Group of Schizophrenias.* New York: International Universities Press.

Bliss, E.L. (1986). *Multiple Personality, Allied Disorders and Hypnosis.* New York: Oxford University Press.

Bollas, C. (1987). Normotic illness. Chapter 8 in *The Shadow of the Object. Psychoanalysis of the Unthought Known.* London: Free Association.

Bollas, C. (1989). *Forces of Destiny. Psychoanalysis and Human Idiom.* London: Free Association.

Bollas, C. (1995). The structure of evil. Chapter 7 in *Cracking Up. The Work of Unconscious Experience.* London: Routledge.

Boyd, A. (1991). *Blasphemous Rumours. Is Satanic Ritual Abuse Fact or Fantasy? An Investigation.* London: Fount/HarperCollins.

Braun, B.G. & Sachs, R.G. (1985). The development of multiple personality disorder. Predisposing, precipitating and perpetuating factors. In R.P. Kluft (ed). *Childhood Antecedents of Multiple Personality Disorder.* Washington, DC: Psychiatric Press, pp. 37–64.

Briere, J. (1989). *Therapy for Adults Molested as Children.* New York: Springer.

Briere, J. & Conte, J. (1989). *Self-Reported Amnesia for Abuse in Adults Molested as Children.* Paper presented to the annual meeting of the American Psychological Association.

Broucek, F. (1982). Shame and its relation to early narcissistic developments. *International Journal of Psycho-Analysis,* **63**, 369–378.

Brown, A. & Finkelhor, D. (1986). Impact of child sexual abuse. A review of the research. *Psychological Bulletin,* **99**, 1, 66–77.

Casement, P. (1985). *Learning from the Patient.* London: Routledge.

Ceci, S.J. & Loftus, E.F. (1994). 'Memory work': a royal road to false memories? *Applied Cognitive Psychology,* **8**, No. 4.

Chasseguet-Smirgel, J. (1985). *Creativity and Perversion.* London: Free Association.

Cohen, B.M., Giller, E. & Lynn, W. (eds) (1991). *Multiple Personality Disorder from the Inside Out.* Lutherville: Sidran Press.

Coons, P. (1986). Treatment progress in 20 patients with multiple personality disorder. *Journal of Nervous and Mental Disease,* **174**, 715–721.

Coons, P. (1988). Psychophysiologic aspects of multiple personality disorder: a review. *Dissociation,* **1**, No.1, 47–53.

Coons, P. (1990). Review of: MPD: An exercise in deception, by Ray Aldridge-Morris. *Dissociation*, **111**, No. 2, 123.

Couch, A. (1995). Anna Freud's psychoanalytic technique. A defence of classical analysis. *International Journal of Psycho-Analysis*, **76** (1), 153–171.

Crabtree, A. (1985). *Multiple Man. Explorations in Possession and Multiple Personality.* Toronto: Collins.

Davies, J.M. & Frawley, M.G. (1994). *Treating the Adult Survivor of Childhood Sexual Abuse. A Psychoanalytic Perspective.* New York: Basic Books.

Deutsch, H. (1942). Some forms of emotional disturbance and their relationship to schizophrenia. *Psychoanalytic Quarterly*, **11**, 301–321.

Doe, J. (1991). How could this happen? Coping with a false accusation of incest and rape. *Issues in Child Abuse Accusations*, **3**, No. 3, 154–165.

Dorpat, T. & Miller, M. (1992). *Clinical Interaction and the Analysis of Meaning.* Hillsdale, NJ: Analytic Press.

Eigen, M. (1993). Chapter 16, Demonized aspects of the self. In *The Electrified Tightrope.* New York: Aronson.

Ellenberger, H.F. (1970). *The Discovery of the Unconscious: The History and Evolution of Dynamic Psychiatry.* New York: Basic Books.

Ensink, B. & Van Otterloo, D. (1989). A validation of the dissociative experiences scale in the Netherlands. *Dissociation*, **2**, 221–223.

Fahy, T.A. (1988). The diagnosis of multiple personality disorder: a critical review. *British Journal of Psychiatry*, **153**, 597–606.

Fahy, T.A., Abas, M., Brown, J.C. (1989). Multiple personality disorder: a symptom of psychiatric disorder. *British Journal of Psychiatry*, **154**, 99–101.

Fairbairn, R. (1944). Endopsychic structure considered in terms of object-relationships. In *Psychoanalytic Studies of the Personality.* Routledge: London, pp. 82–132.

Fairbairn, R. (1952). *Psychoanalytic Studies of the Personality.* London: Routledge.

Feldman-Summers, S. & Pope, K.S. (1994). The experience of 'forgetting' childhood abuse: a national survey of psychologists. *Journal of Consulting and Clinical Psychology*, **62**, 636–639.

Ferenczi, S. (1988; written 1933). *The Clinical Diary of Sandor Ferenczi*, ed. J. Dupont. Cambridge, MA: Harvard University Press.

Fine, C. (1992). Multiple personality disorder. In A. Freeman & F.M. Dattilio (eds). *Comprehensive Casebook of Cognitive Therapy.* New York: Plenum, pp. 347–360.

Fine, C., Luber, M., Paulsen, S., Puk, G., Rouanzoin, C., Young, W. (undated document): *EMDR Dissociative Disorder Task Force Position Paper.* Available from: EMDR Institute Inc. PO Box 51010, Pacific Grove, CA, 93950.

Fink, D. & Golinkoff, M. (1990). Multiple personality disorder, borderline personality disorder and schizophrenia: a comparative study of clinical features. *Dissociation*, **111**, No. 3, 127–143.

Finkelhor, D., Williams, L. & Burns, N. (1988). *Sexual Abuse in Day Care. A National Study.* Durham, NC: University of New Hampshire.

Fish-Murray, C.C., Koby, E.V. & van der Kolk, B.A. (1987). Evolving ideas. The effect of abuse on children's thought. In *Psychological Trauma*, ed. B.A. van der Kolk. Washington, DC: American Psychiatric Press.

Franklin, J. (1990). Dreamlike thought and dream mode processes in the formation of personalities in MPD. *Dissociation*, **111**, No. 2, 70–80.

Freud, A. (1936). *The Ego and the Mechanisms of Defence.* London: Hogarth.

Freud, A. (1967). Comments on trauma. In *Psychic Trauma*, ed. S. Furst. New York: Basic Books, pp. 235–245.

Freud, S. (1892–94). Preface and footnotes to the translation of Charcot's *Tuesday Lectures.* Standard Edition, vol. 1. London: Hogarth.

Freud, S. (1893–95). (with J. Breuer) *Studies on Hysteria*. Standard Edition, vol. 2. London: Hogarth.

Freud, S. (1896a). *Extracts from the Fliess Papers*. Standard Edition, vol. 1. London: Hogarth.

Freud, S. (1896b). *Further Remarks on the Neuropsychoses of Defence*. Standard Edition, vol. 3. London: Hogarth.

Freud, S. (1905). *Three Essays on Sexuality*. Standard Edition, vol. 7. London: Hogarth.

Freud, S. (1906). *My Views on the Part Played by Sexuality in the Aetiology of the Neuroses*. Standard Edition, vol. 7. London: Hogarth.

Freud, S. (1908). *The Sexual Theories of Children*. Standard Edition, vol. 9. London: Hogarth.

Freud, S. (1911a). *Formulations on Two Principles of Mental Functioning*. Standard Edition, vol. 12. London: Hogarth.

Freud, S. (1911b). Psycho-analytical notes on an autobiographical account of a case of paranoia (dementia paranoides). Standard Edition, vol. 11. London: Hogarth.

Freud, S. (1914). *On the History of the Psycho-analytic Movement*. Standard Edition, vol. 14. London: Hogarth.

Freud, S. (1916–17). *Introductory Lectures on Psycho-analysis*. Standard Edition, vol. 16. London: Hogarth.

Freud, S. (1917). *On Transformations of Instinct*. Standard Edition, vol. 17. London: Hogarth.

Freud, S. (1919). *Introduction to Psycho-analysis and the War Neuroses*. Standard Edition, vol. 17. London: Hogarth.

Freud, S. (1920). *Beyond the Pleasure Principle*. Standard Edition, vol. 18. London: Hogarth.

Freud, S. (1923). *The Ego and the Id*. Standard Edition, vol. 19. London: Hogarth.

Freud, S. (1926). *Inhibitions, Symptoms and Anxiety*. Standard Edition, vol. 20. London: Hogarth.

Freud, S. (1939). *Moses and Monotheism*. Standard Edition, vol. 23. London: Hogarth.

Freud, S. (1940a). *An Outline of Psycho-analysis*. Standard Edition, vol. 23. London: Hogarth.

Freud, S. (1940b). *Splitting of the Ego in the Service of Defence*. Standard Edition, vol. 23. London: Hogarth.

Freyd, J. (1993). Theoretical and personal perspectives on the delayed memory debate. A presentation for the Center for Mental Health at Foote Hospital's Continuing Education Conference: Controversies around recovered memories of incest and ritualistic abuse. 7 August. Ann Arbour, Michigan.

Friesen, J. (1991). *Uncovering the Mystery of MPD*. Nashville, TN: Thomas Nelson.

Frischholz, E.J., Braun, B.G., Sachs, R.G., Hopkins, L., Schaeffer, D.M., Lewis, J., Leavitt, F., Pasquatto, J.N. & Schwartz, D.R. (1990). The dissociative experiences scale: further replication and validation. *Dissociation*, **111**, No. 3, 151–153.

Furst, S. (1967). *Psychic Trauma*. New York: Basic Books.

Gannaway, G.K. (1989). Historical versus narrative truth: clarifying the role of exognenous trauma in the etiology of MPD and its variants. *Dissociation*, **2**, No. 4, 205–220.

Gelinas, D. (1993). Relational patterns in incestuous families, malevolent variations and specific interventions with the adult survivors. In P. Paddison (ed), *Treatment of Adult Survivors of Incest*. Washington, DC: American Psychiatric Press.

Glass, J. (1993). *Shattered Selves. Multiple Personality in a Postmodern World*. Ithaca, NY: Cornell University Press.

Goodwin, J.M. (1988). Munchausen's syndrome as a dissociative disorder. *Dissociation*, **1**, No.1, 54–60.

Goodwin, J.M. (1994). Credibility problems in sadistic abuse. *Journal of Psychohistory*, **21**, (4), 479–496.

Goulding, R.A. & Schwartz, R.C. (1995). *The Mosaic Mind. Empowering the Tormented Selves of Child Abuse Survivors*. New York: Norton.

Greenacre, P. (1953). *Trauma, Growth and Personality*. London: Hogarth Press.

Greenacre, P. (1971). *Emotional Growth*, vol. 1. New York: International Universities Press.

Greenberg, M. S. & van der Kolk, B. (1987). Retrieval and integration of traumatic memories with the 'painting cure'. In van der Kolk, B., *Psychological Trauma*. Washington, DC: American Psychiatric Press.

Grotstein, J. (1979). Demoniacal possession, splitting, and the torment of joy. A psychoanalytic inquiry into the negative therapeutic reaction, unanalyzability, and psychotic states. *Contemporary Psychoanalysis*, **15**, No. 3, 407–453.

Grotstein, J. (1981). *Splitting and Projective Identification*. New York: Aronson.

Grotstein, J. (1982). Newer perspectives in object relations theory. *Contemporary Psychoanalysis*, **18**, 43–91.

Gunderson, J.G. (1984). *Borderline Personality Disorder*. Washington, DC: American Psychiatric Press.

Halleck, S.L. (1988). Which patients are responsible for their illnesses? *American Journal of Psychotherapy*, **42**, 338–353.

Halleck, S.L. (1990). Dissociative phenomena and the question of responsibility. *International Journal of Clinical and Experimental Hypnosis*, **38**, 293–314.

Hardy, D.W., Daghestani, A.N. & Egan, W.H. (1988). Multiple personality disorder: failure to diagnose and the potential for malpractice liability. *Psychiatric Annals*, **18**, 543–548.

Harper, A. (1990). *Dance With the Devil*. Eastbourne: Kingsway.

Healy, D. (1993). *Images of Trauma. From Hysteria to Post Traumatic Stress Disorder*. London: Faber.

Hedges, L.E. (1994). *Remembering, Repeating and Working Through Childhood Trauma. The Psychodynamics of Recovered Memories, Multiple Personality, Ritual Abuse, Incest, Molest and Abduction*. New York: Aronson.

Herman, J.L. (1992). *Trauma and Recovery*. New York: Basic Books.

Herman, J.L. & Shatzow, E. (1987). Recovery and Verification of Memories of Childhood Sexual Trauma. *Psychoanalytic Psychology*, **4**, 1–14.

Herman, J. & van der Kolk, B.A. (1987). Traumatic antecedents of borderline personality disorder. In *Psychological Trauma*. ed. B.A. van der Kolk. Washington, DC: American Psychiatric Press.

Hilgard, E.R. (1977). *Divided Consciousness. Multiple Controls in Human Thought and Action*. New York: Wiley.

Hilgard, E.R. (1994). Neodissociation theory. In S.J. Lynn & J.W. Rhue (eds) *Dissociation. Clinical and Theoretical Perspectives*. New York: Guilford Press.

Horevitz, R. & Loewenstein, R.J. (1994). The rational treatment of multiple personality disorder. In S.J. Lynn & J.W. Rhue (eds) *Dissociation. Clinical and Theoretical Perspectives*. New York: Guilford Press.

Horowitz, M.J. (1986). *Stress Response Syndromes*. New York: Aronson.

Howitt, D. (1995). *Paedophiles and Sexual Offences Against Children*. Chichester: Wiley.

Ireland, S.J. & Ireland, M.J. (1994). A case history of family and cult abuse. *Journal of Psychohistory*, **21**, No. 4, 416–428.

Janet, P. (1889). *L'Automatisme psychologique*: Essay de psychologie expérimentale sur les formes inférieures de l'activité humaine. Paris. Felix Alcan. Reprint: Société Pierre Janet/Payot, Paris, 1973.

Janet, P. (1909a). *Les Névroses*. Paris: Flammarion.

Janet, P. (1909b). Problems psychologique de l'émotion. *Rev. Neurol*, **17**, 1551–1687.

Janet, P. (1919). *Les Médications psychologique* (3 vols). Paris: Alcan.

Janet, P. (1935). *Les Débuts de l'intelligence*. Paris: Flammarion.

Kelley, S.J. (1985). Ritualistic abuse of children in day-care centres. In M.D. Langone (ed.), *Recovery from Cults*. New York: Norton.

Kernberg, O. (1975). *Borderline Conditions and Pathological Narcissism*. New York: Aronson.

Khan, M. (1963). The concept of cumulative trauma. In *The Privacy of the Self*. London: Hogarth Press (1974), pp. 42–58.

Kihlstrom, J.F. (1984). Conscious, subconscious, unconscious: a cognitive perspective. In K.F. Bowers & D. Meichenbaum (eds), *The Unconscious Reconsidered*. New York: Wiley.

Kingdon, D.G. & Turkington, D. (1994). *Cognitive-Behavioural Therapy of Schizophrenia*. Hillsdale, NJ: Erlbaum.

Klein, R.M. & Doane, B.K. (eds), (1994). *Psychological Concepts and Dissociative Disorders*. Hillsdale, NJ: Erlbaum.

Klimo, J. (1991). *Psychics, Prophets and Mystics. Receiving Information from Paranormal Sources*. London: Aquarian Press.

Kluft, R.P. (1987). An update on multiple personality disorder. *Hospital and Community Psychiatry*, **38**, 363–373.

Kluft, R.P. (1992). A specialist perspective on multiple personality disorder. *Psychoanalytic Inquiry*, **12** (1), 112–123.

Kluft, R.P. (1994a). Multiple personality disorder: observations on the etiology, natural history, recognition, and resolution of a long-neglected condition. In R.M. Klein & B.K. Doane (eds) *Psychological Concepts and Dissociative Disorders*. Hillsdale, NJ: Erlbaum.

Kluft, R.P. (1994b). Countertransference in the treatment of multiple personality disorder. In J.P. Wilson & J.D. Lindy (eds), *Countertransference in the Treatment of PTSD*. New York: Guilford.

Koch, K. (1972). *Christian Counselling and Occultism*. Berghausen/Bd: Ev. Verlag.

Kohut, H. (1971). *The Analysis of the Self*. New York: International Universities Press.

Kohut, H. (1977). *The Restoration of the Self*. New York: International Universities Press.

Kolb, L. (1987). Neuropsychological hypothesis explaining post-traumatic stress disorder. *American Journal of Psychiatry*, **144**, 989–995.

Krystal, H. (ed.) (1968). *Massive Psychic Trauma*. New York: International Universities Press.

La Fontaine, J. (1994). *The Extent and Nature of Organised and Ritual Abuse*. London: HMSO.

Lacan, J. (1977). *Ecrits*. London: Tavistock.

Laibow, R. (1986). Birth recall: A clinical report. *Pre- & Perinatal Psychology*, **1**, 78–81.

Langs, R. (1978). *The Listening Process*. New York: Aronson.

Lanning, K. (1992). A law-enforcement perspective on allegations of ritual abuse. In D.K. Sakheim & S.E. Divine (eds), *Out of Darkness*. New York: Lexington.

Laub, D. & Auerhahn, N.C. (1993). Knowing and not knowing massive psychic trauma: forms of traumatic memory. *International Journal of Psycho-Analysis*, **74** (2), 287–302.

LeDoux, J. (1989). Cognitive-emotional interactions in the brain. *Cognition and Emotion*, **3**, 267–289.

LeDoux, J., Romanski, L. & Xagoraris, A. (1991). Indelibility of subcortical emotional memories. *Journal of Cognitive Neuroscience*, **1**, 238–243.

Levine, H.B. (ed.) (1990). *Adult Analysis and Childhood Sexual Abuse*. Hillsdale, NJ: Analytic Press.

Lifton, J. (1971). Existential Evil. In N. Sanford & C. Comstock (eds), *Sanctions for Evil*. San Francisco: Jossey Bass, pp. 37–48.

Lindsay, D.S. and Read, J.D. (1994). Psychotherapy and memories of childhood sexual abuse: a cognitive perspective. *Applied Cognitive Psychology*, **8**, No 4, 281–338.

Lineham, M.M. (1993). *Cognitive-Behavioural Treatment of Borderline Personality Disorder*. New York: Guilford.

Loewenstein, R.J. (1991). An office mental status examination for chronic complex dissociative symptoms and dissociative identity disorder. *Psychiatric Clinics of North America*, **14**, 567–604.

Loftus, E. & Ketcham, K. (1994). *The Myth of Repressed Memory. False Memories and Allegations of Sexual Abuse*. New York: St. Martin's Press.

Loftus, E.F., Polonsky, S. & Fullilove, M. (1994). Memories of childhood sexual abuse: remembering and repressing. *Psychology of Women Quarterly*, **18**, 67–84.

Loftus, E. & Rosenwald, L. (1993). Buried Memories. Shattered Lives. *ABA Journal*, November.

Lyon, K.A. (1992). Shattered mirror. A fragment of the treatment of a patient with a multiple personality disorder. *Psychoanalytic Inquiry*, **12**(1), 71–94.

Mack, J. (ed.) (1975). *Borderline States in Psychiatry*. New York: Grune & Stratton.

Mancia, M. (1981). On the beginning of mental life in the foetus. *International Journal of Psycho-Analysis*, **62**, 351–357.

Martin, J. (1994). *Who Am I This Time? Uncovering the Fictive Personality*. New York: Norton.

Meloy, J.R. (1988). *The Psychopathic Mind. Origins, Dynamics and Treatment*. New York: Aronson.

Meltzer, D. (1973). *Sexual States of Mind*. Edinburgh: Clunie Press.

Mendel, M.P. (1995). *The Male Survivor. The Impact of Sexual Abuse*. Thousand Oaks, CA: Sage.

Merskey, H. (1992). The manufacture of personalities: the production of multiple personality disorder. *British Journal of Psychiatry*, **160**, 327–340.

Merskey, H. (1995). Multiple personality disorder and false memory. *British Journal of Psychiatry*, **166**, 281–283.

Midgley, M. (1984). *Wickedness. A Philosophical Essay*. London: Routledge.

Mitchell, D., Osborne, E.W. & O'Boyle, M.W. (1985). Habituation under stress: shocked mice show non-associative learning in a T-maze. *Behavioral Neurology and Biology*, **43**, 212–217.

Modestin, J. (1992). Multiple personality disorder in Switzerland. *American Journal of Psychiatry*, **149**, 88–92.

Mollon, P. (1993). *The Fragile Self. The Structure of Narcissistic Disturbance*. London: Whurr.

Mollon, P. (1994). The impact of evil. In V. Sinason (ed.) *Treating Survivors of Satanist Abuse*. London: Routledge.

Morton, J., Andrews, B., Bekerian, D., Brewin, C., Davies, G. & Mollon, P. (1994). *Recovered Memories. A Report of the British Psychological Society.* Leicester.

Ney, T. (1995). *True and False Allegations of Child Sexual Abuse. Assessment and Case Management.* New York: Brunner/Mazel.

North, C.S., Ryall, J.-E.M., Ricci, D.A. & Wetzel, R.D. (1993). *Multiple Personalities, Multiple Disorders. Psychiatric Classification and Media Influence.* New York: Oxford University Press.

Paulson, S. (in press). Eye Movement Desensitization and Reprocessing: its use in dissociative disorders. *Dissociation.*

Pearlman, L.A. & Saakvitne, K.W. (1995). *Trauma and the Therapist. Countertransference and Vicarious Traumatization in Psychotherapy with Incest Survivors.* New York: Norton.

Perry, J.C. & Klerman, G. (1980). Clinical features of the borderline personality disorder. *American Journal of Psychiatry,* **137,** 165–173.

Perry, M. (1987). Deliverance. *Psychic Disturbances and Occult Involvement.* London. SPK.

Piaget, J. (1945). *Play, Dreams and Imitation in Childhood.* New York: Norton.

Pine, F. (1985). *Developmental Theory and Clinical Process.* New Haven, CT: Yale University Press.

Piontelli, A. (1988). Pre-natal life and birth as reflected in the life of a two year old psychotic girl. *International Review of Psycho-Analysis,* **15,** 73–81.

Piontelli, A. (1989). A study of twins before and after birth. *International Review of Psycho-Analysis,* **16,** 413–426.

Piper, A. (1994). Multiple personality disorder. *British Journal of Psychiatry,* **164,** 600–612.

Piper, A. (in press). 'Truth serum' and 'recovered memories' of sexual abuse: A review of the evidence. *Journal of Psychiatry and the Law.*

Poole, D.A., Lindsay, D.S., Memon, A. & Bull, R. (in press). Psychotherapy and the recovery of memories of childhood sexual abuse: US and British practitioners' opinions, practices and experiences. *Journal of Consulting and Clinical Psychology.*

Pope, H.G. & Hudson, J. (1995). Can memories of childhood sexual abuse be repressed? *Psychological Medicine,* **25,** 121–126.

Price, G. (1994). Abjection and relational cruelty. Unpublished paper.

Prince, M. & Peterson, F. (1908). Experiments in psycho-galvanic reactions from co-conscious (sub-conscious) ideas in a case of multiple personality. *Journal of Abnormal Psychology,* **3,** 114–131.

Putnam, F. (1989). *Diagnosis and Treatment of Multiple Personality Disorder.* New York: Guilford Press.

Putnam, F. (1991). Dissociative phenomena. In Tasman, A. & Goldfinger, S.M. *American Psychiatric Press Review of Psychiatry,* Vol. 10. Washington, DC: American Psychiatric Press, pp. 145–160.

Putnam, F. (1994). The switch process in multiple personality disorder and other state-change disorders. In R.M. Klein & B.K. Doane (eds) *Psychological Concepts and Dissociative Disorders.* Hillsdale, NJ: Erlbaum.

Putnam, F. W., Loewenstein, R. N., Silberman, E.J. et al. (1984). Multiple personality disorder in a hospital setting. *Journal of Clinical Psychiatry,* **45,** 172–175.

Putnam, F.W., Post, R.M. & Guroff, J.J. (1986). One hundred cases of multiple personality disorder. *Journal of Clinical Psychiatry,* **47,** 285–293.

Ramsey-Klawsnik, H. (1990). Sexually abused boys: indicators, abusers and impact of trauma. Paper presented at the Third National Conference on The Male Survivor, Tucson, AZ. Quoted in M.P. Mendel, *The Male Survivor.* Thousand Oaks, CA: Sage (1995).

Read, J.D. & Lindsay, D.S. (1994). Moving towards a middle ground on the 'false memory debate': reply to commentaries on Lindsay and Read. *Applied Cognitive Psychology*, **8**, 407–435.

Rockwell, R.B. 1994. One psychiatrist's view of satanic ritual abuse. *Journal of Psychohistory*, **21**(4), 443–460.

Rosenfeld, H. (1971). A clinical approach to the psychoanalytic theory of the life and death instincts: an investigation into the aggressive aspects of narcissism. *International Journal of Psycho-Analysis*, **52**, 169–178.

Ross, C. (1989). *Multiple Personality Disorder. Diagnosis, Clinical Features and Treatment*. New York: Wiley.

Ross, C. (1990). Multiple personality disorder (letter). *British Journal of Psychiatry*, **161**, 415–416.

Ross, C. (1994). *The Osiris Complex. Case Studies in Multiple Personality Disorder*. Toronto: University of Toronto Press.

Ross, C., Miller, S.D., Reagor, P., Bjornson, L., Fraser, G.A. & Anderson, G. (1990). Schneiderian symptoms in multiple personality disorder and schizophrenia. *Comprehensive Psychiatry*, **31**(2), 111–118.

Roth, S. (1992). A psychologist's perspective on multiple personality disorder. *Psychoanalytic Inquiry*, **12**(1), 112–123.

Ryder, D. (1992). *Breaking the Circle of Satanic Ritual Abuse*. Minneapolis: CompCare.

Salter, A.C. *Transforming Trauma* (1995). Thousand Oaks, CA: Sage.

Sandler, J., Dreher, U. & Drews, S. (1991). An approach to conceptual research in psychoanalysis illustrated by a consideration of psychic trauma. *International Review of Psycho-Analysis*, **18**, 133–141.

Scott Peck, M. (1988). *People of the Lie. The Hope for Healing Human Evil*. London: Rider.

Seinfeld, J. (1990). *The Bad Object. Handling the Negative Therapeutic Reaction in Psychotherapy*. New York: Aronson.

Serban, G. (1992). Multiple personality: an issue for forensic psychiatry. *American Journal of Psychotherapy*, **46**, 269–280.

Shapiro, F. (1989). Eye movement desensitization: A new treatment for post-traumatic stress disorder. *Journal of Behaviour Therapy and Experimental Psychiatry*, **20**, 211–217.

Shapiro, F. (1995). *Eye Movement Desensitization and Reprocessing*. New York: Guilford Press.

Share, L. (1994). *If Someone Speaks It Gets Lighter. Dreams and the Reconstruction of Infant Trauma*. Hillsdale, NJ: Analytic Press, Erlbaum.

Shephard, K.R. & Braun, B.G. (1985). Visual changes in multiple personality. In B.G. Braun (ed), *Proceedings of the Second International Conference on Multiple Personality/Dissociative States*, p. 85. Chicago: Rush-Presbyterian-St Luke's Medical Center.

Sherwood, V.R. & Cohen, C.P. (1994). *Psychotherapy of the Quiet Borderline Patient. The As-If Personality Revisited*. New York: Aronson.

Simon, B. (1992). 'Incest – See Under Oedipus Complex.' The History of an Error in Psychoanalysis. *Journal of the American Psychoanalytic Association*, **40**, pt 4, 955–988.

Sinason, M. (1993). Who is the mad voice inside? *Psychoanalytic psychotherapy*, **7**, 207–221.

Sinason, V. (ed.) (1996). *Memory in Dispute*. London: Karnac.

Smith, B.L. (1989). Of many minds. A contribution on the dynamics of multiple personality. In M.G Fromm & B.L. Smith (eds) *The Facilitating Environment*. New York: International Universities Press.

Sohn, L. (1985). Narcissistic organisation, projective identification and the formation of the identificate. *International Journal of Psycho-Analysis*, **66**, 201–214.

Spanos, N.P. & Burgess, C. (1994). Hypnosis and multiple personality disorder: a sociocognitive perspective. In S.J. Lynn & J.W. Rhue (eds) *Dissociation. Clinical and Theoretical Perspectives*. New York: Guilford.

Spence, D. (1982). *Narrative Truth and Historical Truth*. New York: Norton.

Spencer, J. (1989). *Suffer the Child*. New York: Pocket Books/Simon & Schuster.

Spiegel, H. (1974). The grade 5 syndrome: the highly hypnotizable person. *International Journal of Clinical and Experimental Hypnosis*, **22**, 303–319.

Steinberg, M. (1991). The spectrum of depersonalization: assessment and treatment. In Tasman, A. & Goldfinger, S.M., *American Psychiatric Press Review of Psychiatry*. Washington, DC: American Psychiatric Press, pp. 223–247.

Steinberg, M. (1993a). Advances in detecting dissociation. Structured clinical interview for DSM-IV dissociative disorders (SCID-D). *Psychiatric Times*, April.

Steinberg, M. (1993b). *Interviewer's Guide to the Structured Clinical Interview for DSM-IV Dissociative Disorders (SCID-D)*. Washington, DC: American Psychiatric Press.

Stern, C.R. (1984). The etiology of multiple personalities. *Psychiatric Clinics of North America*, **7**, 149–159.

Stern, D. (1986). *The Interpersonal World of the Infant*. New York: Basic Books.

Stolorow, R.D., Brandchaft, B. & Atwood, G. (1987). *Psychoanalytic Treatment: An Intersubjective Approach*. Hillsdale, NJ: Analytic Press.

Stolorow, R.D., Atwood, G.E. & Brandchaft, B. (1994). Masochism and its treatment. In R.D. Stolorwow, G.E. Atwood & B. Brandchaft (eds), *The Intersubjective Perspective*. Northvale, NJ: Aronson.

Stone, L. & Stone, D. (1992). Ritual abuse. The experience of five families. In D. Sakheim & S. Devine (eds). *Out of Darkness. Exploring Satanism and Ritual Abuse*. New York: Lexington.

Stone, H. & Winkelman, S. (1987). *Embracing Our Selves*. San Rafael, CA: New World Library.

Tate, T. (1990). *Child Pornography. An Investigation*. London: Methuen.

Terr, L.C. (1988). Case study. What happens to early memories of trauma? A study of twenty children under age five at the time of documented traumatic events. *Journal of the American Academy of Child and Adolescent Psychiatry*, **27**, 96–104.

Terr, L.C. (1990). *Too Scared to Cry. Psychic Trauma in Childhood*. New York: Basic Books.

Terr, L.C. (1991). Childhood traumas: an outline and overview. *American Journal of Psychiatry*, **148**, 10–20.

Terr, L.C. (1994). *Unchained Memories. True Stories of Traumatic Memories Lost and Found*. New York: Basic Books.

Thigpen, C. H. & Checkley, H.M. (1984). On the incidence of multiple personality disorder: a brief communication. *International Journal of Clinical and Experimental Hypnosis*, **32**, 63–66.

Tillman, J.G., Nash, M.R. & Lerner, P.M. (1994). Does trauma cause dissociative pathology? In S.J. Lynn & J.W. Rhue (eds), *Dissociation*. New York: Guilford.

Tozman, S. & Pablis, R. (1989). Further skepticism (letter). *Journal of Nervous and Mental Disorders*, **177**, 708–709.

Trickett, P.K. & Putnam, F.W. (1993). Impact of sexual abuse on females: toward a developmental, psychobiological integration. *Psychological Science,* **4**(2), 81–87.

Tudor, T. (1994). Healing the heart. EMDR in post-unification MPD therapy. *EMDR Network Newsletter,* Issue 1, 8–9.

Ulman, R.B. & Brothers, D. (1988). *The Shattered Self. A Psychoanalytic Study of Trauma.* Hillsdale, NJ: Analytic Press.

van der Hart, O. & Friedman, B. (1989). A reader's guide to Pierre Janet on dissociation: A neglected intellectual inheritance. *Dissociation,* **II**, No. 1, 3–16.

van der Hart, O & Horst, R. (1989). The dissociation theory of Pierre Janet. *Journal of Traumatic Stress,* **2**, No. 4, 399–414.

van der Kolk, B.A. (ed.) (1987). *Psychological Trauma.* Washington, DC: American Psychiatric Press.

van der Kolk, B.A. (1994). The body keeps the score: Memory and the evolving psychobiology of posttraumatic stress. *Harvard Review of Psychiatry,* Jan/Feb, 253–265.

van der Kolk, B.A., Brown, P. & van der Hart, O. (1989). Pierre Janet on post-traumatic stress. *Journal of Traumatic Stress,* **2**, No. 4, 365–378.

van der Kolk, B.A. & Fisler, R.E. (1994). Childhood abuse and neglect and loss of self-regulation. *Bulletin of the Menninger Clinic,* **58**, No. 2, 145–168.

van der Kolk, B.A. & Greenberg, M.S. (1987). The psychobiology of the trauma response. Hyperarousal, constriction and addiction to traumatic reexposure. In *Psychological Trauma,* ed. B.A. van der Kolk. Washington, DC: American Psychiatric Press.

van der Kolk, B.A., Greenberg, M.S. & Boyd, H. (1985). Inescapable shock, neurotransmitters and addiction to trauma: towards a psychobiology of post traumatic stress. *Biological Psychiatry,* **20**, 314–325.

Vanderlinden, J., Van Dyke, R., Vandereycken, W., Vertommen, H. & Verkes, R.J. (1993). The dissociation questionnaire: development and characteristics of a new self-report questionnaire. *Clinical Psychology and Psychotherapy,* **1**(1), 21–27.

Van Leeuwen, K. (1988). Resistances in the treatment of a sexually molested 6-year-old girl. *International Review of Psycho-Analysis,* **15**, pt 2, 149–156.

Waites, E.A. (1993). *Trauma and Survival. Post Traumatic and Dissociative Disorders in Women.* New York: Norton.

Waterman, J., Kelly, R.J., McCord, J. & Oliveri, M.K. (1990). *Reported Ritualistic and Nonritualistic Sexual Abuse in Preschools: Effects and Mediators.* Executive Summary submitted to National Center on Child Abuse and Neglect. Washington, DC.

Whitfield, C.L. (1995). *Memory and Abuse.* Deerfield Beach, FL: Health Communications Inc.

Williams, D. (1992). *Nobody Nowhere.* London: Doubleday.

Williams, L.M. (1994). Recall of childhood trauma: a prospective study of women's memories of childhood sexual abuse. *Journal of Consulting and Clinical Psychology,* **62**, 1167–1176.

Williams, N. (1994). *Psychoanalytic Diagnosis.* New York: Guilford.

Winnicott, D. (1960). Ego distortion in terms of true and false self. In *The Maturational Processes and the Facilitating Environment.* New York: International Universities Press, pp. 140–152.

Wolff, L. (1995). *Child Abuse in Freud's Vienna. Postcards from the End of the World.* New York: New York University Press.

Wolff, P.H. (1987). *The Development of Behavioural States and the Expression of Emotions in Early Infancy.* Chicago: University of Chicago Press.

Wyre, R. (1986). *Women, Men and Rape.* Oxford: Perry Publications.

Wyre, R. (1987). *Working with Sex Offenders.* Oxford: Perry Publications.

Wyre, R. (1989). Working with the paedophile. In M. Farrell (ed.), *Understanding the Paedophile.* London: ISTD/The Portman Clinic, pp. 17–23.

Wyre, R. (1990). Why do men sexually abuse children? Appendix in T. Tate, *Child Pornography. An Investigation.* London: Methuen, pp. 281–288.

Wyre, R. & Tate, T. (1995). *The Murder of Childhood.* London: Penguin.

Young. W.C. (1994). EMDR treatment of phobic symptoms in multiple personality disorder. *Dissociation,* **111**, No. 2, 129–133.

INDEX

Note: MPD/DID stands for multiple personality disorder/dissociative identity disorder

Index compiled by Liz Granger

The Wiley Series in

CLINICAL PSYCHOLOGY

Martin Herbert	Clinical Child Psychology: Social Learning, Development and Behaviour
David Peck and C.M. Shapiro (Editors)	Measuring Human Problems: A Practical Guide
Roger Baker (Editor)	Panic Disorder: Theory, Research and Therapy
Friedrich Fösterling	Attribution Theory in Clinical Psychology
Anthony Lavender and Frank Holloway (Editors)	Community Care in Practice: Services for the Continuing Care Client
J. Mark G. Williams, Fraser N. Watts, Colin MacLeod and Andrew Mathews	Cognitive Psychology and Emotional Disorders
John Clements	Severe Learning Disability and Psychological Handicap

Related titles of interest from Wiley...

Disorders of Personality
2nd Edition: DSM-IV and Beyond
Theodore Millon and **Roger D. Davis**
This revised edition incorporates changes in the new DSM and reviews all relevant recent research in the personality field.
0471 01186 X   768pp   1996   Hardback

Cognitive Therapy for Delusions, Voices and Paranoia
Paul Chadwick, Max Birchwood and **Peter Trower**
Guides professionals towards better practice by treating the individual symptoms of delusions, voices and paranoia, rather than by the categorisation of schizophrenia.
Wiley Series in Clinical Psychology
0471 93888 2   224pp   1996   Hardback
0471 96173 6   224pp   1996   Paperback

Cognitive Behaviour Therapy for Psychosis
Theory and Practice
David Fowler, Philippa Garety and **Elizabeth Kuipers**
Focuses on the four main problems presented by people with psychosis: emotional disturbance, psychotic symptoms like delusions and bizarre beliefs, social disabilities and relapse risk.
0471 93980 3   212pp   1995   Hardback
0471 95618 X   212pp   1995   Paperback

Personality Disorders: Clinical and Social Perspectives
Assessment and Treatment based on DSM-IV and ICD-10
Jan Derksen   Foreword by **Theodore Millon**
Describes each DSM-IV and ICD-10 personality disorder in detail, illustrated by the use of case examples.
0471 94389 4   374pp   1995   Hardback
0471 95549 3   374pp   1995   Paperback